The child in Spanish cinema

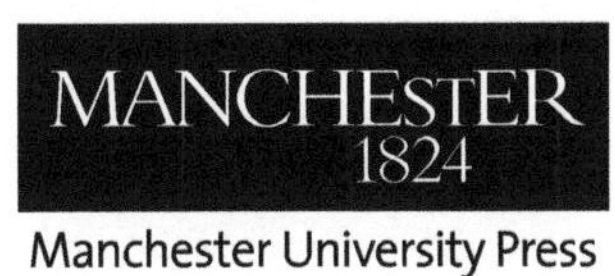

Manchester University Press

The child in Spanish cinema

Sarah Wright

Manchester University Press

Published by Manchester University Press
Altrincham Street, Manchester M1 7JA, UK
www.manchesteruniversitypress.co.uk

British Library Cataloguing-in-Publication Data is available

Library of Congress Cataloging-in-Publication Data is available

ISBN 978 1 7849 9379 5 *paperback*

First published by Manchester University Press in hardback 2013

This edition first published 2016

Printed by Lightning Source

Contents

List of illustrations   *page* vi
Acknowledgements   vii

Introduction   1

1   Auratic encounters with the child of the *cine religioso*   23

2   Coming of age with Marisol   59

3   Memory and the child witness in 'art-house horror'   89

4   Angels and devils: embodiment and adolescence in recent Spanish
    films   129

Conclusion   156

Bibliography   160
Index   179

List of illustrations

1 Pitusín (Alfredo Hurtado) in *La buenaventura de Pitusín* (Luis R. Alonso, 1924), courtesy Filmoteca Española, Madrid. 7

2 Daniel Brühl, Claudia Vega and Sara Rosa Losilla in Kike Maíllo's *Eva* (2011), ESCAC, Escándalo Films and Ran Entertainment. 12

3 Pablito Calvo in *Marcelino, pan y vino* (Ladislao Vajda, 1955), Vanguard Cinema. 29

4 Pablito Calvo in *Marcelino, pan y vino* (Ladislao Vajda, 1955), Vanguard Cinema. 43

5 Marisol (Pepa Flores) in *Un rayo de luz* (Luis Lucia, 1960), Tribanda Pictures. 67

6 Ana Torrent in *El espíritu de la colmena* (Víctor Erice, 1973), Elías Querejeta Producciones Cinematográficas. 91

7 Manuel Lozano in *La lengua de las mariposas* (José Luis Cuerda, 1999), Warner Sogefilms, S.A. 110

8 Poster for Bayona's *El orfanato* (2007), Wild Bunch Distribution. 113

9 Sergi López in *El laberinto del fauno* (Guillermo del Toro, 2006), Estudios Picasso. 121

10 Francesc Colomer in *Pa negre* (Agustí Villaronga, 2010), Alfama Films. 126

11 Achero Mañas's *El Bola* (2000), Film Movement. 138

12 Nerea Camacho in Javier Fesser's *Camino* (2008), Media Pro and Películas Pendleton. 152

Acknowledgements

This book has been profoundly shaped by the assistance of several people: Duncan Wheeler, who read the whole manuscript and whose comments and suggestions go unacknowledged throughout the book but have improved its content immeasurably; Laura Gómez Vaquero, who was swift, efficient and creative in her location of many of the materials which form the basis of the book, and María Delgado, who has always been extraordinarily generous with her time, expertise and support but on this occasion went out of her way on all counts and was instrumental in bringing this book together. Valeria Camporesi has been an inspiration and has provided practical help and insights. I am also extremely grateful to Robin Fiddian who generously afforded his time in abundance at very short notice and finally to Jo Labanyi who provided last minute support when it was most crucial. I am very grateful to the AHRC for the Fellowship in 2010–11 which gave me time and space to devote to the project. Kerry Jarman stepped in with her expertise on visual images at short notice. Matthew Frost at Manchester University Press has been extraordinarily patient and supportive.

Ruth Aedo Richmond, Cristina Amich Elías, Peter Beardsell, Matilde Conesa, Ann Davies, Stephanie Donald, Dru Dougherty, Jonathan Ellis, Sally Faulkner, Polly Fox, María Dolores Gispert, Julián Gutiérrez-Albilla, Rhian Harris, Jessamy Harvey, Fiona Huggett, José Manuel Alonso Ibarrola, Valerie Lobban, Frank Lough, Alex Lowe, Karen Lury, Dave McCall (BFI), Olya Melnitchouk, Lidia Merás, Tatjana Pavlović, Brian Powell, Ana María Sánchez-Arce, Alison Sinclair, Paul Julian Smith, Helena Taberna, Sarah Thomas, Sélica Torcal, Ana Torrent, Horacio Valcárcel, Isabel Valcárcel, Robert Vilain, Elisa Costa Villaverde, Tom Whittaker and James Williams all provided practical or intellectual support.

I am particularly grateful to Emma Wilson and Karen Lury for discussions about the child in cinema and to Laura Mulvey, who was keynote speaker at our Postgraduate Conference at Royal Holloway and discussed cinema and time with me over dinner after the lecture. I am also grateful to Federico Bonaddio, Jo Evans and Ann Davies who very kindly read sections of the book.

I would like to thank my postgraduate students, Madori Nasu and Judith Meddick, for discussions which have fed into this book. I am also grateful to my colleagues in the School of Modern Languages at Royal Holloway, University of London, and especially, to Ann Hobbs, Cathy Thorin, Helen Thomas, Sarah Midson, and, *in memoriam*, to our colleague David Vilaseca who was killed tragically in a road accident in 2010.

My students at Royal Holloway, particularly the finalists on the 'Seducing the Nation' course, have provided a lively forum for the discussion of ideas, as have attendees (teachers and A and AS level pupils) at the 'Through the Eyes of a Child: The Child as Protagonist in Spanish Film' workshops that I led at the BFI. I am grateful to Christine James (BFI Education) for her creative input at these events. I benefitted from feedback at the following papers and presentations: the Ferens Annual Lecture at the University of Hull on 'The Child in Spanish Film' in 2011 (I am particularly grateful to Neil Sinyard, Iris Kleinecke-Bates, Jenny Rumble and John and Mary Jones); 'Spain's First Child Stars' at the Child Actors/Child Stars: Juvenile Performance on Screen' at the University of Sunderland in 2011; the inaugural lecture for the Masters programme in Literaturas Hispánicas: Arte, Historia y Sociedad at the Universidad Autónoma, Madrid; 'El as más pequeño. Estrellato y orfandad en el primer cine español', at the Consejo Superior de Investigaciones Científicas at the invitation of Pilar Nieva-de-la-Paz and María Francisca Vilches-de-Frutos; a seminar at the University of Newcastle and a workshop at the University of Aberdeen with Fiona Noble on child stars as part of a 'Performance and Visual Culture' workshop. I gave the paper, 'Dubbing the Child Star' at the 'Sonic Futures' NECS annual conference at King's College London in 2011 and spoke on embodiment in recent Spanish cinema at the PCA/ACA Popular Culture Association annual conference in Texas in 2011 (Debbie Olson) and on 'Skin, Adolescence and Embodiment' at the AHGBI conference in Stirling in 2012.

I benefited from expert assistance from Marga Lobo, Trinidad del Río and José Luis Fernández Guardón at the Filmoteca de Madrid; Antonio Duato at the Filmoteca de Valencia; Rosa Saz Alpuente, Filmoteca de Barcelona; Javier Campillo, Instituto Cervantes, Toulouse. I thank staff at the Biblioteca Nacional, Madrid, the Hemeroteca de Madrid, the British Library, the Founders and Bedford Libraries at Royal Holloway (and in particular Russell Burke) and the staff of Roehampton University Library where I was lucky enough to gain access to their marvellous collection on children's literature.

During a research trip to Madrid I was extremely lucky to be looked after by Carmen Ramiro, José Vila and Maruja Rincón.

Finally, I thank Carmen Gutiérrez Olóndriz, RON, Girma Olóndriz, the Escobars, the Smalls, Isabel Wright and Alejandro Escobar, for his seemingly unending patience and support.

This book is dedicated to my children, Inés and Tomás, and the memory of my mother, Stella Wright.

Introduction

In Kike Maíllo's film *Eva* (2011), it is 2041 and cybernetic engineer Álex Garel (Daniel Brühl) returns to his snow-covered home town to resume a project he had abandoned ten years before: the construction of a child robot. In hushed tones, and in a secluded space behind curtained glass in the university laboratory, Julia, his old professor, shows him the prototype. The robot's skin glistens as if it was real but its eyes are blank. Álex is to give the robot life, constructing the artificial memory of a machine that should be 'fun but safe' (a reference, doubtless, to Isaac Asimov's three laws on robotics and which foreshadows the film's theme of created rising up against creator).[1] He and Julia watch a show-reel of children taking the 'marshmallow test'[2] but Álex deems these children to be 'too boring' as models for his child-robot. Later, his car turns into a street beside a school and he begins his search for the perfect child, his eyes scouring the playground, the car cruising alongside the pavement. A tracking shot – his point of view from the car – follows some children out of the school gate and is arrested by the sight of a pair of legs belonging to a girl walking on her hands. The legs appear above some bill boarding whilst the rest of the child's body is, for the moment, hidden. The child who emerges on the other side is dressed in a red coat and she twirls in the snow before resting her gaze on Álex. He is attracted by this child's 'otherness', her difference, her originality, her self-absorption and her capacity for play (all attributes of 'childhood' in the collective imagination). We were all children once, as Julia later reminds him, but as Álex's relationship with this child, Eva, bears witness, constructions of the child or the child's experience are so often 'a form of anthropomorphism' (Lury, 2010: 109) in the sense that they reveal adult investments in the child. In the film's final twist, it will be revealed that Eva is also a robot, having been created by David (Álex's brother) and Lana (his former lover) after Álex left town. Eva overhears a conversation which reveals to her the truth of her mechanical origins – she had no knowledge of this, it had been omitted from her implanted, 'prosthetic memory'. Traumatised at this discovery, she will run away, and later will rebel against her creator.

'¿Qué miras?' (what are you looking at?) asks Eva, '¿te gusta mirar a los niños? (do you like looking at children?) and '¿eres un pervertido?' (are you a pervert?) as Álex holds out his hand with sweets. Maíllo has cited Little

Red Riding Hood and the relationship between a child (Natalie Portman) and a man (Timothy Hutton) in Ted Demme's *Beautiful Girls* (1996) as influences for the relationship between Eva and Álex (Arce, 2011) and the film shifts, undecidedly, between depictions of Eva as a latter-day Lolita, and suspicions as to a sinister ulterior motive for Álex's interest in the child. The film observes Eva's face in close-ups.[3] Seduced by Eva – as journalist Toni García (2011) would be in his critique for *El País*, describing ten-year-old Claudia Vega in this role as possessing 'trazos de *femme fatale*, con una capacidad de seducción francamente apabullante' (traces of *femme fatale* with a frankly overwhelming capacity for seduction) – Álex takes out his phone and captures her image as she skips away. Later he will use this image as a model for his robot.

Eva prided itself on its cutting edge special effects, but the fascination with animating the inanimate returns us to the origins of cinema. Early cinema developed from Marey and Muybridge's photographic documentation of the human form in motion (Doane, 2002: 46–68) and the earliest film projections would begin with a projected still image that would begin to move. Louis Lumière's' *Repas de bébé* (Feeding the Baby, 1898) (featuring Louis's brother Auguste, and his wife and child) delighted in the very ability to show the child in motion.[4] The image of Auguste, his wife and child, resembles a family photograph and Lebeau notes how the film engenders, 'the shuddering into motion of the still photograph' (Lebeau, 2008: 23). Segundo de Chomón (Spain's answer to George Méliès and expert in the trick-shot) made *Metempsychose* in 1907 (in collaboration with the French film-maker Ferdinand Zecca), a film which drew on the coming to life of the still image of a child.[5] The crying baby appears to be a drawing like the cabbage it emerges from. But then suddenly it comes to life, revealed to be a real baby, as it is picked up and carried in a woman's arms. Chomón's *Magic Bricks* (1908), meanwhile, playfully projects the face of a laughing girl onto some bricks. When the bricks are removed one by one, dismantling the image as the child continues to laugh, the image is now revealed as no more than a projection. Chomón's *El teatro eléctrico de Bob* (Bob's Electric Theatre, 1906) meanwhile, begins with three children who set up a miniature stage on a table before their toys are magically brought to life in their imaginations and for the viewer to see, drawing a parallel between the puppets brought to life and the children animated on screen. Gaby Wood (2002) draws links between early automata and the new cinematic medium; Noel Burch (1990: 6–22) has noted the 'Frankensteinian dream' underlying early cinema; whilst for Michelle Bloom early film activates a 'Pygmalionesque imagination' (Bloom, 2000).[6] Kike Maíllo's *Eva* references *Pygmalion*, E. T. A. Hoffman's 'The Sandman' and Villier de l'Isle's 'Tomorrow's Eve' in its tale of a man who falls in love with a woman without realising that she is mechanical (the undercurrent of eroticism in the relationship between Álex and Eva). The film also clearly refers to 'Pinocchio' – by way of Kubrick/Spielberg's *A.I.* (2001) – as Eva rebels when she discovers that she is not a real child. Resonances of James Whale's *Frankenstein* (1931) are clear in Álex's search for the child to conduct his experiment through the 'marshmallow test' that, in its ability to predict intellectual prowess, implies a search for a perfect brain. Pinocchio, the child who wants to become a real boy, might seem like an apt metaphor for the child's will to come to life on screen, but the creature, that 'child' of Frankenstein, born out of an unholy alliance between the human and the scientific/ technological, is perhaps the most appropriate model for the cinematic child.

The Child in Spanish Cinema recognises Stephen Connor's observation that cinema 'wants to come to life'. Cinema has 'thematised this ambition', Connor explains, 'through the many stories it tells of automata endowed with life: Frankenstein's monsters, robots, computers, puppets, ventriloquists dummies [which tell] the story of its own power' to animate (Connor, 2000: n.p.). The cinematic children in this book betray traces of their mechanical origins. Dolls, ventriloquists' dummies and cyborgs populate the Spanish films under discussion. Moreover, film, in this book, wants to have a body. Sound, vision and touch work together with spectatorship to make this body felt.[7] Furthermore, themes ushered in by *Eva* carve out a framework of reference to which the chapters return: the child and his/her creator; the child and the monster; the monstrous child.

If this book explores the way that film brings children to life on screen, it will also examine the ways that films featuring children bring the past to life on screen. In this sense, if film has a (mechanical) body, it also has a (prosthetic) memory. Laura Mulvey's *Death 24 x a Second* is instructive in the way that it draws attention to the potential that new technologies bring for us to get closer to our icons. 'Delayed cinema', for Mulvey, refers in the first place to the slowing down of film but also 'to the delay in time during which some detail has lain dormant, as it were, waiting to be noticed' (Mulvey, 2005: 8). But delayed cinema also refers to the capacity of film to bring the past to life: cinema has a 'privileged relation to time, preserving the moment at which the image is registered, inscribing an unprecedented reality into its representation of the past' (Mulvey, 2005: 8–9). New technologies revive old Spanish films whilst old reel-to-reels at several Filmotecas in Spain provide access to a wealth of material that is not otherwise available for viewing. Certain films are periodically released with a short print-run. But there are many cinematic children, referenced in newspaper clippings, but whose films are presently unavailable, that make up a background of 'lost children' and which haunt attempts to achieve anything like a comprehensive picture of the child in Spanish cinema. Studies of Spanish early film are particularly fraught with difficulties: it is estimated that some 90 per cent of film stock has been lost or destroyed, complicating the notion that we can revive the Spanish past through film (Arnau, 2007). Nevertheless, film will be seen to have traits of the archive and this book will move forwards and backwards in time in order to trace influences and developments. Finally, film itself has a memory which works intertextually to produce themes, resonances and intensities that recur over time.

The child in Spanish cinema

El laberinto del fauno (Pan's Labyrinth, Guillermo del Toro, 2006) recently established in audience's minds the associations of Spanish cinema (sub-titled and with glorious visuals) with transnationalism in the context of child-centred film.[8] Del Toro was seen as spiking a renewed interest in the (child-centred) 'genre film' with his endorsement of Bayona's *El orfanato* (The Orphanage, 2007) (Alejandro Amenábar's English-language *The Others* (2001) might also be seen as another variation on this transnational trend). Critics also drew attention to the intertextual reliance of Guillermo del Toro's film on another globally famous Spanish film: Víctor Erice's *El espíritu de la colmena* (The Spirit of the Beehive, 1973) (Smith, 2007; Miles, 2011). Erice's iconic film has transcended the limits of national cinema to be seen as paradigmatic of an 'international child film format' (Martin-Jones, 2011: 81) as well as of the image of the child on screen *per se* (Lebeau, 2008). The film circulates on the art cinema circuit, through international film festivals, independent cinema chains and specialist DVD distributors in world cinema. Ana Torrent's contribution to Carlos Saura's *Cría cuervos* (Raise Ravens, 1976), which is also periodically revived in international film festivals, has confirmed her status as a palimpsest for filmic investigations of memory as well as for discussions which broach childhood as poised between innocence and monstrosity.[9]

Torrent's mute gaze might be seen as a reaction to the excesses of the *película con niño* (child-centred films) which had dominated in Spain during the 1950s and 1960s from the sentimentality of Pablito Calvo's perform-ance in *Marcelino, pan y vino* (The Miracle of Marcelino, 1955), through the extraordinary vocals of Joselito, the 'singing nightingale', to the riot of colour and noise in the musical extravaganzas of blonde-haired singing sensation Marisol.

The Child in Spanish Cinema will start with the 1950s in Spain and travel forwards in time towards the present day. But as no book has yet traced a genealogy of the child in early cinema, I will begin with a brief, imperfect, potted pre-history of the child in Spanish cinema up to the 1950s. Jean-Claude Seguin's unpublished thesis (1990) has been instrumental to this plotting and is, to my knowledge, the only work to date which traces the child in (early) Spanish cinema through time.[10] There is, however, much work still to be done on the child in Spanish cinema, perhaps particularly in the period prior to the 1970s.

Child stars have been present in Spanish cinema since its inception. Segundo de Chomón's experiments with the image of the child as part of a cinema of attractions were soon followed by Angel García Cardona's picaresque adventure *El ciego de la aldea* (The Blindman of the Village,

1906) which opens with a close-up of a girl's laughing face before following her adventures as she traps some thieves before neatly dispatching them to the cops. This resourceful *pícara* portrays a girl in an active role. The same cannot be said of the girl's worldview as presented in *La secta de los misteriosos* (The Mysterious Sect, Alberto Marro, 1917), an adventure about a kidnapped child and a stolen necklace, starring child star Alexia Ventura. The film uses parallel editing and jump-cuts to express the chaos and threat of modernity as Alexia is carried around, strapped to train tracks and rescued in the nick of time before the train comes thundering past the screen.[11] Alexia expresses her anguish through the wringing of hands and upturned face, the shadows of the bars in the basement where she is imprisoned, falling across her face. Alexia Ventura had been dubbed the 'Spanish Mary Pickford' by the Spanish press although she did not usher in the 'more emancipated and youth-oriented images of women during the years of World War I' as Kirby has found of Pickford and her contemporary Helen Homes in Hollywood film (Kirby, 1997: 77). (Unlike Ventura, Pickford was, in fact, an adult playing a child, a phenomenon observed in José Buchs's *El abuelo* (The Grandfather) some years later in 1925).[12] There are more interesting female roles in the film, such as that of the female ruffian, La Garza, dressed in black satin, balaclava and high heels, who steals Alexia in the night. The prince, meanwhile, in the Moorish fantasy sequence (the backstory to the stolen necklace at the heart of the drama), is obviously played by a woman and indulges in a long kiss with the princess of the harem. Ventura, meanwhile, is carried around and dressed up in bows: a more disappointing paradigm for female subjectivity.[13]

If Ventura was the 'Spanish Mary Pickford', then Pitusín (Alfredo Hurtado) was created in response to the success of Jackie Coogan in Chaplin's *The Kid* (1921). *La buenaventura de Pitusín* (Pitusín's Good Fortune, Luis R. Alonso, 1924) was a show-reel organised by Hurtado's mother, Prudencia, with the two thousand pesetas left to her by her dead husband. In the opening sequence, a curtain extends over the screen. A lady, dressed in 1920s style, with white hair tied in a loose bun, strides towards the separation in the curtain and pulls it aside. Behind we glimpse a boy, sitting at a writing desk, short bobbed hair and sailor suit with white socks and 'Alice' style shoes. The woman waves to the boy and gestures out towards the audience: he should come to greet us, the cinema spectators. She has to beckon him again, and now he advances, somewhat cautiously at first, but then stands smiling out from the screen, head bobbing from side to side as he greets his implied audience before drawing the curtain closed, an action echoed in the iris-fade to black. The circumstances surrounding the film's production, coupled with the opening scene which hints at coaxing and cajoling, may remind us of Vicky Lebeau's comments at the opening of her book *Childhood and Cinema*. Noting that 'from its inception, cinema lays claim to the child' (Lebeau, 2008: 7), she cites the image of a child, the frontispiece to C. Francis Jenkins's *Animated Pictures* (1898) in which a little girl is naked, head buried in her hands, whilst a photographer attempts to coax her into posing for him for a photograph. Lebeau calls attention to the scene's articulation of a 'pro-filmic crisis' and notes that it suggests 'the level of connivance between (early) cinema and the spectacle of the child' (2008: 7). Throughout the 1890s and early 1900s, she maintains, 'the new phenomenon of the moving pictures *moved in on* the child' (2008: 7), displaying a fascination with animating the child on screen. Early Spanish cinema was no exception with the visual representations of children on illustrations, paintings, newspaper cartoons and picture postcards now transposed onto films.[14] The name 'Pitusín' (little thing) had been chosen for its similarly to 'chiquilín' (little kid), which was how Jackie Coogan was known in Spain.[15] Mention of Coogan suggests to us now the exploitation of child stars (the famous Coogan Law which came into being as a result of the purloining of Coogan's assets by his family). But if Coogan's 'naturalism' owed a lot, at the very least mythically, to cruelty (his father famously told him, according to different accounts, that his dog had died, or that he was going to be sent to a workhouse, to get him to cry on cue), Pitusín's acting style suggests to the spectator the hard work involved in the perfection of his art. Pitusín's preparation in a Madrid acting academy charts the move of most cinematic production from Barcelona to Madrid in the 1920s. Pitusín's films draw on the potential of the child as the focaliser of emotion. *La buenaventura de Pitusín* blends comedy and pathos, melodrama and the picaresque to present the drama of a child who becomes an orphan. In *La buenaventura de Pitusín*, Pitusín is the result of the philandering ways of Jaime, a source of distress to his sister, the Marquesa de Bradomín, who eventually takes him in following the death of his mother.[16] During his adventures, he will dress as a girl to read fortunes and steal scraps from beneath a table where men are playing cards (complete with knowing wink to the audience). In a key scene of *La buenaventura de Pitusín*, Pitusín sits at the feet of his mother in a rendition of the Madonna and Child, gazing upwards at her in a way which may remind us of Janet Staiger's investigations into the acting styles of early cinema in which emotion is now conveyed through the eyes and lips (Staiger, 1985). Pitusín looks up and then casts his gaze downwards. He has short, bobbed hair (somewhat reminiscent of Baby Peggy), cute sailor suits and large, expressive eyes, designed to mobilise feelings of nurture in the viewer whilst comparisons in the press to Coogan attempted to encourage patriotic sentiment in his potential fan-base. By emphasising Prudencia's back-story of poverty alongside the sense that Pitusín's wide-eyed glances and superior acting skills are the result of hard work and professionalism on the part of Pitusín, Pitusín became the self-reflexive cinematically constructed orphan, whilst his framing in close-up consolidated the fetishised face of the child on the Spanish screen.

If Pitusín was the most popular star of the 1920s,[17] we also find evidence in press cuttings of Antoñito Cabero – who had made six films by 1927 (Anon, 1927a: 6) – and Alicia Nuri. Four-year-old Luisita Gargallo (daughter of the scriptwriter Francisco Gargallo) made Nick Winter's *La tía*

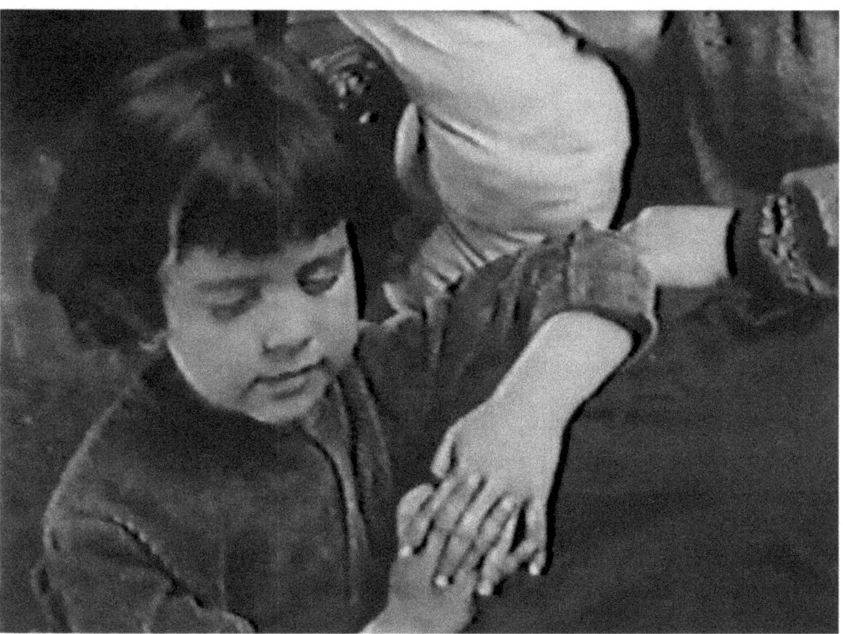

1 Pitusín (Alfredo Hurtado) in *La buenaventura de Pitusín* (Luis R. Alonso, 1924).

Ramona (Aunt Ramona) in 1927 – press pieces show her dressed in a tutu and ballet slippers (Anon, 1927b) – and Pepito España starred in *La calumnia* in 1928 (Seguin, 1990: 45). Seguin also notes Valeria de la Fuente's contribution to *Estudiantes y modistillas* (Students and Seamstresses, Juan Antonio Cabero, 1927) and the son of Francisco Beringola who starred in a propaganda film against tuberculosis, *Corazón de reina* (Heart of a Queen, 1926). *¡Muñecas!* (Dolls!, Mario Roncoroni, 1926) and *La virgen del mar* (The Virgin of the Sea, Roncoroni, 1926) were very popular films of the time starring Avelina, but they also appear to be currently unavailable.[18]

The cinema of the Republic in the 1930s produced Adolfo Aznar's *Pupín y sus amigos* (Pupin and His Friends, 1931) whilst Miguel Silvestre's *Los niños del hospicio* (The Children of the Poorhouse, 1933) was steeped in Christian lachrymosity. *Niños* (Children, 1934) by Alfonso Ponce de León and *Los héroes del barrio* (The Heroes of the Neighbourhood, Armando Vidal, 1937), inspired by Mickey Rooney's 'our gang', are other films cited by Seguin (1990: 49). *Sor Angélica* (Sister Angelica, 1934) by Francisco Gargallo was a tremendous success and starred the child star Arturito Girelli whilst also inscribing Lina Yegros as the 'dulce llorona' (weeping woman). Girelli and Paquito Alvarez were the victims of a story of child substitution (a cautionary tale against adultery) in *Vidas rotas* (Broken Lives, 1935) by Eusebio Fernández Ardavín, based on a short story by Concha Espina. In the 1930s a competition was held to find the 'Spanish Shirley Temple'.[19]

Luis Buñuel agreed to work on films for Ricard Urgoitia's Filmófono on the condition that his name did not appear on the credits for any of the films produced under his supervision, despite the fact that he directed films with Sáenz de Heredia and worked on scripts with Ugarte (Abajo de Pablos, 1996: 24). Nowadays, Buñuel is not well known as the man who attempted to introduce the 'Spanish Shirley Temple' to the world (in interviews Mari Tere speaks of her relationship to director Sáenz de Heredia although there is no mention of Buñuel).[20] Blond, blue-eyed Shirley Temple clone Mari Tere appeared in the pro-divorce film *¿Quién me quiere a mí?* (Who Loves Me?, Sáenz de Heredia, 1935) and the *españolada*-influenced *¡Centinela Alerta!* (Attention on the Watch!, Jean Grémillón, 1937), both co-directed by Buñuel – his previous depiction of children on screen had been the dead baby carried upstream and the diseased child who the narrator tells us died some days after filming in his surrealist documentary *Tierra sin pan* (Land Without Bread, 1933).[21] *¿Quién me quiere a mí?* was a commercial flop ('a film that is Spanish and European' was the tag-line and Labanyi views it as a little too high-brow for contemporary tastes), but Mari Tere's innocent face, played against the tenderness of the faces of her male leads (there is a subtext articulated here of adult actors encouraging the young star with her lines), went a long way to diffuse the implicit eroticism of scenes where Mari Tere danced for a gallery of adult male admirers: in some ways she was a critical response to the 'paedophilic gaze' that Temple inspired.[22] Labanyi also finds that this pro-divorce story has progressively 'maternal' male characters (Labanyi, 2004: 300). *¡Centinela, alerta!*, meanwhile, displayed sympathy for a single mother and victim of rape. *Carne de fieras* (Wild Beasts, Armando Guerra, 1936), a tale of adoption against a circus act, was completed under the auspices of the CNT (Confederación Nacional de Trabajadores) left-wing propaganda filmic production.

Further, 1936 saw the child used as propaganda in the anarchist CNT produced *¡Nosotros somos así!* (That's How We Are!, Valentín R. González), a surprising mosaic of set-pieced dances and songs by children interspersed with scenes of the outbreak of fighting – the main narrative is a story about the conscience-raising of Alberto, a boy who has been taught to look down on those of inferior class but who help him out when his father is arrested. A piece of left-wing propaganda for the CNT, it was produced as war was breaking out in 1936 (although filming began earlier). It begins with an array of Shirley Temple clones, including a close-up of one little girl who orders, 'Attention!': 'the tragic-comedy is about to begin/the children with their gestures/singing and dancing are looking for passion/to show the world that there is no deeper error than that of a false education'. Cinema of the time was saturated by musicals from Spain and Hollywood and this film features set pieces from children including tap dances and synchronised arrangements of their bodies to form flowers. But the film also references Betty Boop and Popeye (in blow-up figures at the back of the stage) whilst the opening credits, three men bashing anvils over a fire, recalls the Soviet cinema which Urgoitia was responsible for distributing in Spain (alongside the works of Disney). The film is a strange mixture of dance sets combined with propagandistic monologues and inserted reconstructions and actualité footage from the outbreak of war. The musical set-pieces seem mannered and contrast with the scenes of war. In one scene, children dance together in a slow local dance, dressed in folkloric costumes, the boys in caps, the girls with shawls, like miniature adults. The theme of children assuming the roles of adults is continued when the children form a mini-courtroom and spout adult rhetoric. The aim may be to compare left-wing politics to the innocent justice of children but it has an unsettling effect. As Karen Lury has noted of child actors called upon to play mini-adults, the effect is uncanny, 'the child-as-object is doing something – acting, dancing, talking – in a manner they are not meant to be able to do, thus disturbing the boundaries between child and adult and troubling the seemingly fixed distinction between animate and inanimate, object and subject. The status of the child and its body "as a thing" rather than as a subject is exposed' (Lury, 2010: 66). Adults are not seen in these sets, but their presence is felt and the effect is of the manipulation of children by adults, for ideological purposes.

¡Nosotros somos así! is quite different in tone from the Soviet-style *Aurora de esperanza* (Dawn of Hope) by Antonio Sau (1937) which focuses on poverty and civil unrest and shows the dramatic passage of Juan (Felix Pomes) from comfortable family man to leader of anarchist revolutionaries and finally to his decision to join the militia. In an early scene, Juan's son Antoñito ('Chispita') asks his father to tell him a bedtime story. A close-up of Juan's son Antoñito, clasped in Juan's arms, shows him dropping off to sleep whilst Juan tells him that:

> erase una vez un país donde existían unos hombres muy buenos que muchos llamaban malos, que veían que algunos tenían juguetes muy bonitos y otros no [...] y aquellos hombres tan buenos quisieron arreglar las cosas y la gente los insultó, los persiguió, hasta los metieron en la cárcel. [...] pero un día los hombres buenos pudieron salir de la cárcel, quitaron los juguetes a aquellos niños que tenían demasiados y los repartieron entre los otros niños pobres, que no tenían ningino. Y desde entonces en aquel país todos los niños tenían juguetes.

> (once upon a time there was a country where there were some good men that everyone called bad who saw that some children had very nice toys and others had none [...] and those good men wanted to fix things and the people insulted them, chased them and even put them in jail [...] But one day the good men got out of jail, took the toys away from the children who had too many and distributed them to the poor children who had none. And since that day in that country all the children had toys).

'Why don't we go to that country, Dad?' asks Antoñito. 'No need', Juan responds, 'there are some good men here, too, who will share out the toys'. But after months of searching for work (his wife finds work displaying underwear in a shop window but after becoming a laughing stock her husband flies into a rage), Juan will finally decide to join the Marcha de Hambre (Hunger March) and the militia. His wife stands clutching her children to her whilst her children look up towards her, signifying the future.

The outbreak of war saw propaganda films on both sides charting the progress of child evacuees. Titles such as *Nuevos amigos* (New Friends, 1937) recording the arrival of Republican refugees in the USSR and *Children of Spain* (1937) were produced by Soviet-made newsreel and British Movietone News. Similar films were *Llegada de niños españoles a Veracruz* (Arrival of Spanish Children in Veracruz, 1937) and *Niños españoles en Méjico* (Spanish Children in Mexico, 1938). *Guernika* (1937) and *Elai-Alai* (1938) by Nemesio M. Sobrevila, featuring dancing, singing children, were the most outstanding examples of these films. Other child-centred films of the period were Sáenz de Heredia's *¡No me mire usted!* (Don't Look At Me, 1941), about a teacher who hypnotises his students, *Forja de almas* (Forging Souls, Ardavín, 1942), which retold the life of a priest, Andrés Manjón, and *Lluvia de hijos* (Raining Kids, Fernando Delgado, 1947), a story of woman who attempts to pass off someone else's child as her own when her husband returns after a long journey abroad. Florián Rey's *La aldea maldita* (The Cursed Village, 1942) was an excessive, mawkish remake of his starkly beautiful silent film of the same name of 1930 (I will return to this film in the next chapter). The child here is representative of the male family line and when his mother is forbidden to see him for her sins, she turns mad. Luisito Martínez was the star of *Cristina Guzmán* (Delgrás, 1943). Most indicative of the 1940s, once censorship and state control were established, was Sáenz de Heredia's epic *Raza* (Race), released in 1941 and described as Francoism's *Potemkin* (Gubern, 1977). The iconic *Raza*, famously based on a script written by Franco himself, depicts the life of a family and the differing fortunes of the three children as war breaks out. Yarza (2004) examines the scene where the patriarch sits in the garden and tells his children about their ancestors, whilst, as Marsha Kinder eloquently notes, 'When Don Pedro solemnly tells his children, "When death calls, one must go proudly … such was your forefathers' beautiful death," his eldest son asks, "how can any death be beautiful?" The rest of the film is rhythmically punctuated with a series of aesthetic answers to this question' (Kinder, 1993: 151–152).

If this has been a tale, to some extent at least, of Hollywood clones and ideological drones, from the 1950s the *cine con niño* comes into its own. In the 1950s the angelic faces of Pepito Moratalla, Pablito Calvo, Miguelito Gil and Marco Paoletti endorsed the values of National Catholicism in the *cine religioso* (religious cinema). *Surcos* (Furrows, Nieves Conde, 1951) was promoted by García Escudero, who would later promote the New Spanish Cinema. In its neo-realist depiction of poverty and Spanish slums, it shocked the authorities and García Escudero was sacked from his post as moderator general of cinema. In the 1960s, Joselito was a singing sensation and his films negotiated the passage between the moral tones of *cine religioso* and the colour and light ushered in by Marisol's films later that decade. The 1960s also saw Rocío Durcal, Ana Belén, Estrellita and Pili and Mili as singing/dancing sensations, whilst Cristina Galbó and Pedro Díez del Coral were the stars of Manuel Summers's masterpiece *Del rosa al amarillo* (From Pink … To Yellow, 1963). The 1970s saw Lolo García's cherubic face feature in *La guerra de papá* (Daddy's War, Antonio Mercero, 1977) and in the pseudo science-fiction *Tobi, el niño con alas* (Tobi, the Boy With Wings, Antonio Mercero, 1978) at a time when cinema was enjoying the *destape*, or nakedness characteristic of films from that era. 1973 also saw the release of Víctor Erice's *El espíritu de la colmena* and Carlos Saura's *Cría cuervos* both starring the iconic Ana Torrent. Juan José Ballesta (star of *El Bola* (Ball-bearing), Achero Mañas, 2000), Nerea Camacho (*Camino*, Javier Fesser, 2008), Ivana Baquero (*El laberinto del fauno*), Fernando Tielve (*El espinazo del diablo* (The Devil's Backbone), Guillermo del Toro, 2001), Francesc Colomer (*Pa negre* (Black Bread), Agustí Villaronga, 2010) are just some of the faces fetishised on the Spanish screen in recent years.

The child, memory and cinema

Eva blends a 1970s aesthetic, evident in the clothes, cars and furniture, with a combination of retro-styled robots (the cat, Gris, who gives the impression of being assembled from old metal, the butler, Max (Lluís Homar) with reassuringly clunky efficiency) and futurism expressed as blue rays and clinking crystals. *Eva*'s 'retrofuturism' is partly a product of the director's nostalgia for the robots of his youth (*Dr Who, Close Encounters of the Third Kind, E.T.*) (Lijtmaer, Maíllo and Fernández, 2011: 6). It also has to do with Maíllo's desire to show that Spain can enter into dialogue with Hollywood science-fiction to present a new Spanish 'genre' film (publicity made much of the fact that this was 'Spain's first film with robots'). *Eva*, then, is Maíllo's cinematic 'baby'. The film's stars are Spanish and also transnational: Lluís Homar is known internationally for his work with Pedro Almodóvar, whilst Daniel Brühl, whose Spanish is as impeccably flawless as his German, was the adolescent in Wolfgang Becker's retro-inspired *Goodbye Lenin* (2003).[23] The special effects of the film won awards at the Spanish Oscars, the Goyas. Box-office takings were low but now the rights to distribute the film in the English-speaking world have been bought by media moguls the Weinstein brothers who presumably hope to capitalise on the success of recent Spanish child-centred 'genre' films such as Bayona's *El orfanato* and Guillermo del Toro's *El laberinto del fauno*. Aesthetically, the aim of retrofuturism is to allow us to imagine robots in our own homes (the discourse begun by Capek on the labour provided by robots continues now as a discussion as to whether robots serve humans or provide companionship).[24] Max dexterously prepares coffee and cleans the house but when Álex later is in need of sympathy he asks Max to turn up his 'emo-level': Max does so and gives him a seemingly heartfelt hug. The film's retrofuturism also

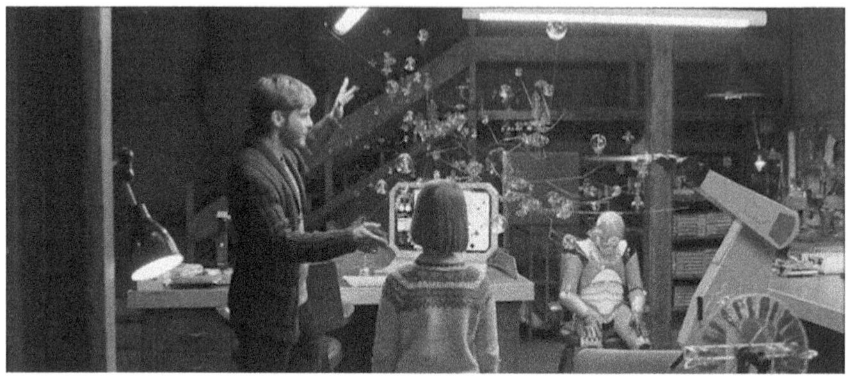

2 Alex creates a prosthetic memory for a child robot prototype in Kike Maíllo's *Eva* (2011).

underlines the melancholy of the film's protagonist. We do not know what led Álex to leave town so abruptly – an undisclosed trauma which had him cease all communications. But it will turn out that Eva is so attractive to Álex precisely because she represents the memory of his relationship with Lana and with his brother David. The film flirts with the red herring that Eva is actually Álex's daughter (it is the robot prototype which notices the similarity through facial recognition) but Eva is, of course, a blend both of her implanted memory (created by Lana and David and presumably in part therefore a product of their desires and longings over Álex), her experiential memory and finally her programmed response to Álex's own desires. Through the prototype robot, we get to see what Eva's memory might look like: this is the 'hand-up', a dazzling structure of crystal cogs, which was apparently based on the nineteenth-century diagrammatical pictures which, according to the theories of phrenology, might correspond to an imaging of memory (Lijtmaer, Maíllo and Fernández 2011: 86). This 'crystal sculpture' also resembles Robert Fludd's seventeenth-century imaging of memory, cited by Draaisma in his book *Metaphors of Memory* (2000), as one illustration of the way we are fascinated with the visual conceptualisation of memory. Eva, too, is the product of an intricate structure of interlocking, artificial memories. Eva, then, represents prosthetic memory.[25]

Alison Landsberg first put forward her theory of prosthetic memories in an article on *Blade Runner* and *Total Recall* in 1995 and she developed this in her book *Prosthetic Memory: The Transformation of American Remembrance in the Age of Mass Culture* (2004). Science-fiction, she remarks, shows a preoccupation with prosthetic memories, that is memories that are implanted but which may bear no relation to a person's lived experience (Landsberg, 1995). In the sense that memory is constitutive of identity, we all might incorporate elements of the cyborg, for mass media (and Landsberg's main discussion centres around cinema) can alter our conception of what constitutes an experience in the sense that through it a person can 'take [...] on a more personal, deeply felt memory of a past through which he or she did not live' and watching a film can add to our personal archive of experience (2004: 2). Films like *Blade Runner* allegorise this relationship between individual and prosthetic memory as they show the impossibility of distinguishing between real and prosthetic memories. In *Eva* we have similar confusions between the real and the prosthetic. In one scene, as Álex and Eva climb up a snow-covered hill, Álex tells her, 'entre tu madre y yo' (between your mother and I), 'no hay nada' (there's nothing), finishes Eva, and she continues, 'tu madre es una gran persona y muy guapa, pero lo nuestro acabó hace mucho y aunque cambio la cara cada vez que oigo hablar de ella es solo por el bueno recuerdo de los momentos que vivimos juntos (your mother is a great person and very beautiful but we separated some time ago and even if my face changes every time I hear someone mention her it's just because of the good memories of old times). 'What are you talking about?' asks Álex, 'Nothing, just saying what you would say if you were in a film', responds Eva, with a smirk. Álex assumes her knowingness comes from precociousness: in fact it has to do with her prosthetic memory. Retrofuturism also signals a memory-lapse, a gap where memory should be. The DVD extras to *Eva* contain footage (cut from the final edit), which are the back-stories of Álex, David and Lana, prosthetic memories that can be activated at the click of a button or computer-mouse.[26] At the end of the film, Eva has rebelled against her mother, Lana (she discovered by accident that she is a robot instead of a child) and pushes her off a cliff where Lana falls to her death. Eva suffers from memory loss and then, on recovering her memory, confesses to her crime. Álex de-activates Eva and the film lingers over the capacity of a robot to create feelings of love, empathy or desire. But the DVD extras also provide an alternative ending where Eva, Álex and Lana are together on an idyllic beach. Whether this dream belongs to Eva, Álex or even Lana it is clearly prosthetic. As in Landsberg's work, memory is problematised as 'essential, stable or organically grounded' as well as being 'transportable' and not necessarily related to lived experience (1995: 176).

Eva takes place in a snow-covered chronotope, distanced in space and time from contemporary Spain (although the linguistic markers suggest that this is, indeed, Spain). But preoccupations with memories lost and implanted gesture towards contemporary Spanish 'memory wars'. Spain is currently immersed in a memory boom, begun in the 1990s as a response to the sense that if a 'Pact of Silence' was tacitly agreed upon after the death of General Francisco Franco for the sake of moving peacefully towards democracy, it is now incumbent to go back and revisit the past. If the Franco regime represented the institutionalisation of the Francoist victory (the 1939 Law of Political Responsibilities, for example, enshrined the criminalisation of all those who were retroactively deemed to have been Republican supporters), the Transition saw the 1977 Amnesty Law shield any Franco era crime from being brought to trial. The 'spirit of the Transition' was based on a fear of a return both to the war and to the Second Republic which preceded it, but even as it allowed democracy to be established it also endorsed a culture of amnesia. What is now needed, according to some critics, scholars and historians, is a 'culture of memory', a process by which Spanish society confronts the legacy of its traumatic past of war, exile and repression (Ferrán, 2007: 14). The Law of Historical Memory, passed in 2007, took a step forward towards this goal, but the recuperation of historical memory is also stubbornly resisted by right-wing politicians and journalists who argue against 'reopening the wounds of the past' and breaking 'the accord among Spaniards embodied in the transition to democracy' (Escudero Alday, 2013: xii). Meanwhile, the unearthing of mass graves by volunteers takes place at weekends even as rows erupt over the rights of dead bodies. Debates rage over the politics of memory and who has the clearest purchase on the past.[27] The fabrication of a false historical consciousness in Spain (the culture of nostalgia which reproduces schoolbooks from the regime and re-releases Francoist films) is set against a desire to recuperate traumatic memory through oral testimony (and countering this, historians who believe that history can only be located in the revelation of previously known 'facts') (Labanyi, 2008).[28] Meanwhile, following the 2007 Law of Historical Memory, Francoist monuments and symbols are systematically being dismantled. At the same time, certain traumatic aspects of Spain's history have recently come to light, with more sure to follow. The child has emerged as a central figure in the politics of memory. Those who remember their dead were the children or grandchildren of those who died in the war or its aftermath which means that the child, flexibly, becomes symbolic not just of the loss of memory but also of its recuperation. At the same time, the child is often deeply implicated in the stories which are emerging. Evacuees or children orphaned by war meant that the 'niño perdido' [lost child] was a motif which circulated from the end of the war.[29] Stories of child abuse by Catholic clergy have recently begun to emerge, but also the shocking stories of how children, born to Communist families, were taken from their families and adopted by other, right-wing parents.[30] Even after the notion of the 'red gene' conceived by chief psychiatrist of the Franco regime, Vallejo Nágera, had long since failed to have any currency, orphanages and hospitals continued to practise kidnappings to use in the trade of adoptions, well into the 1980s.[31] The child is therefore symbolic not only of the loss of historical memory and its recuperation after a time-lag but also it is often a site of trauma in contemporary memory wars. We might be reminded that Landsberg's theories of prosthetic memories identify artificial memory as being like a prosthetic limb that masks a trauma. The resonances Landsberg's theories also bring of implantation seem particularly apt not just in the light of stories of child adoption for ideological reasons but also for a nation trying to come to terms with years of cultural brainwashing.

Landsberg's theories have been criticised for their optimistic portrayal of the ethics of being 'sutured' into history, where the word 'suture' may also suggest an implantation of memory (see, for example, Burgoyne, 2009). There is also the sense that film itself may substitute for cultural memories which were repressed for so long. Over time, prosthetic memories may come to take the place occupied by memory. A friend tells me that she does not remember drinking Cava on Franco's death, but the image of a celebrating nation has been so reproduced now as to make her feel that she must have done.[32] Memories of the death of Admiral Carrero Blanco are now fixed in time through images of the car bomb which were shown on Spanish television.[33] These are cathartic reconstructions of collective memory.[34] The suggestion of implantation is also useful for discussion of a regime which censored all cinematographic material in an attempt to present a seamless endorsement of the regime's ideology. It may also be an apt metaphor for children who grew up subject to Francoist ideologies. Prosthetic memory may speak to the impossibility of reaching a 'truth' about the past: memories are always already 'sutured' to some extent, and always already prosthetic.

Since the 1990s, facsimiles of childhood artefacts from the Franco regime, retro-styled *aides de memoire*, have enjoyed a surge of public interest. Films from the Franco era have been released on DVD. Whilst the DVD releases have provided a boon to the scholar of Spanish film, they also raise interesting questions about their production and reception. As Jessamy Harvey notes in her excellent review piece on some of the reproductions of schoolroom artefacts, 'as retro-cultural products they exploit their status as shared history and shared iconography'. However, she notes that, 'uncontextualised, they can elicit, therefore, any number of unchecked responses, nostalgia, anger, surprise. The onus is on the reader to be the critic' (Harvey, 2001: 115). The releases on DVD, as a response to public demand, display evidence of a nostalgia/critique for the culture of the Franco regime (or, through disavowal, a combination of the two). The aim of this book is not to analyse the memories people hold of the films under discussion.[35] Drawing on Landsberg, this book will acknowledge the potential of these films to create memories for the viewer of a time which (due to temporal or geographical restrictions), may or may not have been part of a spectator's archive of experience. It will also address questions of the relationship of the past to the present and to our sense of a place within history/memory. History and memory tend to be seen as opposites, with history implying the partial accounts of the archive and memory relying on testimony to approach the truth. Prosthetic memory implies the impossibility of truth, but through engagement prosthetic memories can nevertheless offer sites for reflection on the past.

As Neil Sinyard points out in *Children in the Movies*, the child that reaches us in the twentieth century is a shifting amalgam of the Romantic and the Freudian views of childhood (Sinyard, 1992: 7).[36] But if Ariès's groundbreaking study *Centuries of Childhood* showed us how childhood only emerged as a distinct age to be treasured in recent times (1965),[37] cinema has revealed the potential of the child to act as a motif not just for the 'other', but also for the self. Pop psychology speaks of the 'inner child', whilst psychoanalysis presents the imbrication of memory and the child in the constitution of the self (I will return to this in Chapter 3). Above all, 'we were all children once' as children's geographer Philo reminds us (2003: 7). The child therefore can be a potent motif of memory. Recent work on children's films stress the need for a 'new [cinematic] politics of childhood' (Wilson, 2005: 332) in which films or interpretations of them 'make use of cinema's potential to evoke touch, the tactile, the haptic, drawing attention to space' (2005: 332).[38] Drawing on children's geographies, scholars of film can heed the ways that films recreate the experience of childhood, through touch, sound, motor sensory movement or spatial awareness.[39] As Wilson notes, the recreation of the child's experience can impact on an adult spectator, creating a sense of 'lack of mastery'. 'Emotions felt, remembered by an adult temporarily dispossessed, also recall a child's (more extensive) lack of control over its circumstances, its environment, even at times over its own body' (Wilson, 2005: 330). The adult, 'involuntarily returns to the child's state of helplessness (motor, emotional or political)' (Wilson, 2005: 330). Or, through film, we can (inter-subjectively) return to childhood 'haunts' (Weiss, 1999: 35). David Martin-Jones compares the 'lack of mastery' in some cinematic incarnations of the child's experience to Deleuze's description of the child in neo-realism, in which, 'the child is affected by a certain motor helplessness, but one which makes him all the more capable of seeing and hearing' (Deleuze, 2005: 3). This child for Deleuze is the witness to history. But his/her wide-eyed gaze is open to suggestions of passivity in the face of history. Martin-Jones suggests that it is through the disjuncture between past and present (the adult remembering the child), in other words, through memory, that critical reflection can take place: 'this is the power of the "adult-child-seer" in these films, to at once be overwhelmed (to paraphrase Wilson, in motor, emotional and political terms) by the limit situation, and yet [...] to be aware of its historical resonances, even if the child character is not' (Martin-Jones, 2011: 81).

However, if recent scholarship has noted cinema's attempts to recreate the experience of childhood, it has also noted cinema's fascination with the child as a visual entity. Vicky Lebeau, in *Childhood and Cinema* (2008), notes how cinema has gazed at the image of the child from its inception. Cinema drew on a plethora of visual imagery of the child circulating in paintings, advertisements and postcards.[40] The child's face in particular is fetishised. It is not so much that the child is 'to-be-looked-at' (Mulvey, 1975) but rather, as Lebeau notes, that 'cinema moves in on the child' (with all the negative connotations such a phrase suggests) (Lebeau, 2008: 7). In her ground-breaking *Cinema's Missing Children*, Emma Wilson explores the ways that cinema at base expresses a desire to animate the dead child with melancholia and loss. Like Wilson (2003), I want to explore the way the cinematic image of the child comes to life. Like Karen Lury, in her excellent book *The Child in Film: Tears, Fears and Fairy Tales* (2010), I will explore the framing, construction and performance of the child on screen. In this book, the child returns us to childhood haunts, recreating the past on screen, but the child here is also at once looked at and looking, representing the self and other. It is also a story about cinema itself.

In the chapters that follow, the child will be brought to life on screen. The cinematic children in these chapters retain traces of their mechanical origins: thus they are dolls, ventriloquists' dummies, cyborgs or automata. Moreover, developing the monstrous undertones evoked by these mechanical traces (cinema as 'Frankensteinian dream'), these films, in different ways, return repeatedly to a central motif: the child's confrontation with a monster and, derivatively, the theme of the monstrous child. Through their obsessive recreation over time, the themes of the child and the monster and the monstrous child come to stand in metonymically for the confrontation of the self with the horrors of Spain's recent past.

These films thematise, then, cinema's 'desire to bring the past to life', as the prosthetic nature of cinema's confrontation with the past. There is a meta-discursivity about the theme of the child and the monster which engineers a critical distance, thereby transcending Deleuze's sense of the passivity of the cinematic child and allowing for critical reflection of the representation of the past and of the child's (our) place within it. Moreover, the return to the motif of the monstrous child allows for reflection on the legacy of the Spanish past on a nation who for so long were the 'children' of a patriarchal fantasy. Prosthetic memories, with all the negative connotations of inauthenticity and implantation that the term implies, but also the positive, ethical connotations of a spectator's ability to transcend time and space to acquire understanding, provides an interesting way to approach one's position with regard to Spanish cultural memory.

Chapter 1 will focus on the *cine religioso* (religious cinema), in particular, *Marcelino, pan y vino*. Ostensibly about the miraculous coming to life of a life-size crucifix I will explore the ways that the film explores in parallel the animation of the child on screen. The children of the *cine religioso* appear like automata, programmed to love unconditionally an absent mother. I extend this discussion into the dubbing of the child and the ways we might see this practice as a form of ventriloquism. Chapter 2 examines the Marisol films from the 1960s and the way that she was groomed by her creators to respond to and engineer the economic and cultural changes of the consumerist Spain of the 1960s. The films of Rocío Durcal, Ana Belén, Pili and Mili and Estrellita will serve as counterpoint to her tale from innocence to coming of age as she continues to make films in the period of *destape* in the freedoms of the 1970s. Chapter 3 begins with Víctor Erice's *El espíritu de la colmena* and works through cinematic memories of this film in later works such as *El laberinto del fauno*, *El orfanato* and *El espinazo del diablo*. The films are seen to gesture towards the imaginary creation of a missing child. This missing child is prescient of the recent revelations and scandals concerning missing children in the Spanish press. Chapter 4 explores adolescent embodiment through touch and fantasy and returns the spectator to the powerlessness of childhood. It also examines violence and oppressive religion as legacies of Francoism in two recent Spanish films, *El Bola* and *Camino*.

Repeatedly, then, Spanish cinema animates the child on screen and in doing so brings alive periods of Spanish history as prosthetic memories. As Spain emerges from a period of cultural amnesia towards remembrance, cinema has an important role to play in cultural memory. The cinematic child is a potent image with which to reassess our relationship to the past, and also to the present.

Notes

1 The three laws of robotics are that a robot may not injure a human being or, through inaction, allow a human being to come to harm; it must obey orders given to it by human beings except where such orders would conflict with the First Law; and it must protect its own existence as long as such protection does not conflict with the First or Second Laws (Asimov, 1983).

2 The film uses footage from a famous experiment in Stanford University of the 1960s where children were given a marshmallow and told that they could eat it but that if they chose not to, when their interlocutor returned they would be rewarded with five more. The study concluded that those who could wait would do better academically, although, conversely, those who did not wait might be happier.

3 The repeated close-ups of Claudia Vega's face replicate cinema's fetishisation of the child's face on screen. In reviews, the success of the film is seen to have depended to a large extent on the charisma of Claudia Vega.

4 Cabero (1949: 30) records that the film was shown in Barcelona in 1896. Antonio Promio was responsible for the distribution of the Lumière films in Spain.

5 Chomón is best known for *El hotel eléctrico* (The Electric Hotel, 1908).

6 Georges Méliès's 1908 *Pygmalion* has been seen as 'a metaphor for the image-maker, in other words the film-maker: the one who tries to give life to the simulacra engendered by his imagination' (Stoichita, 2008: 237n).

7 Although not strictly phenomenological, readings of spectatorship are influenced by the work of Vivian Sobchack (1991, 2004), Jennifer Barker (2009) and Elsaesser and Hagener (2010).

8 Del Toro is Mexican but *El laberinto del fauno* was a Spanish/Mexican co-production filmed in Spain with Spanish actors, thereby complicating traditional views of national cinemas defined by the nationality of the director.

9 I discuss Ana Torrent as palimpsest of memory in Wright (2013a).

10 Three recent books on representations of the child in cinema devote some attention to Spanish film: Vicky Lebeau's *Childhood and Cinema* (2008) examines Erice's *El espíritu de la colmena* (The Spirit of the Beehive, 1973) whilst Karen Lury's book *The Child in Film: Tears, Fears and Fairytales* (2010) draws on that film and *El laberinto del fauno* for her discussion of the child and memory in film. Emma Wilson's *Cinema's Missing Children* (2003) contains a chapter on the theme of the missing child in Pedro Almodóvar's *Todo sobre mi madre*

(All About My Mother, 1999). A special edition of the journal *Archivos de la Filmoteca* of 2001 presented a series of articles on the child in Spanish film in the first half of the twentieth century. It presented research on Spanish child stars of the Franco period (Camporesi, 2001; Elena, 2001; Estivill, 2001; Gubern, 2001); the portrayal of the child in the films of the *Frente de juventudes* (Cruz, 2001) and the child in the seminal *Marcelino, pan y vino* (Vajda, 1955) (Jolivet, 2001). Whilst some scholars have begun to focus attention on child protagonists such as Marisol (Evans (2004), Triana-Toribio (2003)), Joselito (Elena (2001), Seguin (1990)) or Pablito Calvo (Jolivet (2004); Harvey (2004)), considerably more attention has been accorded to Ana Torrent, star of *El espíritu de la colmena* and *Cría cuervos* (Smith (2000a); Martín-Márquez (1996); Stone (2001), etc.). A number of critics have examined children in the films of Pedro Almodóvar (Wilson (2003), Gutiérrez Albilla (2012), etc.). Santiago Fouz-Hernández (2007) has addressed 'youth culture' in films of the late twentieth and early twenty-first centuries. Some critics have begun to suggest the significance of the continued presence of the child on the Spanish screen. Rob Stone (2001) devotes a chapter of *Spanish Cinema* to 'Spirits and Secrets: Four Films about Childhood', focusing on *El espíritu de la colmena*, *El sur* (The South, Erice, 1983), *Cría cuervos* and *Secretos del corazón* (Secrets of the Heart, Armendáriz, 1997). Marsha Kinder (1993), in her seminal *Blood Cinema*, makes the claim that the preoccupation with child protagonists (and, by extension, with Oedipal plots) in cinema of the Transition, reveals unresolved tensions concerning Spain's traumatic past.

11 Admittedly attempts at generalisations as to Ventura's star persona are thwarted by the lack of material. Ventura starred in her own vehicle, *Alexia o la niña del misterio/Alexia or the child of mystery* (1914), in which a count loses his daughter in an accident and believes her to be dead, but she has survived: after many adventures she will find her father thanks to the assistance of a hypnotist (Seguin, 1990: 40). Seguin notes a later film, *Elva* (1916) about a girl suffering from meningitis, but this film is not included in the database of the Filmoteca in Madrid, which does give us *El beso de la muerta* (The Kiss of the Dead Woman, Alberto Marro, 1915), *Los misterios de Barcelona* (The Barcelona Mysteries, Alberto Marro, 1915), *El testamento de Diego Rocafort* (Diego Rocafort's Will, Alberto Marro, 1917) and *Tenacidad* (Tenacity, Baltasar Abadal, 1920). Unfortunately none of these films is available for viewing at Madrid's Filmoteca Española. Studies of Spanish early film are fraught with difficulties: it is estimated that some 90 per cent of film stock has been lost or destroyed, complicating the notion that we can revive the Spanish past through film.

12 Gaylin Studlar (2001) has observed how the woman who was really a child neutralised the threat represented by Pickford's sexuality. Sally Faulkner notes the use of adult stars playing children in Buchs's film (Faulkner, 2013).

13 For a reading of this film, see Wright (2013b), an article which compares Alexia Ventura to Pitusín.

14 For some of these images, see Borrás Llop (1996) and Charnon Deutsch (2000).

15 See Wright (2013b).

16 The Marquesa's name is presumably a reference to Valle-Inclán's Don Juan type.

17 After *La buenaventura de Pitusín*, Pitusín made a series of films as a child actor including *La chavala* (The Lass, Florián Rey, 1924), *Los Granujas* (The Rogues, Fernando Delgado, 1924), *La medalla del torero* (The Bulrighter's Medal, José Buchs, 1924), *La revoltosa* (The Mischief Maker, Florián Rey, 1924), *Amapola*

(Poppy, José Martín, 1925), *El Lazarillo de Tormes* (Lazarillo of Tormes, Florián Rey, 1924), *Malvaloca* (Hollyhock, Benito Perojo, 1926), *El pilluelo de Madrid* (The Urchin from Madrid, Florián Rey, 1926), *En la tierra del sol* (In the Land of the Sun, Ramón Martínez de la Riva, 1927), *Corazones sin rumbo* (Drifting Hearts, Benito Perojo, Gustav Ocicky, 1928), *La pata del muñeco* (The Doll's Foot, Javier Cabello Lapiedra, 1928), *Agustina de Aragón* (Agustina of Aragon, Florián Rey, 1929), *Sombras del circo* (Circus Shadows, Adelqui Millar, 1931), *Sierra de Ronda* (The Ronda Mountains, Florián Rey, 1933), *El novio de mamá* (Mum's Boyfriend, Florián Rey, 1934), *Paloma de mis amores* (Paloma of My Heart, Fernando Roldán, 1936) and *La Dolores* (Dolores, Florián Rey, 1940) (see Sánchez Vidal, 1991). He had a successful career touring with recitals of poetry and playlets and this enabled him to make the transition into talkies. He then moved into production, working as assistant director on Orson Welles's *Chimes After Midnight*, amongst others, and then directed his own films, including *Un abrigo a cuadros* (A Checked Suit, 1956).

18 See Seguin (1990: 46).

19 An article in *Proyector de Cine* in 1936 asked, '¿Existe una Shirley Temple en España?', and launched a competition organised by Films Selectos-Hispano Fox 'para la elección de la niña española más parecida a la pequeña gran estrella' (for the election of the Spanish girl who looks most like the great star). The advert which appeared in press alongside a photo of Temple agreed that Temple look-alikes would be selected by region until the final 'gran fiesta infantil' in Barcelona in February where the winner would be announced and offered either a trip to Hollywood or 5000 pesetas (Anon, 1936). Gubern and Hammond note that the prize originally went to a girl called Mary Carmen Lopez in February (Gubern and Hammond, 2012) but by May the press were announcing that Antoñita Barboso (later named Mari Tere) had won the prize-money. A picture of the contract signed by Antoñita's parents accompanied the article alongside a photograph of the seven finalists: 'it makes us think we are looking into a shop window at a parade of dolls at Christmas-time', as the article explains (Gibert, 1936: 5). For the relationship between Buñuel, Sáenz de Heredia and Filmófono, see Mortimore (1975: 180–182).

20 Mari Tere says, 'pregúntale a José Luis, y ya verás lo que te dice' 'José Luis Sáenz de Heredia?' 'Sí, mi director. Dice que hablo por los codos' ('ask Jose Luis, and see what he says', 'Jose Luis Saenz de Heredia?' 'Yes, my director. He says I talk nonstop') (Jaen, 1936: n.p.) Another interview mentions Enrique Herreros and Urgoiti, both of whom are greeted by Mari Tere, but there is no mention of Buñuel (Aguilar, 1936: n.p.).

21 See Labanyi (2004) and Gubern and Hammond (2012).

22 I will discuss Grahame Greene's revelation of the eroticism present in Temple's films in Chapter 2.

23 Pedro Almodóvar's global success has proven difficult to imitate. Alex de la Iglesia's *Balada triste de trompeta* (The Last Circus, 2010) is symptomatic of a national cinema that can have difficulty in finding international markets. Transnational star Penélope Cruz has suggested she may make films in Spain to aid the Spanish film-making industry (Anon, 2012).

24 Capek devised the word for robot from the Czech for drudgery or slave labour.

25 Sherry Turkle reflects on the way that robots' ability for companionship is changing our personal relationships. In *Alone Together: Why We Expect More*

from Technology and Less from Each Other (2011), she describes the Hasbro doll which has experiential memory allowing it to grow and learn.

26 Publicity reports that the back-stories of Alex, Lana and David will be re-inserted into the film for distribution in the US.

27 For the memory wars, see Labanyi (2006) and Ferrán (2007). Santos Juliá was instrumental in debating the repression of memory practised during the Franco regime which played havoc with the rich cultural heritage of the 1930s, and the amnesia of former Falangists who became liberals without self-criticism. But he argues that memory should be kept out of the political debates because it is subjective and private, not objective nor political (see Mate, 2010: 16–17) and Labanyi (2006).

28 See also Cenarro (2008a) on 'Francoist nostalgia' affecting certain Spanish historians who she compares to those who deny the Nazi Holocaust. See also Paul Preston's comprehensive account of the 'Spanish Holocaust' (Preston, 2012).

29 An exhibition on publicity and propaganda of the Franco era held at the Círculo de Bellas Artes, Madrid, in 2007, showed how the 'niño perdido' was used as a motif to sell insecticide in 1940. See, for example, Richards (2005) who has investigated the overlapping categories of detailed civil-war children, including those considered 'morally abandoned' (usually, the children of 'Reds') and placed into state institutions, and those who were repatriated after exile to other countries

30 On sexual abuse in Spain see Mitchell (1998).

31 See Serrano (1996), Bandrés and Llavona (1997) and González Duro (2008). Under Francoism, the children of political prisoners were given new surnames and repatriated with Nationalist families. See Vinyes, Armengou and Belis (2003) and Vinyes (2010). 'What started as a business for taking children from families deemed to be politically damaging to the regime became an illicit business that continued until the 80s' (Tremlett, 2011a).

32 See, for example, Carlos Saura's recent comments to *The Guardian* (Tremlett, 2011b).

33 We might draw parallels with the prosthetic memories of the death of J. F. Kennedy, as discussed by Elsaesser (1996) and Sturken (1997).

34 Compare the cathartic reconstruction of events leading to Franco's death in Albert Boadella's *!Buen viaje, Excelencia!* (Have a Good Trip, Your Excellency!, 2003) (Wright, 2007).

35 Jo Labanyi's oral history project is currently working towards this goal (Labanyi, 2005a).

36 For Freudian accounts see Zornado (2006) and Castañeda (2002). For the Romantic child, see Heywood (2001: 24–27). Whilst a large corpus of works devotes attention to the child as spectator (which lies outside the bounds of this study), representations of the child in cinema have a more limited bibliography. Included here are a selection: Jenkins, *The Children's Culture Reader* (1998); Ian Wojcik-Andrews, *Children's Films: History, Ideology, Pedagogy, Theory* (2007); Adrian Schober's *Possessed Child Narratives in Literature and Film: Contrary States* (2004).

37 Aries revealed how childhood began to be thought of as separate to adulthood only in the seventeenth century (1965).

38 I take the notion of this new cinematic politics of childhood from Stephanie Hemelryk Donald's excellent work on the child and migration in world cinema (2012).

39 I am grateful to Sarah Thomas for drawing my attention to the work of Owain Jones (2003) and Chris Philo (2003) and for talking to me about her work on the child and Spanish film. Kuhn (2010) uses Winnicott to recreate the space of childhood while David Martin-Jones (2011) uses a Deleuzian sense of the motor-sensory experience of cinema.

40 For the visual image of the child, see Higonnet (1998) and Holland (2004).

1

Auratic encounters with the child of the *cine religioso*

Marcelino, pan y vino (The Miracle of Marcelino, Ladislao Vajda), a pious feature about an orphan who finds a statue of Christ in an attic and takes it some bread and wine, was the surprise hit of 1955. It was based on the best-seller by José María Sánchez-Silva which had sold one hundred editions in three years and had been serialised in the publication *Ya* as well as on radio.[1] Nevertheless, when Hungarian émigré Ladislao Vajda started production on a film version no one quite predicted the runaway success it would prove to be: the film's artistic and technical teams were offered a small salary in exchange for a cut of the profits (Arconada and Velayos, 2006: 12).[2] In fact, the film was a global phenomenon, hugely popular at home and abroad, winning acclaim at the Berlin, Venice and Cannes film festivals.[3] Pablito Calvo, its child star, shot to instant fame and created the craze for what became known as the *película con niño* in which child stars became hot property to be 'fabricated, exploited or revered' (the musicals of the 1960s featuring Marisol and Joselito are the most spectacular examples of this phenomenon) (Pavlović, 2011: 118). In 1991 *Marcelino, pan y vino* inspired an Italian/Spanish remake by Luigi Comencini and a Japanese/Spanish/French anime version (scripted by Jaime de Armiñán) was released in 2000 and a version set against the Mexican Revolution in 2010 (José Luis Gutiérrez). Vajda's film now enjoys a healthy afterlife on Spanish and Spanish-language television at Easter (Prout, 2005: 71).

In the film, Marcelino (Pablito Calvo) is brought up in rural Spain in the mid-nineteenth century by twelve friars who find him as a baby on the friary steps. The friars make some half-hearted attempts to find a family to look after the child, but in the end decide to care for him themselves. One day, aged about five, Marcelino finds a life-size effigy of Christ and, deciding it looks hungry, takes it some bread and wine. The statue materialises into a flesh and blood Christ who comes off the cross and sits with the boy. When asked what he wishes for, Marcelino expresses a desire to be reunited with his dead mother. At the end of the film one of the friars finds him dead, in a wooden chair at the foot of the statue, presumably having joined his mother in Heaven. As an outer frame to the narrative, the story of Saint Marcelino is told by a friar (Fernando Rey) to a sick girl to comfort her anxious parents.

In her excellent book on the film, Anne-Marie Jolivet suggests that international interest in child-centred films after World War II (examples include Rossellini's *Rome, Open City*, 1945; de Sica's *Shoeshine*, 1946; Radvanyi's *Somewhere in Europe*, 1947 and Rossellini's *Germany Year Zero*, 1948) might have inspired Vajda to choose a child protagonist for his film (Jolivet, 2004: 26–27). These neo-realist films about the fall-out of war had transnational appeal and created a niche for films of artistic merit featuring child protagonists. *Marcelino, pan y vino* used filmic techniques (chiaroscuro tonalities, crane shots, dollies and deep focus) which were technically more advanced than other Spanish films of the era. But far from the social commitment of European neo-realism, Vajda's film fits easily with the mawkish sentimentality that defined the Spanish *cine religioso* of the 1950s. These were melodramas with religious themes which often featured child protagonists. In these films, boys (for they were always boys) were often longing for their absent or dead mothers (*El maestro* (The Teacher, Eduardo Manzanos and Aldo Fabrizi, 1957); *Cerca de la ciudad* (Close to the City, Luis Lucia, 1952) and *Un traje blanco* (The Miracle of the White Suit, Rafael Gil, 1956) follow this model) in a genre largely designed for female cinema-goers and their children. But *Marcelino, pan y vino*, the most successful of these films, was unique in its celebration of child death. In this film, the death of a child is not purported to be the tragedy that is feared by the parents of the sick girl in the story that frames the narrative proper, but rather, 'a triumphant experience for the individual and an affirmation for the community' (Avery and Reynolds, 2000: 7). Marcelino's miraculous tale survives through the generations, drawing the community together (even if, as the narrator informs us, the locals have forgotten the reason for their festivities). The Franco regime loved to institute commemorations, as 'a way to install a sense of tradition for their ideologies, and to reinforce the identity of a community through the re-enactment of master narratives' (Connerton, 1989: 70), in this case, death as a sacred and regenerative act.[4] In early Francoism, death was construed, at least for those on the winning side of the Spanish Civil War, as a glorious sacrifice against Republican barbarians (Vincent, 1999; Anderson, 2011). The orphaned children of those who had died in the war were 'often cited as symbolising the pride of the "race" and the saving of Christianity and civilisation' (Anderson, 2011: 558). Marcelino's story makes no reference to the Spanish Civil War which had ended in 1939 (in fact its cyclical view of history returns the viewer to the aftermath of the War of Independence). But the close relationship it depicts between Church and state has more to do with the 1950s than the nineteenth century. In 1953 a Concordat had been signed by the Vatican to make Spain into a 'confessional state'. If the child is central to Catholic belief,[5] it was also central to Francoist ideology, which aimed for longevity through the education of its children. By 1955 the orphan was no longer a socio-historical reality, but the rhetoric of the child orphan and child martyr continued to hold sway. Child death featured prominently in children's reading matter in the 1950s – not only were children exposed to the lives of child saints in didactic material, but such stories featured regularly in comics of the time (Harvey, 2004: 63). Books such as Gros and Raguer's *Niños santos: siluetas de vidas edificantes para la infancia y la juventud* (1954), whose frontispiece has an illustration of crowds the children being guided by child angels on their way up a celestial staircase, were standard fare. *Marcelino, pan y vino* not only fits into this context but might be said to enhance and perpetuate this worldview.

Ladislao Vajda was the son of Hungarian scriptwriter Lazlo Vajda, whose most famous collaboration had been Pabst's *Pandora's Box* (1929). But if Vajda's choice of a child protagonist concerned his efforts to emulate the artistic merit of the neo-realists of the time (such as, for example, Rosselini's *Germany, Year Zero* and *Rome, Open City*), it appears that he would not have wished to recreate the controversy inspired by, for example, Rossellini's *Il Miracolo* (The Miracle, co-scripted by Fellini, 1948) about a man calling himself Saint Francis (played by Federico Fellini) who villain-ously impregnates Nanni (Anna Magnani) who then believes that the baby she is carrying is Christ – the film was highly controversial internationally with accusations of blasphemy, although the Vatican saw it as a modern version of the miracle of the Virgin (Johnson, 2009: 249).[6] But Román Gubern posits the success of Maurice Cloche and Ralph Smart's Anglo-Italian co-production *Peppino e Violetta* (Never Take No for an Answer, 1951) as a possible inspiration for Vajda.[7] This film might provide a bridge between the socially committed neo-realist films and *Marcelino, pan y vino* in that the protagonist, Peppino (Vittorio Manunta) has been orphaned by the war and his loneliness means that he idolises his donkey (Violetta). When the donkey falls ill, he takes her to see Saint Francis, but when the authorities refuse to allow him access to the Saint he takes the donkey to the Vatican to see the Pope. Cloche's previous film, *Monsieur Vincent* (1947), a chronicle of the life of St Vincent de Paul, had won an Oscar for Best Foreign Film. Vajda once declared that his decision to make *Marcelino, pan y vino* derived from his desire not to aggravate the censors. State endorse-ment brought preferential distribution opportunities and financial prizes. But where Jolivet hints that the religious ideology behind this film might not have been shared by its director, Valeria Camporesi has revealed that Vajda had suffered from anti-Jewish legislation in Italy, after fleeing Hungary at the start of World War II – it was quite possible that Vajda wanted to produce films which would allow him to become smoothly integrated into the contemporary Spanish context where Catholic censors adjudicated on each film (article 4 of the *Boletín Oficial de Estado* of 19 July 1946 had declared ecclesiastical presence on censorship boards established in the same year and moreover these were the only members of the board to enjoy com-plete veto [Gutiérrez Lanza, 2011: 307).[8] Catholic ideologues at the time pronounced on the perceived possibilities of cinema to promote religion – as I have noted elsewhere (Wright, 2005).[9]

In *Marcelino, pan y vino*, Christ comes to life and Marcelino's life is taken away. The death-bound Marcelino and the resurrected Jesus present an eloquent dialectic of animate and inanimate, of becoming alive and leaving life, of motion and stillness. On one level, the spectator is returned to the childhood delight in animating dolls and Marcelino, a lonely orphan, is cast as the child with a big imagination who brings the effigy to life through fantasy (indeed the story suggests that the Christ figure might be seen on a par with Marcelino's other imaginary friends, the goat and Manuel (Sánchez-Silva, 1969: 44). This is a game with scale in reverse: dolls are usually miniatures but here the statue is much larger than Marcelino and he has to stand on a table and reach up to the statue in order to offer it food. As a life-size toy, Winnicott would call the effigy a transitional object (and the attic a transitional space) whose function is to manage the absence of Marcelino's mother (Winnicott, 1980). The film leaves the question of whether Marcelino is imagining things or whether he really is experiencing a miracle open until the end. But, conversely, children who saw visions were often accused of having over-active imaginations and here the miraculous is confirmed. The sense that Vajda might know the story of the moving crucifix at Limpias near Santander is suggested by the scene where Marcelino opens the window of the dusty attic and light streams through onto the face of the crucifix, illuminating its features. In a series of visions beginning in 1918, at Limpias, a crucifix was seen to move its eyes and even an arm – the first visions were by girls, aged thirteen and twelve respectively. Later, Father Antonio López, who, in a parallel to Rosellini's film, was a teacher at the local St Vincent de Paul school, was changing an electric light and was at eye-level with the crucifix, light streaming onto its face, when he saw the crucifix close its eyes (Christian, 1992: 38, 44).[10] Thus, the film might be seen as a parable encouraging devotion to material objects. Caroline Walker Bynum has shown how in the history of Christianity pilgrims visited places where material objects – paintings, statues, relics – allegedly erupted into life by such activities as bleeding, weeping and walking about. Christians were later challenged both to seek ever more frequent encounter with miraculous matter and to turn to inward piety that rejected material objects of devotion (Walker Bynum, 2011). But Franco's Spain had few such qualms about 'idolatry': Franco himself had an 'amulet': the arm of Saint Teresa which he kept on his bedside table (when he died he was surrounded by the arm of Saint Teresa, the cloak of the Virgen del Pilar and other reliquaries).

The shifting polysemy which turns in *Marcelino, pan y vino* between the secular tale of a child's fantasy and the sacred devotion to an idol establishes the magical life of things (Kuznets, 1994). Just as the love of a child is what animates the doll, it is Christ's 'divine love' that takes away the life of Marcelino. This is the Grimm view of the fairy tale: wish-fulfilment as the granting of desire to give the subject exactly what it asks for, in spite of the dire consequences. Or, conversely, the glorious display of divine power.

This is also the metaphor of cinema itself: film's ability to animate stillness and to create an aura (Benjamin, 1968a).

This chapter will concentrate on the ways that *Marcelino, pan y vino* brings the child to life on screen. The film creates an aura around the child which is very much in keeping with National Catholic ideology but, as we shall see, also prepares the nation for the commodity fetishism of the emerging period of consumerism which was 'desarrollismo' (developmentalism), known as the 'miracle years'. The child emerges here as an automaton tailor-made to activate the desires of female cinema goers and their children. In the second part of this chapter I will develop the idea of the child of the *cine religioso* as automaton by focusing on the dubbing practices which saw the child voiced by an adult female actress. The mysterious blend of the eerie in the familiar ushered in by voice is seen to corroborate recent subversive readings of *Marcelino, pan y vino* which view its aesthetics as more in keeping with the horror genre than with religious cinema – indeed this may account for the immense popularity of the film for a nation bored by the clichéd iconography of National Catholicism. The film returns us not just to childhood fear of the dark and the monsters that emerge from the shadows, but also to the game of 'Grandmother's Footsteps' or 'What's the Time Mr Wolf', which in Spanish is known as 'que viene el Coco'.[11] Marcelino's visits to the effigy draw him closer to the 'monster' before being 'caught' by him at the end of the film. As a corroboration of this subversion of the film's 'official' meanings, the voice, then, might open up a small space from which to negotiate alternative readings to the apparently seamless face of Francoism's totalitarian kitsch aesthetics.

The child's face on screen

Walking along the Gran Vía, Madrid's main cinema strip, huge billboards announced the *Marcelino, pan y vino*: one extracted Marcelino's head and had it floating in the air, suspended, rather like the image of Franco's head above the crowds in the photo-composition, 'Franco y la muchedumbre' (Franco Above the Crowds).[12] Inside the *Coliseum* cinema, watching the screen, the scale of the billboards was matched by the enormous close-ups of the child's face that the film employs, what Anne-Marie Jolivet has referred to as the 'epifanía de un rostro en la pantalla' (epiphany of a face on the screen) (Jolivet, 2004: 179).[13] Charles Affron, in his book on acting, notes that cinema is 'breathtakingly perched between the unequivocal reality of the photographic process and a style that is by definition magnifying, hyperbolic. It is as if some great mannerist canvas were suddenly animated with breathing, moving, speaking creatures' (Affron, 1977: 3–4). He reminds us that a spectator may engage as much with an actor's performance as with a character's situation. Karen Lury writes that the child actor is valued more for 'who or what they *are* – inevitably or inherently – than what they can *do*' (Lury, 2010: 150). Béla Balázs, writing of silent film star Asta Nielsen, remarks that her facial expressions are, 'like those of small children … Her face is not only the bearer of her own expression, but barely detectable (although always palpable) it reflects the expression of the other as if in a mirror' (Balázs, 1952: 65). In interview, Vajda explained that his technique with Calvo was to use mimicry, showing the boy what posture or facial expression to adopt: in fact it is Vajda's arm that we see as Christ's reaching out to Marcelino and the look of delight may have resulted from the sweets that Vajda liberally handed out (Arconada y Velayos, 2006: 18).[14] But on screen, the innocence of a child's face is mobilised to suggest the 'truth' of the materialisation of the flesh, which is never seen, but takes place off screen. The epiphanic face of Marcelino, the look of innocent delight in what Jolivet terms the 'metafísica sagrada del rostro y de la luz' (sacred metaphysics of the face and light) Jolivet (2004: 179) is used in a key scene to confirm the material presence of Christ as, hidden from our view, Christ comes down off the wooden cross to sit with Marcelino. Calvo's face fills the frame, a play of light and shadow. For Balázs, it is the close up of the child that 'brings their facial expressions and gestures so close to us that we can delight in them as a natural phenomenon independently of their role' (Balázs, 2010: 62). This is a case of 'behold the child' as much as 'ecce homo'. The close-up embodies the pure fact of representation, of manifestation, of showing 'here it is' (Doane, 2003: 91). For Deleuze, the close up 'abstracts it from all spatio-temporal coordinates, that is, it raises it to the state of Entity' (Deleuze, 1986: 95–6). This is Walter Benjamin's aura, 'the unique phenomenon of a distance however close it may be' (1968a: 224). Pablito Calvo's face on screen appears to have been 'pr[ied] from its shell' (Benjamin, 1968a: 225) in the sense that the edges dissolve and soften, surrounding the face in a halo which in turn throws light onto the spectators sitting in the auditorium.

Mary Ann Doane has noted how the discourse on the close up may eclipse its actual use in films, but here scale seems an apt way to introduce not just the monumental success of Pablito Calvo and this film, but also the 'cult of the child' of 1950s Spain with which the image of Calvo might be seen to intersect. Once *Marcelino, pan y vino* was a hit, gigantic scale was matched by ubiquity, with Calvo appearing meeting journalists, children, actresses, at Cannes – where he famously threw a bunch of flowers into the face of Grace Kelly, cried when the scissors reserved for press-cuttings were confiscated from him and carried out a photo-shoot at the beach (Deslaw, 1955) – waved to crowds from airplane steps and even received an audience with the Pope – a build up of aura outside the studio, what Benjamin would term the 'phony spell of a commodity' (1968a: 231). Calvo's face appeared on postcards, posters, sticker books, long-playing records and, according to a special edition of NO-DO, the state newsreel, devoted to 'el fenómeno de Marcelino' (the Marcelino phenomenon), on a doll manufactured in response to the popularity of the film. Before filming even began, we are told that children, their mothers and 'también la tía y la vecina' (auntie and the

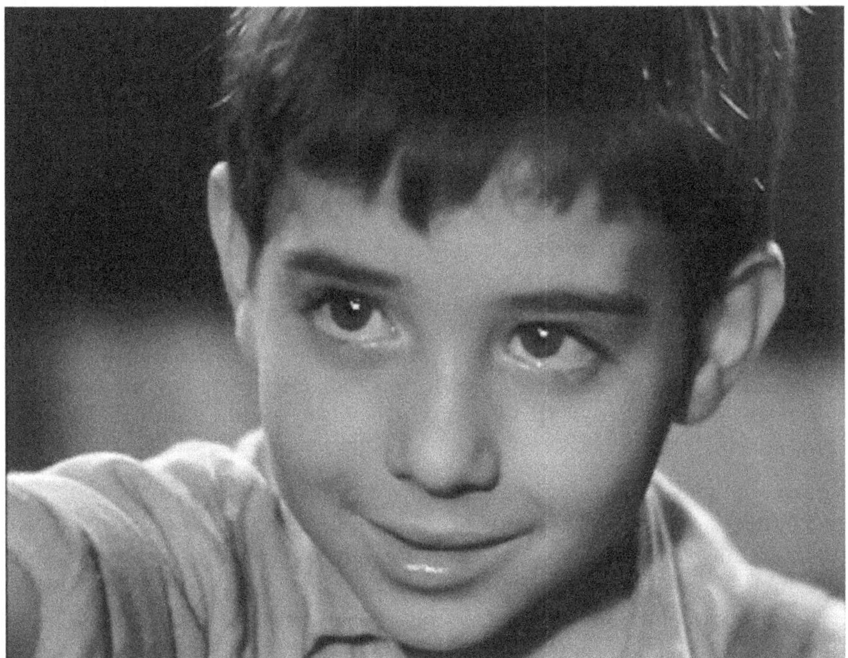

3 Marcelino's epiphanic look of delight in *Marcelino, pan y vino*
(Ladislao Vajda, 1955).

next-door neighbour, too) accompanied 2000 children (other accounts have
it at 5000 as the epic nature of this film infects accounts of it) to auditions,
all hoping to be plucked from obscurity for the starring role. The schizophrenic nature of the close-up, its counter-posing of distance and closeness
(Doane (2003) notes the desire to express the gigantic, but also to get hold
of a subject in the close-up) suggests, on the one hand, the exaltation of
the child, its special, fragile status, and on the other, that children were to
be found everywhere, providing manifold opportunities for child worship.
What it also expresses is the schizophrenia of a nation poised in the mid-
1950s between the conservative promotion of the child as a figurehead for
the National Catholic values of *primer franquismo* (pro-natalism, family
and religion) and the emergence of new opportunities for consumerism in
the era of *desarrollismo* (spending power, fame and commodification).

The cult of the child in early Francoism

A propaganda photograph, designed to celebrate thirteen years of peace
under the Franco regime, appeared alongside film articles and publicity
materials in the Francoist cinema journal *Primer Plano* on 28 September
1952. This photograph is similar to many images of Franco enjoying family
vacations with his grandchildren (or other invited children) circulating in

press and magazines and on the state newsreel. The photograph depicts the Generalísimo in a laughing embrace with his grand-daughter Carmen under the slogan, 'El día del caudillo' (The Day of Our Leader). The by-line invokes the outbreak of war in 1936 and Franco's role as 'el liberador' (Franco the liberator) against the 'sombras del terror marxista' (the shadows of Marxist terror):

> La distancia entre los días de 1936, batidos por los vientos de la lucha, y los días de 1952, queda reflejada en esta sencilla fotografía. Significativa como ninguna otra. Es una imagen para grabarla en nuestras corazones, donde la fidelidad a Franco se mantiene en un arca de constancia y lealtad.

> (The distance between those days of 1936, battered by the winds of struggle, and these in 1952, is reflected in this simple photograph. More meaningful than any other. It is an image to be engraved on our hearts, in which fidelity to Francisco Franco is maintained in an arc of constancy and loyalty).

Franco created a 'personality cult' through his messages to his subjects through, for example, the frontispieces to children's schoolbooks. Here, the infant reinforces Franco's status as patriarch and protector of the nation. The myth of childhood innocence, for James Kincaid, empties the child of its own political agency, so that it may more perfectly fulfil the symbolic demands we make upon it (Kincaid, 1992). Henry Jenkins reminds us that 'culture imagines childhood as a utopian space, separate from adult cares and worries [...] beyond historical change, more just, pure and innocent, and in the end, waiting to be corrupted or protected by adults' (Jenkins, 1998: 3–4). The impermanence of childhood is surely what associates it so firmly with the constant threat of its disappearance/corruption. Peace under Francoism was fragile because, as Paloma Aguilar Fernández (1996) has explained, it was based on the covering over of schisms. It had to be continually reinforced as time went on and the past became more distant as the replaying of the division between victor and vanquished. In this Manichean infantilising of history, childhood represents the fragility of peace obtained by Francoism, a peace that, like an innocent child, and for the sake of the child, must be constantly protected against the threat of its corruption.

Mary Nash (1994) notes that the project of pro-natalism established in the immediate post-war years to populate a flagging nation (aligning natalism with empire-building) had been abandoned by the 1950s. Conversely, access to greater economic prosperity meant a rise in fertility levels in the mid-1950s, but the continued use of contraception and the overall decline in birth rates meant that pro-natalism was considered to have failed as a policy. But the annual concession of prizes (paraded regularly on NO-DO) given to the largest families 'came to form part of the propagandist ritual attached to the figure of Franco even when pro-natalism was no longer part of official policy' (Nash, 1994: 172). The cycle of comic films beginning with *La gran familia* (The Great Family, Fernando Palacios, 1962), continuing with *La familia y uno más* (The Great Family Plus One, Palacios, 1965) and

La familia bien, gracias (The Family's Fine, Thanks, Pedro Masó, 1979), which celebrated the traditional Francoist large family, continued until the late 1970s and even if by the final film the family was having to adapt to the ideological changes post-Franco, nevertheless, the notion of the large family harked back to the *Fuero de los Españoles* of 1945, which declared that 'El Estado protegerá particularmente a las familias numerosas' (The State will particularly protect large families) (Evans, 2000: 79) with concessions and prizes. *Operación plus ultra* (Pedro Lazaga) of 1966, also starring Alberto Closas as *pater familias*, was based on the radio programmes which awarded children from around the world prizes for bravery, talent or excellence, and depicted the children as forming one very numerous, gifted, international family (in the film Spanish is the *lingua franca* which performs the important function of bringing different nations into a Francoist fold). In the 1950s, if pro-natalism was now a utopian dream, Francoist religious cinema appears to respond to its failure with a corresponding build-up of the figure of the child. In the sense that Francoism was based on conservative family values, bolstered by religious imagery, as a way to sustain patriarchy, the aura surrounding the child fitted in perfectly.

If Francoism had to do with a yearning to recover a lost mythical state of grace now brought into the realm of politics, then the child, always caught between nostalgia and the future, encapsulated this longing.[15] Children were equally well suited to the Fascist and Catholic variations of this myth ensuring continuity through the various power struggles within Francoism. Lee Edelman has shown how successive political regimes have aligned themselves with the child (his example is recent US political policy) for, as he puts it, 'We're fighting for the children, whose side are you on?' displays 'such "self-evident" one-sidedness – the affirmation of a value so unquestioned, because so obviously unquestionable, as that of the Child whose innocence solicits our defense' (Edelman, 2004: 2). In the case of Francoism, political views might be accepted by the status quo according to a Gramscian logic by which the 'naturalness' of the child made it impossible to dissent, in the sense that, 'what, in that case, would it signify *not* to be fighting for the children? How could one take the *other* "side," when taking any side at all necessarily constrains one to take the side of, by virtue of taking a side within, a political order that returns to the Child as the image of the future it intends?' (Edelman, 2004: 3). The child as the future of Francoism's future was one of the central tenets of National Catholic ideology. Franco once stated that unity and solidarity were brought about by 'the total education of children in a political creed that is based on eternal truths: the law of God, service to the Fatherland and the general wellbeing of the Spanish people' (Tusell, 1988: 135). The child was the symbol of the new Spanish state and schoolbooks were designed to aid the education of the child into National Catholic ideology to ensure the perpetuation of the new regime.[16]

If Francoist cinema might be described as an exercise in the 'mass mobilisation of affect', then the child rose up as an affective key, twinning culture and politics, exhorting the nation to protect its children at all costs (hygiene and breastfeeding campaigns used shame to discipline mothers against the threat of child mortality).[17] Meanwhile, the *Auxilio Social*, the state social welfare system, had always used images of children on its publicity posters: here the sense of working for the good of the child helped to neutralise the working classes' potential rejection of the regime by creating a cheap welfare infrastructure, whilst offering indoctrination and propaganda in exchange. As Angela Cenarro explains, it also 'fulfilled a proselytizing function by insisting that all "good Spaniards" should contribute to the care of the needy through donations, thus building the "national community" or "New Spain." According to this totalitarian scheme, welfare sought to incorporate the masses into the state; individuals were not conceived as subjects entitled to social rights but as members of a hierarchically ordered, state-controlled "national community"' (Cenarro, 2008b: 41). Thus, what was sold as a campaign to ask the public to help needy children (the orphan was the image most favoured by the *Auxilio Social*) in fact aimed to turn the nation into obedient subjects.[18]

The 'cute aesthetic'

Marcelino pan y vino is just one of many films which deploy what Jessamy Harvey has termed the 'adorable orphan' phenomenon (2004). As Harvey astutely points out, 'adorable' contains with it the notion of child worship within a Christian tradition, but it also draws on notions of 'cuteness' which Lori Merish has convincingly described in relation to Shirley Temple. Cute is designated aesthetically by 'roundness of form and thickness of limbs; roundness and flatness of face; largeness of eyes; and especially by largeness of head in proportion to the body – all attributes of the human infant' (Merish, 1996: 187). As Merish explains, the modern cult of the cute child is pure spectacle, pure display, but nevertheless 'designates a commodity in search of its mother', mobilising feelings of nurture in the viewer and 'is constructed to generate maternal desire' (Merish, 1996: 186). Thus, 'valuing cuteness entails the ritualized performance of maternal feelings' (Merish, 1996: 186), a 'peculiarly feminine proprietary desire' (Merish, 1996: 188) which stages a need for adult care. (Merish cites the advertising campaigns of Carl Naether of the 1920s who used children in advertisements to transfer maternal sentiments from the child to the commodity.)[19] The child stars of the *cine religioso* – Pablito Calvo, Miguelito Gil, Marco Paoletti, Pepe Moratalla – all children in search of mothers – correspond to the cute aesthetic. In this sense they stage the drama of maternal desire.

The films of the *cine religioso* depict all male worlds where men take over the nurturing roles for their offspring. Jo Labanyi (2001) explains that this had to do with the repatriation of men who had returned from war, by reintegrating them into family life. Thus, Marcelino is brought up by twelve friars, including Fray Papilla who stands in as mother-figure. Chispa

(Pepe Moratalla), one of two altar boys (latter day Laurel and Hardy with music Mickey-Mousing their shambolic gait) intent on securing a new bell for the church tower, is being brought up by the parish priest in *Sucedió en mi aldea* (It Happened in My Village, Antonio Santillán, 1956). In *El golfo que vio una estrella* (The Good-for-nothing Who Saw a Star, Iquino, 1955), about some children who write to God to raise money for their sick mother, Colilla (Pepe Moratalla) is cared for by the nightwatchman. In *Cerca de la ciudad*, the missionary priest sent to Madrid's shanty-towns distributes the roles of nanny, nurse, teacher and father-figure amongst his male friends and acquaintances (including a comic but tender turn from Pepe Isbert). In *El maestro*, the art teacher cooks and cares for his son before being punished for a night out dancing to jazz by his son's death. In the final scene of *Cerca de la ciudad*, the camera closes in on 'the repentant criminal father (the "good thief") in a male version of the weeping Magdalen image [...] For this is an all-male world where men redeem themselves and others by taking on the maternal caring function, literally and figuratively writing women out of the picture' (Labanyi, 2001: 37).[20]

The caring males, taking on the maternal roles, were not an invention of Francoism. Marsha Kinder has found that Florián Rey's original 1930 film *La aldea maldita* offers a variation on José de Ribera's painting *La mujer Barbuda (Magdalena Ventura, con su marido)* (The Bearded Woman, Magdalena Ventura with her Husband) (1631) which features a bearded woman with breast exposed, nursing her baby (Kinder, 1993). *La aldea maldita* is a starkly beautiful silent film which features the 'fallen mother' as a threat to the crumbling patriarchy as Acacia (Camen Viance) becomes a prostitute in town after a mass exodus in the village following a particularly harsh harvest. Her husband Juan (Pedro Larrañaga) permits her to return to the family home only so that he can maintain his honour before his blind father, but he tells Acacia that she may not even look at their son. The film relies on religious motifs to get its message across: Acacia is stoned by some children in a village when she is banished from the family home after the death of the old patriarch, but when she goes mad, trying to talk to any children she meets on her travels, her husband relents and allows her to return to her son. Rey made a remake of his own film under early Francoism in 1942 and the remake underlines the kitsch aesthetic of Francoism as the film indulges in its religious iconography. Juan's (Julio Rey de la Heras, who would later play the patriarch in *Raza*) forgiveness is depicted through his washing of Acacia's (Alicia Romay) feet. If Rey's silent version allowed for criticism of the question of honour, the remake glorified it, casting Acacia's husband as the benevolent patriarch who offers forgiveness to his fallen wife. The 'bad mother' would also feature in the 'superproducción' (lavish film production) by Cifesa in 1950, *Pequeñeces* (Little Trifles, Juan de Orduña) in which Currita Albornoz (Aurora Batista), neglects her duties to her family and, moreover, her responsibilities to provide an education for her only son (Carlitos Larrañaga, the son of Pedro, star of *La aldea maldita*).

The child in Rey's 1942 remake of *La aldea maldita* was played by a girl but the role was that of male child, representing the legacy of the patriarchal lineage. The child emerges from the *cine religioso* as a spectacle to be adored but these images are repeatedly of male children. Thus in *Marcelino, pan y vino*, a story told to a dying girl frames the narrative, but the fascination with Marcelino is revealed through the repeated close-ups of his face, scenes of him playing, resting, watching. *Cerca de la ciudad*, the aforementioned missionary film in which a priest (Adolfo Marsillach) travels to Madrid's shanty-towns to perform missionary work with the local orphans, presents a conspicuous absence of female figures, in 'an all male world' (Labanyi, 2001: 36) where the five orphans are joined by a class-full of males, are cared for by males and where, apart from a girl glimpsed behind the credits, women are largely absent. Another child star of the era was Marco Paoletti, the Italian-speaking star of *El Lazarillo de Tormes* (César Fernández Ardavín, 1959) (an adaptation of the eponymous book) and *El maestro*, in which a teacher loses his son and then meets Gabriel, a young boy who turns out to be none other than the boy Christ himself. Pepito Moratalla, meanwhile, starred in *El golfo que vio una estrella* and *Sucedió en mi aldea*, whilst Miguelito Gil found fame with *Un traje blanco* (and later *Recluta con niño* (Recruit with Child, Pedro Luis Ramírez, 1956).[21] The male child was 'watched, written about and wanted' (Steedman, 1995: 9) whilst the female child is overridingly absent.[22]

The films extol the benefits of educating boys, seeing them as 'buena tierra a sembrar' (fertile land for sowing), as Father José explains in *Cerca de la ciudad*, but girls are nowhere to be seen in that film. The regime instituted segregation of the sexes in the classroom and it is no surprise from these films to learn that illiteracy amongst women was much greater than that of men (Harvey, 2008). Co-education was morally pernicious owing to the precocious sexuality of girls. In the 1950s, in fact, arguments in favour of co-education were quashed as:

> al niño se le educa para potenciar sus facultades y prepararle para la vida dura y luchadora que ha de exigirle la formación de una familia. A la niña se la educa para ser femenina, intensificar su feminidad y ser una mujer de su casa, esposa fuerte y madre amorosa e inteligente con sus hijos.[23]

> (boys should be educated to make the most of their faculties and to prepare them for the hard struggle that will be demanded of them in the forming of a family. Girls should be educated to be feminine, to intensify their femininity and to be housewives, strong wives and loving and intelligent mothers to their children).

The relationship between the male teacher and his class of male boys is fetishised in these films. Furthermore, *Cerca de la ciudad* engages with the theme of delinquency (promotion for the film featured stills of the film's boy-protagonists, with the by-line, 'scallywag' or 'ragamuffin'). Labanyi explains that *Cerca de la ciudad* shows the regime's displacement of its colonising onto the metropolis, 'by 1952 the regime had dropped its overt imperialist rhetoric in order to court US dollars, while retaining its repressive domestic policies which conceived of the regions as colonies and of the working classes as "savages" to be pacified' (Labanyi, 2001: 31). If *Cerca de la ciudad* saves boys from the perils of 'delincuencia juvenil' (juvenile delinquency), then the boys of these films are not examples of what Francoist psychologist and eugenicist Nágera described as 'niños amorales' (amoral children) (Nágera, 1941: 247), although interestingly they do share some of the traits of his 'niños difíciles' (difficult children) (Nágera, 1941: 258), for example the 'niño mimoso' (spoilt child) who 'no tiene otra finalidad que asegurarse la satisfacción de sus instintos y deseos mediante la aparente necesidad de ternura' (has no aim other than satisfying his instincts and desires through the apparent need for tenderness) (Nágera, 1941: 266) – in the sense that these children are desirous only of reunion with their mothers. The exaltation of the male child has to do with reproductions of the Madonna and Child paradigm as an aesthetic hook, but it also means that the films practise a sort of soft eugenics. Nágera, the state psychiatrist to whom I shall return later, believed that 'race' was a 'complejo psicoafectivo' (psycho-affective complex) and that given the right environment, a child could flourish (Nágera, 1941: 228).

Overridingly in these films, these are men coping without absent, neglectful women. The appeal of Pepe Moratalla (who starred in *El golfo que vio una estrella*, *Sucedió en mi aldea* and *Cerca de la ciudad*) appears to be based on the notion that he is old before his years – he is often pictured with a cigarette hanging out of his mouth, attempts to steal the communion wine in *Sucedió en mi aldea* and indulges in all sorts of picaresque attempts to trick adults – the insinuation is that it is lack of maternal care which leads him to these practices. In *Cerca de a ciudad*, a film which deals specifically with juvenile delinquency, working mothers leave their children in Father José's crèche at the end of the film, supplying a cause (maternal neglect). The five boys in the film named José are left motherless and hungry. The priest's mother meets his many letters with stony silence.

These films return obsessively to the mother as lost object. The absent mother turns the children of the *cine religioso* into automata, programmed to love endlessly. They are like Sigmund Freud's memories of his childhood fears that his mother would disappear: he searched for her endlessly, only to finally find her in a wardrobe.[24] In these films we are not able to put a face to the mother. Yet the films address mothers through the cute aesthetic (the performance of maternal desire) and through their narratives of maternal loss. Removed from the scene, we have the sense that the mother is watching events unfold from a (celestial) position. In the aforementioned close-up of Calvo's face in *Marcelino, pan y vino*, the look on Marcelino's face confirms the presence of Christ but also confirms that of the spectator – the halo of light bathes us in light which literally brings us in from the dark. The light touches us as we caress the image of the child. In an impossible embodiment the spectator is locked in a celestial embrace with the child on screen. This is 'appropriation in the guise of an embrace' (Merish, 1996: 186), for the cute aesthetic ensures that this is a maternal spectatorship (whatever the class or gender of the spectator), activating an 'erotics of maternal longing'. The religious paradigm invoked is that of the Madonna and Child and several films depict this visually, particularly *El maestro*, in which a child takes up a position beneath a statue of the Virgin. But here the mother has ducked 'out of the frame and out of the framework of motherhood' (Mavor, 1996: 60), emphasising maternal absence as neglect. These are orphans (motherless children) and so the child is already lost to the spectator, and suffused with longing and desire.

Marcelino, pan y vino contains a sequence in which we see Marcelino at play, up to mischief or sleeping, which recalls the obsession with photographing the child. There is a poignancy about these images: perhaps Mavor is right when she suggests that 'both the photograph and childhood accept their shape and their poignancy from death' (Mavor, 1996: 5). In the sense that the child stars of the *cine religioso* are already lost to the spectator, their images become attempts to animate them through celluloid (Wilson, 2003). There is the sense that the image of the child is a fleeting capturing of an image in motion: the child is constantly changing, perpetually moving towards death – the practical problems facing the growing child star would be later addressed in a press article by Jaime Blanch and Pepe Moratalla (Morales, 1961).[25] The loving gaze directed at Marcelino and the other child stars as they sleep recalls the old funerary tradition of photographing dead children. This tradition attempts to make the child seem alive once more and, within a Christian tradition, suggests everlasting life (Mavor, 1996; Wilson, 2003). Marcelino is a child who is always already dead, the images of him are shot through with poignancy.[26] The mother invoked here is the *Mater dolorosa*, weeping for her suffering child, which suffuses these films with lachrymosity.

The films of the *cine religioso* are awash with tears. Alejandro Yarza (2004) has written convincingly of Francoist films' brand of kitsch, its bank of crosses and tears. Using the example of *Raza*, the film scripted by Franco himself, he argues that Francoism employed kitsch to get across ideological messages. Yarza cites Milan Kundera's definition of kitsch as 'two tears flowing in quick succession, the first tear says: How nice to see children running on the grass! The second tear says: How nice to be moved, together with all mankind, by children running on the grass! It is the second tear that makes kitsch kitsch' (Kundera, 1987: 251). All crying, arguably, involves a sense of the performative, but it is the second tear that joins one with the rest of humankind and in the sense that Francoism represents a desire to regain an originary state of grace, it is the second tear that performs a recognition of this. Kitsch, then, was fundamental in the Francoist attempts to sway its populations ideologically. As Yarza writes, 'Francoism understood, to its advantage, the fetishistic nature of the cinematic apparatus, whose ultimate goal was to produce a submissive and unified cinematic subject who, by identifying with the camera's point of view, would identify with the state's ideology' (Yarza, 2004: 51). For Kundera, 'the feeling induced by kitsch must be a kind the multitudes can share. [...] it must derive from the basic images people have engraved on their memories: the ungrateful daughter, the neglected father, children running on the grass, the motherland betrayed, lost love' (Kundera, 1987: 251). The films of the *cine religioso* mobilise kitsch through their child protagonists. This is kitsch as stock reference, as cliché. Tomas Kulka writes that 'children in tears' are one of the clichés of kitsch, carrying an emotional charge: 'this emotional charge does not just typically occur in kitsch: it is a sine qua non' (Kulka, 1996: 27). Kulka offers some advice to the painter who attempts to paint a crying child:

> Our painter should be advised to choose a nice and cute little child rather than a wicked or ugly-looking one. The cry shouldn't be hysterical, but rather a sob of the soft and quiet variety; the child should elicit a sympathetic response. The painter should avoid all unpleasant or disturbing features of reality, leaving us only with those we can easily cope with and identify with. Kitsch comes to support our basic sentiments and beliefs, not to disturb or question them. [...] Typical consumers of kitsch are pleased not only because they respond spontaneously, but also because they know they are responding in the right kind of way. [...] Kitsch always plays on the lowest common denominators. (Kulka, 1996: 27).

Kulka goes on to cite John Morreall and Jessica Loy on cuteness in kitsch: 'eyes set low in the head, a large protruding forehead, round protruding cheeks, a rounded body shape, short, thick extremities, soft body surface, and clumsy behaviour. The manufacturers of dolls, children's books and greeting cards exaggerate all these features to elicit positive response from customers' (Morreall and Loy, 1989: 68). This is the brand of kitsch mobilised by the *cine religioso*, a kitsch aesthetic in the feminine mode, which recalls the cute, Romantic images of the child which circulated on advertisements and postcards of the time.

These *tableau vivant* from religious paintings serve almost to freeze the action, framing the child as an image of beauty. Thus *Un traje blanco*, about a boy's attempts to procure a suit for his first communion, features a scene in which Marcos and Polonio, the two child protagonists, sit, heads in arms in the eaves of a barn – a recasting of the cherubs from Raphael's *Sistine Madonna*, which, as Higonnet has written, became 'detached from the theological context, extracted from a religious painting and turned into single or double cherub portraits. Reproduced on their own, they were transformed from adoring sacral witnesses into adorable roly-poly babies' (Higonnet, 1998: 39). The dimpled boys in *Un traje blanco* discuss whether Polonio looked like an angel when he took first communion in a white suit: 'te faltaban las alas pero esas van detrás' (you're missing wings but they go behind), remarks Marcos. This is a self-conscious reference to the rendering of the child protagonists as religious cherubs. The culmination of this cliched reproduction of the child comes in *El maestro* when the final, startling, scene in which the teacher is led by the boy, Gabriel (who we have been told is the son of a carpenter), to a church. Upon entering he finds the boy having assumed a position beneath the statue of the Virgin Mary, thereby converting it into a portrait of Madonna and Child. This is 'sweet kitsch', which is sentimental, associated with 'superficiality, saccharine sweetness and the manipulation of mawkish emotions' (Solomon, 2004: 236). Notably, a review of *El maestro* speaks of its being 'slow as molasses and twice as sticky' (sweetness is associated with this imagery, in Bourdieu's sense of taste, a point made by Merish about the cute aesthetic).

Writing about 'cuteness' in relation to dolls and other merchandise, Daniel Harris questions our desire for the 'aura of motherlessness' (Harris, 2001: 5) which surrounds cuteness. He remarks on the tendency towards cute dolls who have suffered some deformity: 'cuteness is not something we find in our children but something we do to them. Because it aestheticises unhappiness, helplessness and deformity, it almost always involves an act of sadism on the part of its creator' (Harris, 2001: 5). Cuteness, then, is not based on ideals of beauty, but is grotesque. It is interesting to note, therefore, that cuteness relies on similar images in the *cine religioso*. In *Un traje blanco*, for example, Marcos loses his arm in an accident when he is working picking slag to make money to buy his communion suit. In the final scene of glory as he parades down the aisle of the church, resplendent in his communion suit, part of the sympathy he elicits is achieved through the sight of his empty sleeve trailing beside him. The repetition of these images of helpless, mutilated boys hints at the grotesque nature of Francoism's desire for its subjects: parents and children are locked into a grotesque state of prolonged and infantilised longing.

The child and commodity culture

The cute aesthetic presents the child as aesthetically already lost, and yet provides practical solutions as to how to rescue the child. In a nation portrayed as existing in a perpetual state of longing, the solution seems to be to go out and shop. Thus, *Sucedió en mi aldea* toys with the notion of buying goods on credit (but the altar boys discover that it is not possible to buy a church bell on credit – moreover this is a world that is closed to them without the signature of an adult) and then proposes the buying of a lottery ticket as a way to solve economic hardship. Finally, it is the boys' goodness which reaps rewards: they buy the church bell with the lottery winnings and donate the rest to charity, but when one of the boys falls ill it is the connections they have made and the way that their story touches others which ensures that the medical bills will be paid. In *El golfo que vio una estrella*, Colilla is a sceptic ('el catecismo – así no hay progreso' (there's no progress with the Catechism) – he remarks at one point) but eventually experiences a religious conversion due to the guilt he feels at not having helped the two children to find money to pay for their sick mother's medicine. His guilt is expressed through a nightmare (a montage of close-ups of the face of the little girl, superimposed with flickering candles) whilst his conversion relates back to a scene of the nativity that he saw in a shop window. When the children receive help, Colilla suggests that it means that God has forgiven him, but notably the solution is provided by secular means: the children write a letter to God (the plot focuses on their attempts to raises enough money on the Madrid streets to pay for the stamp) and when it is read by the postal workers, the post office gathers together enough money to present the children with the necessary funds (notably they were impressed not just by the children's faith in God, but also by their faith in the postal service). In *Cerca de la ciudad*, it is likewise the charitable act of an individual which provides the necessary funds for the priest to open a school, nursery and orphanage – the spinster donates her mansion to the cause. This view of childhood is similar to that suggested by Holland about images of children on advertisements for charitable causes: orphans whose innocence appeals for help from prosperous benefactors (Holland, 2004: 148). Interestingly, none of the films endorses wholeheartedly the hand of God in the working of miracles. Rather, religion is presented as something which children in particular, but also adults might believe in to achieve goodness (this is true even of *Marcelino, pan y vino* where his reunion with his mother/God may be a figment of his imagination). Far from having been born into original sin, these children chime with the Romantic view of childhood innocence and goodness: the challenge for society in these films is to maintain goodness in the face of economic hardships.

Un traje blanco starring Miguelito Gil, famous for the comic-sweet *Recluta con niño*, draws on nascent improvements in the economy in the mid-1950s to encourage its nation to go out and shop, giving a religious affirmation to both splurging on unnecessary commodities and giving in to pester-power. Thus the plot centres on a boy's attempts to buy a white communion suit to fulfil his dead mother's wishes. Rejecting all cheaper versions as inferior, Marcos experiences an epiphany in the changing room of the department store Galerías Preciados, when he views himself in the white suit.[27] The scene articulates the aura which commodity fetishism bestows on products – here the suit appears to glow with its own halo. This is a very different treatment from the attempts to buy a suit in *La gran familia* of 1962. Here, when one of the boys, *el petardista* (the one who sets off fireworks), spills food on his shirt, his sisters mock him by saying that he has already found a communion suit with decorations. Later, in the department store, upon finding that she does not have enough money to buy the suit his mother remarks only that she will return another day to buy them and she tells the children that they will be arriving later. The carnivalesque irreverence of the earlier scene is reinforced when later, after the communion during the family party, *el petardista* goes down to the kitchen and covers his immaculate suit in cake-mixture. Within the film, these scenes are contained as examples of the affectionate anarchy of young children (indeed the film's drama turns on the moment when the youngest child goes missing and the love of a mother who knows exactly what he was wearing in spite of the fact that she has fourteen other children to care for), but when viewed against the reverence shown by *Un traje blanco* towards the white suit, they seem transgressive.[28]

In *Un traje blanco*, Marcos's poor father, at risk of seeming uncaring in the face of the material needs of his son, swallows his pride and attempts to borrow a suit from a local family, but to no avail. When a travelling circus comes to town, Marcos and his best friend Polonio, steal a white suit worn by a circus dwarf but soon reject it as a worthless imitation. They ask the 'Reyes' (Three Wise Men) for a suit but are rewarded merely with a drum and whistle. Finally, Marcos goes out to work, in secret, at night, picking coal from slag, in an attempt to make money for the suit. He is involved in an accident and loses his arm. His story captures the attention of the world media who report Marcos's plight and he is rewarded with thousands of suits, sent from all over the world by sympathetic rich people. In the final scenes we see Marcos enter a room glowing with the merchandise, a consumer's paradise. He then takes first communion in a church bathed in light with accompanying rousing music – as the spectral altar boys from an earlier scene suggest – his mother is watching him and his union with her is now complete.

The film may be readying the evolving commodity culture, preparing nation for the notion of entry into the international economic mainstream and international trade by suggesting sympathetic foreigners all engaged in shopping beyond its frontiers (notably most of the carefully packaged items arrive by plane). But mainly, the film borrows from the pleasures of shopping (in one scene Marcos and Polonio go into raptures over the feel and look of the cloth of the suit, its buttons and lapels), articulates the conferment of value to be had by commodity fetishism (the pleasure of mother and child in the buying of goods). In Marcos's dream on the night before, he hopes to be rewarded with a suit by the 'Reyes' – a spectral, 'orientalist' black and turbaned figure (as in, for example, Murillo's *Adoration of the Magi*, 1660) with his luxurious robes floating around him – who enters through the window and leaves the precious suit for Marcos. This figure resembles a costumed mannequin from a department store window at Christmas (in the 1950s Galerías Preciados organised competitions to write to the Reyes Magos which were later reproduced in the press, documented in photographic exhibitions and visited by huge numbers of people (Toboso, 2000: 241)). It also suggests the exotic possibilities of shopping in department stores which engage in international trade for mothers who wish to bring about magical transformations in the lives of their loved ones. As Merish writes, the cute aesthetic (here mobilised by the child at Christmas time) is a 'feminine mode' which 'demands a maternal response and interpellates its viewers/consumers as "maternal"' (Merish, 1996: 186).

Merish explains cuteness according to Doane's 'commercial structure of "feminine" consumer empathy, a structure that blurs identification and commodity desire' (Merish, 1996: 187, citing Doane, 1989). The film celebrates the city as providing opportunities for commodity culture but more importantly, also implicitly suggests the 'emotionally priceless' status of the child. As Victoria Zelizer has written, children underwent a 'profound transformation' during the nineteenth century, from a family member who went out to work to aid the family economy, to an economically 'worthless' but emotionally 'priceless' figure which supplied love and emotion in return for the money spent (Zelizer, 1985). *Un traje blanco* shows the dangers of allowing the child to work, graphically illustrating the potential emotional costs involved.[29] *Un traje blanco* celebrates commodity culture even as it exalts the pricelessness of the child.

Dubbing Marcelino

As Anne-Marie Jolivet explains, in her extensive guide to the film, *Marcelino, pan y vino* is orchestrated through the voice telling the miracle of Marcelino to a dying girl and her parents:

> cuando empieza a contar y se inicia el *flash-back*, el ritmo de los planos borra las huellas de la enunciación puesto que la voz del narrador diegético pasa *en off* desde el plano cercano de la niña y desaparece luego dejando hablar las imágenes. La *voz en off* estructura el relato y marca hitos narrativos. Conforme avanza la historia se vuelve cada vez más "abstracta"; al final sólo el régimen alocutivo de los pronombres mantiene el recuerdo del narrador diegético y de sus tres oyentes los que se unen e identifican naturalmente los espectadores. (Jolivet, 2004: 50)

> (when he begins to tell the story and the flash-back begins, the rhythm of shots erases the traces of enunciation given that the voice of the diegetic narrator becomes a voice-over from the close-up of the girl and then disappears letting the images speak for themselves. The voice-over structures the story and marks the narrative. As the story advances it becomes more and more abstract, at the end only the alocutive regime of the pronouns retains the memory of the diegetic narrator and of the three listeners thereby uniting and enunciating the spectators).

This voice is not, however, an example of Chion's *acousmêtre*, the disembodied voice that apparently has no origin and yet is powerful and ubiquitous. In this case, we see the origin of the voice in the body of Fernando Rey (who had begun his career as a dubbing actor and who was well known in the 1950s for his voice-overs) – Rey, clad in a black habit, disappears during the telling of Marcelino's story but reappears at the end at the end of the film, offering a connection between body and voice. This is important, because as Chion points out, voices seek bodies, or in other words the impossible embodiment of the acousmatic voice (the voice without a body) produces unsettling, uncanny effects (Chion, 1999).

In the pivotal scenes of *Marcelino, pan y vino*, Marcelino enters the attic (which he had been warned not to enter by Fray Papilla) and discovers the resin statue of the crucifixion. After deciding that the statue's gaunt face means that Christ is hungry, on the second meeting, we watch as the fleshy hand of Christ, which once had been wood, starts to twitch and then move, together with rousing orchestral accompaniment, towards the bread held out for him by Marcelino. On the third meeting this scene of transubstantiation (materialisation of the body of Christ) is reinforced by the timborous voice of Christ (the dubbing artist José María Ovies) which asks Marcelino, '¿No te doy miedo?' (Aren't you afraid of me?). The term 'acoustics' has its origins in the disciples of Pythagoras, who had to listen to the voice of their Master who was concealed behind a curtain, so that the sight of the speaker did not distract from the message (Chion, 1999: 19). Chion explains that 'the interdiction against looking, which transforms the Master, God or Spirit into an acousmatic voice, permeates a great number of religious traditions' (Chion, 1999: 19) and as Dolar writes, 'in the Old Testament God often appears as an acousmatic voice' (Dolar, 2006: 62). The camera-work in the film may echo this impossible embodiment: as we are aligned, on Marcelino's second meeting with the statue, with what is purportedly Christ's point of view. It is more usual for the spectator to 'overhear, unseen' (Doane, 1985: 169) the diegetic action from an extra-diegetic space. But here the as-yet-unseen Christ assumes our frame of vision as his own and embodiment occurs somewhere neither inside nor outside the screen, uniting spectator and divine voice in a sort of spectatorial ventriloquism.

Connor has shown how in cinema the eye can supplement the ear, either in the process of aural asking and visual answering identified by Rick Altman (1980) (the sound says 'where?'; the visuals say 'here'), yet 'it is also possible for the ear to borrow and internalize some of the substantiating powers of the eye, and to mould from them a kind of sonorous depth, a space sustained by and enacted through the experience of sound and hearing alone' (Connor, 2001: 21). As Elsaesser and Hagener have pointed out, sound is a spatial phenomenon (unlike the flat image), which 'gives film a "body"' (Elsaesser and Hagener, 2010: 137). Chion has written that the voice wanders across the screen and demands to be screwed onto a body. The body of Christ is fleshed out by the voice, the 'word made flesh', the disembodied voice allows us to create depth out of the severed hand and shabby chair worn over time with the bulk of successive bodies.

However, there is another voice in this scene, the voice of Marcelino, whose effects have gone unremarked by scholars. Whilst the image is provided by child star Pablito Calvo, the voice is that of the then thirty-year-old female dubbing artist, Matilde Vilariño.

The dubbing of children in cinema in Spain dates back as far as the introduction of 'talkies' and the divisive effects of foreign language films. In 1941 legislation was passed which banned the screening of film in any language

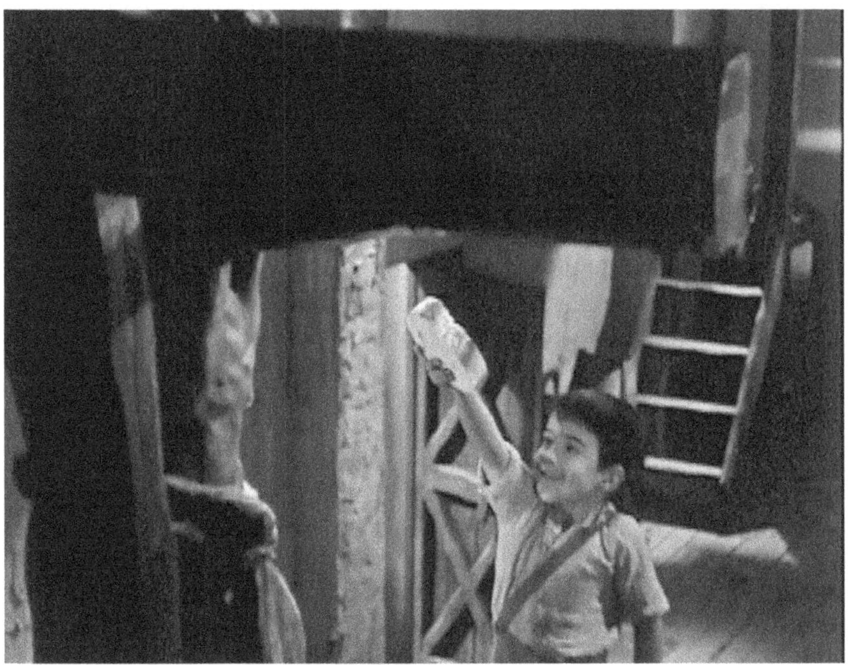

4 Marcelino offers bread to the crucifix in *Marcelino, pan y vino* (Ladislao Vajda, 1955).

other than Castilian (this was an attempt to promote national cinema but also to outlaw films made in languages such as Catalan). This meant the death of subtitling and the hegemony of dubbing. The irony of this was that a law designed to promote national film production functioned to allow foreign films to reach the masses in a way that would not have been possible through subtitling (Ballester Casado, 2001). Ana Ballester Casado suggests that the entrenchment of dubbing in the Franco era in Spain may have been due to economic factors (the creation of jobs for dubbing actors); social factors (a large proportion of the audience was illiterate) and political factors (dubbing allowed censors to manipulate the texts in ideological terms with changes to the script) (Ballester Casado, 2001). Even for Spanish films, the recording of direct sound was expensive, leading dialogues to be post-synchronised in the studio. Children were often chosen for their looks whilst their ability to perform in the dubbing studio could not always be relied on. It was therefore not uncommon for child stars to be dubbed by adult female actresses. In the 1980s, Steven Spielberg famously demanded that *E.T.* be dubbed into Spanish by child stars rather than adult actresses, whilst Ana Torrent captivated audiences with her own voice in *El espíritu de la colmena*. But Lolo García was dubbed in his films in the 1970s and in fact the practice is widespread and continues in the twenty-first century: a production of *El florido pensil* (The Flower-Filled Garden, Juan José Porto) of 2002, for example, used an actress where the voice of a child star was found to be unsuitable in the editing suite.[30]

In *A Voice and Nothing More*, Mladen Dolar explains that we tend to overlook the voice, hearing the message and not the medium. He advocates a concentration on the voice in terms of, 'an object which does not go up in smoke in the conveyance of meaning and does not solidify in an object of fetish reverence, but an object which functions as a blind spot in the call and as a disturbance of aesthetic appreciation' (Dolar, 2006: 24). It is in this sense that the child's voice might be listened to, not in the metaphorical figure of speech connoting agency and power, but in the sense of the disorientating aesthetics produced by the dubbing of a child's voice.

James Lastra notes that far more important than fidelity of sound to source is the *effect* of 'correct' sound produced during synchronisation (Lastra, 2000: 147) (his example is coconut shells for horses' hooves and metal sheets for thunder). But dubbing operates in a different way. The voices are miked for maximum clarity. The audience at a dubbed film is well aware that it has been dubbed in a studio by actors who are mimicking facial expressions, emotions and words (a post-synchronous doubling, whether or not foreign translation is involved).[31] The dubbed sound takes up an ambiguous spatial dimension: its source is knowingly extra-diegetic and yet it inflects what we see in the diegetic fiction.[32] A series of articles in the pro-Franco cinema magazine *Primer Plano* documented the ongoing debates on dubbing (arguments were mainly centred on whether dubbing helped to preserve Castilian) in the 1940s and into the 1950s, suggesting a heightened awareness of dubbing processes.[33] In 1943, an article had shown readers a dubbing studio, noting the incongruity of the cigar-smoking man (who had dubbed Weismuller in *Tarzan*), required to produce the sound of a baby crying: 'El Director: ¡Llore más fuerte! El caballero berrea' (Director: Cry louder! The man howls) (Mejías, 1943: n.p.). The LP released in 1955 featuring songs from *Marcelino, pan y vino* states clearly that Vilariño provides the voice of Calvo. But this seems to be a different case from that of Indian national cinema where, as Neepa Majundar points out, despite anxiety regarding 'ghost voices' (dubbing actors recruited for their singing talents) in the 1940s, during the 1950s the singing voice became recognised in itself. The child star system worked hard in Spain to keep dubbing artists in anonymity (dubbing retains its anonymity today, despite some recognition – there are no awards for dubbing at the Goyas, for instance). Sélica Torcal, for instance, was not credited as having provided the voice of Marco Paoletti in *El maestro*, nor in the commercial success *El Lazarillo de Tormes* (Ardavín, 1959), featuring the same actor, as the Italian-speaking child star Paoletti went on tours to publicise the film. It was only much later that dubbing stars would be recognised as a recent documentary (Alfonso Suárez's *Voces en imágenes*, Verité, 2010) testifies. It is generally assumed that the anonymity of dubbing artists went hand in hand with attempts by Francoist censors to edit Hollywood films through the dubbing of their dialogue (as we have seen, the practice pre-dates Francoism) but anonymity pervades the profession. An episode of the afternoon show *¡Qué vida tan feliz!* (30.01.2011) on Telecinco with María Teresa Campos dedicated to child stars mistakenly attributed the voice of Calvo to Matilde Conesa. Just as dubbing stars today become attached to certain Hollywood stars, so Matilde Vilariño, Sélica Torcal and others are now recognised voices for the portrayal of child stars. In the 1950s they may have had recognisable voices, but these adult female actresses would not be known as stars themselves until much later: thus audiences and critics alike operated in a kind of collective disavowal. Indeed, in an article of 1957 from *Primer Plano*, hidden within a section of Mexican cinema, we find the question, '¿será cierto que no es la propia voz del dulce y tierno Pablito Calvo voz de Marcelino la que escuchamos en la pantalla? Se comenta que es la voz de una mujer la que dobla al famoso niño. Por cierto que ha desilusionado un poco al público' (can it be true that we don't hear Pablito Calvo's own sweet and tender voice on screen? It is rumoured to be the voice of a woman dubbing the famous boy. This certainly has disillusioned the public a little) (M. Ceja, 1957: n.p.). This awareness of the inauthenticity of the sound, which purports to be the phonology and sonicity of the 'grain of the child's voice', is here conceptualised as a fall from grace.[34]

In an article of 1933, 'Les Souffrances du "dubbing"' (The Torments of Dubbing), Antonin Artaud appears to be writing a vindication of the work of French actors forced to sell their voices for a pittance to American film companies preparing their productions for the French market. But a closer reading reveals that his real target is the process of dubbing itself. Artaud had been working on a screenplay called *The Dybbuk* (a folkloric character who inhabits the body of someone who has died and speaks through their mouth) (Yampolsky and Joseph, 1993). Artaud was interested in the split between voice and body articulated in dubbing – he saw in the fanatic attention to the micro-movements of the mouth, which the spectator cannot help but engage in, the way that the actor's body assimilates that of another in a process of devouring. Derrida (1978) glosses Artaud's words to articulate *différance*: there is a delayed repetition involved in dubbing where the voice is both stolen and prompted (Derrida, 1978: 179). Artaud is writing of dubbing that occurs between two languages. But in the lips of the child star, animated by the female voice, we find a similar process of devouring, a similar awareness (however much disavowed) of the assimilation of one body by another, and at once a theft and a prompting of the child's voice. In an attempt to reverse the tyranny of the image in film criticism, Altman has written that in film we should view the soundtrack as the ventriloquist and the image as the dummy (Altman, 1980). In the case of child stars dubbed by female actresses, it is hard to escape the uncanny sense that we are witnessing a ventriloquist throw her voice to a dummy.

Mary Ann Doane explains that film reconstitutes a body, a fantasmatic body composed of the welding of voice and image, she maintains that 'sound carries with it the potential risk of exposing the material heterogeneity of the medium'. She writes of 'attempts to contain the risk' in which sound is 'married' to the image in order 'to make the screen look alive in the eyes of the audience' (Doane, 1985: 163). But in what ways can child-dubbing threaten the integrity of the fantasmatic body, and what lengths do individual films go to in order to contain the risk or to manage the impurity presented by the dubbed child?

In *El Lazarillo de Tormes* (César Fernández Ardavín, 1959), we open to a close-up of a man's face – this is the eponymous Archpriest to whom, in the written tale, Lázaro the man tells his story. It is implied that Lázaro has now become the concubine of the wife of the Archpriest in return for material comfort. Ardavín's film is a Catholic remaking of the picaresque tale, and rather than the sordid tale of adult sexual affairs, the voice-over we listen to is that of the boy, Lazarillo, supposedly telling his life-story to the Archpriest out of a desire to renounce his sinful trickery. The effect of the female voice, purportedly belonging to the boy, over the face of the Archpriest is disconcerting. When we see the boy, Marco Paoletti, the incongruences continue. Paoletti is obviously mouthing words in Italian which are dubbed in Spanish. But the eruptions in the micromovements on Paoletti's face are somewhat contained by the story-line which features two blind characters, one at the start of the film (his first blind master) and one at the end (a blind beggar girl) who verify Lazarillo's identity by his voice. Notably, in the case of the blind master, the story hinges on the success or otherwise of Lazarillo to dupe his master regarding his actions – but his voice manages to screw the voice onto his body.

In *El maestro* meanwhile, the voice of Gabriel (Marco Paoletti) is made to seem more natural in contrast to that of a stuttering boy who is told to place pebbles in his mouth, which only serves to make him even more unintelligible. The odd sense that Gabriel's voice may in fact be that of a woman is also naturalised within the plot. Although religious in theme, the film is a supernatural tale in which Gabriel appears to be sent from the other world, a direct emissary from the teacher's dead wife. Thus, the dubbing merely accentuates the sense that the teacher's wife is speaking to him from the dead, speaking through the body of the child to encourage him to find peace. Finally, any strangeness contributes to the otherworldliness of this character for Gabriel is none other than the child Jesus Christ – at the end of the film he takes up a position as Child to the statue of the Madonna. This in itself is such an uncanny scene that the strange effect of the voice merely adds to the disorientating mood – we cut quickly to a view of the teacher awaking from a deep sleep – perhaps, after all, the whole thing has been no more than a dream.

Un traje blanco presents decoys (a shop-window dummy; the dwarf at a travelling circus) who wear the sought-after white communion suit, but ultimately the sub-text in the context of magical transformations suggested by the Reyes Magos and finally wrought by spending power is a Pinocchio-style search for the real boy embodied in Marcos (played by Miguelito Gil) – one of the posters for the film even shows Miguelito Gil with the shop mannequin. But in one aforementioned scene, Marcos and Polonio go into the eaves of a barn to discuss the miraculous white suit. They discuss it in raptures, recalling the touch and look of the fabric, the buttons and lapels. The sound gives the distinct impression that these are two women in the bodies of children, discussing shopping for their wedding dresses – the search for a specifically white suit is the preoccupation of the film for, 'los chicos prefieren tomar la primera comunión de blanco' (children prefer to take their first communion dressed in white). Shopping is very much presented as the new religion, and the film resolutely focuses on spectacle (the final glittering scene of the boy's entrance into the church) as a way to compensate for the strangeness of the acoustics.

Cerca de la ciudad, a film by Luis Lucia of 1952, a surprising missionary film whose theme is ventriloquism, notably used the child stars themselves to dub their own voices. Coming a couple of years before the Marcelino phenomenon, a contemporary review of the film starts by noting that 'no es frecuente en el cine español que los niños tengan actuaciones destacadas en películas' (it is not frequent for Spanish cinema to feature child protagonists in films), expressing surprise that Lucia should have chosen to work with children 'que hablan y trabajan con categoría de actores' (speaking and working as actors) (García, 1952: n.p.). But despite assurances that they come from 'los suburbios' (the outskirts), the cast features Pepe Moratalla, a child actor who dubbed all of his own films (in Iquino's *El golfo que vio una estrella* Moratalla went on to the starring role but he was never as famous as Pablito Calvo – from the 1960s he worked as a dubbing actor, providing the voice for Mickey Rooney as well as several Jess Franco characters). In the film, the protagonist-priest, Father José, played by Adolfo Marsillach, is sent to the Parish of the Infant Jesus in a shanty-town on the outskirts of Madrid where he establishes a school for the town's orphaned boys. Children in the village are undisciplined and lack mothers, whilst the townspeople have (with the exception of one hard-hearted spinster) forsaken the Church. Father José uses voice-trickery to win over the children by employing a ventriloquist's dummy left to him by his fairground father to great effect. He displays his virtuosity with the putting on of voices as he relates a joke about a stuttering priest and altar boy to local drinkers in a tavern. Finally, he throws his voice to make it appear that the parrot or a bust of her late husband are imparting to the stony-faced spinster the word of God – that she must donate her mansion to the priest for him to realise his dreams of creating an orphanage and school for the village. If the voice is here exposed as fraudulent and persuasive, throwing doubt on the apparently pious intentions of the priest (Torreiro, 1997: 314), this is merely a continuation of the theme introduced in the prologue to the film which not only suggests that this film has been made merely to respond to the pressures of censorship ('las peliculas con curas están de moda' (films with priests are in vogue)) but also overtly parodies the NO-DO style (the film begins with a camera crew looking for a subject to film in much the same way that NO-DO showed camera crews filming different sections of society and industry) and implicitly presents the authority of the voice of the regime as similarly fraudulent. In a key scene of the film, in which Father José tells a joke to listeners in a tavern regarding a stuttering priest, Marsillach (or dubbing actors) adopts different voices for the priest who 'tar- tar- tartamudea' (the stuttering inflecting the narrator of the joke as well as its protagonist) and the high-pitched, stuttering altar boy who the priest initially believes is imitating him before realising that he too suffers from a stutter (the punch-line being 'tenemos misa pa' rato'). As he puts on the voice of the boy, his face distorts to achieve the high pitched required for the child's voice. Later, he adopts a different child's voice for the voice of Pepito, the ventriloquist's dummy, dressed as a young boy. In one scene, in which the boy who is mute has a conversation with the ventriloquist's dummy, the priest is ventriloquising the mute boy (he interprets his words for the onlookers) as well as operating the dummy. The presence of ventriloquism as theme, and specifically the performance of a distorted facial expression to match an obviously false child's voice, arguably precludes the use of anything other than children's voices for the dubbing of this film. Certainly it may have detracted from the important message that the priest is a skilful orator (i.e. his voice-shifting requires authority, not falsity, to work). Furthermore, a sense of falsity may have disrupted the integrity of the film's emotional core (which centres on the innocence of the child protagonists and on the priest's stammering at the end caused by emotion), creating a disturbing symmetry between Marsillach's facial distortions and those of the dubbing artist working in the studio – this may have simply been too much for the film's weaving of sound and image to bear.

We began with the film *Marcelino, pan y vino*. I now want to turn again to that film to see how the dubbing of Pablito Calvo may be seen to affect our reading of that film. If Doane (1985) is correct in her assertion that sound creates a fantasmatic body, then what kind of body is produced by the dubbed child star? For Borges, dubbing engenders monsters whose genealogy goes back to the Greek Chimera, a 'monster with the head of a lion, the head of a dragon, the head of a goat' (Borges, 1988: 62). Later, in the 1960s, a critic dubbed dubbing, 'the schizophrenic stunt of disembodied performances ... grafted voices hemstitched onto other actors' faces' (Nornes, 2007: 208). A short story ('Echoes') by Isek Dinesen (1991, cited by Yampolsky and Joseph, 1993) imagines a female who takes possession of a child's body to house her voice for her own sinister motives. For Kristeva, sound has to do with a pleasurable sense of reunification with the mother (after all, the mother's voice was the first voice we heard in the womb) but as alluring as such a reading would be in the context of this film, which deals with the anxious desire to be reunited with the mother, the disorientating effect of the voice (a woman's voice in a child's body) cuts across this suggestion, making Marcelino's desire for his mother appear less than natural. In fact, what we have here is the 'bodiless voice of an invisible/absent Master, a voice that cannot be attached to any object in the diegetic reality' (Žižek, 1996: 92). The significance of the question of dubbed children must centre, at least partly, on questions of our emotional responses to the voice/ image fusion. Alfred Hitchcock exploited our emotional reaction to unfaithful sounds in *Psycho* (1960) where he used three actors (two female and one male) to produce the disturbing voice of Mother (Rebello, 1990).[35] Žižek writes that the voice 'literally cuts out a hole in the visual reality: the screen image becomes a delusive surface, a lure secretly dominated by the bodiless voice [...] as if the true subject of enunciation of Norman's mother's voice is death itself, that is, the skull that we perceive for a brief moment in the fade-out of Norman's face' (Žižek, 1996: 92). This extraordinary voice, like that of Marcelino, has connotations of death.

Critics have noted the vampiric subtext in *Marcelino, pan y vino.* Purportedly a tale of the joyful reunion between mother and child in the presence of God, the film borrows heavily from the aesthetics of the horror film, from iconographic cobwebs and rusty scythes of the attic, the chiaroscuro effects created by Guerner, to the use of the camera, in which the spectator 'se identifica con la suma alteridad – cabe decir, monstruosa – de un no-muerto que establece con su inocente víctima – aquí el resplandeciente rostro de Pablito Calvo – la misma hipnótica relación que un vampiro mantendría en un film de terror al uso clásico' (identifies with the extreme otherness – that is, monstrous otherness – of a nondead being which establishes with its innocent victim – here the shining face of Pablito Calvo – the same hypnotic relation that a vampire would hold in a classic horror film) (Company, 1997: 355). This film coincides with one definition of the horror film that operates through the occlusion and then revelation of something horrible (Sobchack, 2006) as we strain to see around the chair back to glimpse the Christ-figure. Classic horror often involves a fear of being touched in the dark and this film's scenes in which the Christ figure reaches out for the bread fill us with a mixture of anxiety and pleasure, as does the scene where Marcelino grasps the resin legs of the statue in an embrace.[36] But what of the play of voices? Here the voice of Christ/ God is a coaxing, voice, alluring in its gravelly tones, and through the use of dubbing, Marcelino's voice becomes the voice of a child who has been robbed of his own breath (Artaud, 1978), a dead child.

The demons released by such a combination of voice and image seem monstrous, producing uncanny effects. This is not a revelatory pulling back of the curtain, like Toto in the *Wizard of Oz* (Victor Fleming, 1939), who discovers that the masterful voice belongs to a voice-throwing old man. Shaviro has written of contemporary celebrities that knowledge of the mode of their production merely adds to their allure (2010: 10). One has the sense that audiences accepted the dubbed voices of these child stars in a process of disavowal which acknowledged them as manufactured, kitsch commodities

– that this merely added to their appeal. Dubbing is inscribed into Spanish cinema practice, as Almodóvar's playful symbolism of the separated lovers expressed through sound and lip sync attests in *Mujeres al borde de un ataque de nervious* (1980). Most Spaniards accept dubbing as part of the film-going experience.[37] Even the mythologies surrounding Francoist censorship of film through dubbing focuses on the more comic-absurd aspects of this practice (the rendering of Grace Kelly's relationship with her husband as an incestuous one between brother and sister is a famous example). But where Heredero notes the 'asfixiante vigilancia ideológica' (asphyxiating ideological vigilance) which operated in Francoist censorship and the need to 'rastrear cualquier anomalía o rugosidad' (trace any anomaly or gap) in Spanish films of the 1950s, child dubbing might provide just such an anomaly, a way to open a tiny gap in the 'conformismo dimisionario que abundaba' (resigned conformity which abounded) (Heredero, 1993: 22).[38] We started with a discussion of Benjaminian aura in the close-up of a child. One definition of aura arises from Benjamin's (1968b) reflections on Baudelaire, Proust, the photograph and memory, which led him to muse on the auratic encounter, 'to perceive the aura of an object we look at means to invest it with the ability to look at us in return' (1968b: 188). It is clear that this gaze has to do with reaching through time, investing something/someone with the ability to look back at us which involves an imaginary encounter through time (Hansen, 2008). This returns us to the schizophrenia of our earlier discussions of the aura, but here the distance of time is collapsed into closeness. Interestingly, through the etymological connotations of the word aura (which in Greek and Latin means 'breath'), by looking back at the child and allowing it to return our gaze we metaphorically endow the child star with the breath it was robbed of through the dubbing process. In this way the mute gaze of the child stars in the films of the *cine religioso* speaks to us across time.

As I write this, a YouTube clip is circulating on the Internet under the title 'Franco ventrílocuo'. It is part of a film made in 1937 for international distribution and recuperated in Basilio Martín Patino's *Caudillo* (1973). It shows General Franco with his wife and daughter, Carmencita, in the style of Christmas messages to the nation. Franco asks his daughter if she has anything to say to the children of the world (in an earlier version she was asked to speak to the children of Germany). 'What should I say?', she asks, 'Pues, lo que quieras, nena' (whatever you want), says Franco with an awkward smile. She then proceeds to recite a speech which she is obviously reading from a board whilst Franco mouths the words behind her, the ventriloquist activating his dummy. Apparently the film was not made available for domestic consumption. Other instances of children being made to stand as mouthpieces come to mind, such as Franco's failed attempts to bring up the child Juan Carlos in his image.[39] But it is the recent recovery of new facts about the *Auxilio Social* which puts an entirely new perspective on the theme of the cinematic orphan. In *Los niños perdidos del fran-*

quismo, Vinyes, Armengou and Belis revealed that around 30,000 children, considered to be 'rojos' (reds), were wrenched from their mothers and repatriated with Francoist families. Chief 'biopsychiatrist' to the regime, Antonio Vallejo Nágera, believed that it was possible to isolate a 'red gene'. However, through repatriation, it was possible to re-educate children into National Catholic ideology. This is the most extreme case of ideological ventriloquism and puts a new slant on the cinematic orphan, engendering nurture in spectators for a child in search of a 'better' mother than the one it was born to.[40] It also gives new meaning to the emphasis in these films on education: the child, as *Cerca de la ciudad* has it, is 'tierra para sembrar' (land to be sown). In 1954, Rafael Gil released *Murió hace quince años* (He Died Fifteen Years Ago), an anti-Communist film which dealt specifically with the question of brainwashing and implantation of memories but from the perspective of a Francoist family whose son, Diego, is taken abroad to the USSR as a child to escape the Spanish Civil War. The film begins emotively with a child struggling and screaming out for his father whilst being led alongside crowds of boys to board a ship (the scene recreates images shown on newsreel of the evacuation of children but here with a focus on the anguish of a child). Once abroad, Diego is told to forget his family and receives a form of cultural ventriloquism through education (we see high, drafty industrial-style classrooms, headmistresses in military coats and severe expressions and children repeating by rote). As an adult, Diego (Francisco Rabal) is recruited as a spy to return to his family in Spain where his father is high in the Francoist ranks. At the reunion at the airport with his father and cousin, Mónica, he coldly offers his hand in response to the glistening eyes and warm embrace issued by his father. The house he returns to resonates with memories: his housekeeper puts out the music box and crucifix from his childhood, there is a portrait of his dead mother on the wall – but he appears not to respond. The theme of implantation of ideas runs through the film. In a conversation with Mónica, he speaks about the girlfriend he has left in the Soviet Union, 'ella no quiere más que a sus ideas porque le educaron así' (she loves only her ideas because that is how they educated her), but he tells Mónica, 'tú puedes pertenecer a un hombre de un modo absoluto, quiere decir que él te podría mandar hasta en tus pensamientos' (you can belong to a man completely, which means that he can even order your thoughts). But when he is instructed to have his own father killed, he suffers a crisis of conscience in a hospital bed, under the sign of the cross. He renounces his past and enjoys a tearful reunion (in a replacement of that earlier scene) with his cousin and father.[41]

If this film may have alerted the public to the question of ideological implantation and ventriloquism (complete with the suggestion that the ideal Falangist woman is no more than a mouthpiece for her husband's ideas), then there were other images of children with ventriloquised voices that would have been familiar to audiences of *Marcelino, pan y vino* in 1955. The child, reciting Catechisms or saluting the patria is featured in *Un traje blanco* and *El maestro*, for instance. In Sáenz de Heredia's *¡Ho me mire usted!*, the central conceit had been that the schoolboys are hypnotised to help them to remember their lessons. Children marching across the country-side, with drums, whistles and songs (as we see in *Un traje blanco*) were fea-tured in NO-DO newsreel of the time, turning the countryside into a jubilant marching utopia, as were the children, silently forming patriotic symbols with their bodies in formation. Bodies were disciplined and punished and voices stolen and prompted. Žižek has written that 'the voice displays a spectral autonomy, so that even if we see a person talking, there is always a minimum of ventriloquism at work' (1996: 58). These become errant voices, crossing the screen, reminding us of the suppression of the voices of children (and indeed of a nation) during the long years of the Franco regime.

Coda: the case of Joselito

It was the child's voice that would be central to the development of the Spanish child star. Pablito Calvo went on to make other films (*Mi tío Jacinto*, My Uncle Jacinto Ladislao Vajda, 1956) but none would attain quite the same success. José Jiménez Fernández, born into poverty, made money singing *fandanguillos* until he was heard on a radio show by Antonio Guzmán Merino (a screenwriter for musicals) who created 'Joselito', 'el niño con la voz de oro' (the boy with the golden voice), writing a script for *El pequeño ruiseñor* (The Little Nightingale, Antonio del Amo, 1957) (modelled on the theme of maternal absence of *Marcelino, pan y vino*), the film that was to launch Joselito's career. An article published as pre-release publicity in November 1956, noted the delay in the film's release attributed to the slow recovery of one of the film's stars, Lina Canalejas, after a car accident. She was now ready, the article informs us, to undertake dubbing of her own voice in the film. The same article notes that Joselito has been chosen by recording studios R.C.A. to make a record of the greatest hits of the film: 'en los próximos días los lectores que se interesen por el arte de Joselito ya podrán adquirir sus grabaciones en las tiendas de toda España' (in the next few days those readers interested in Joselito's art can buy his records in shops all over Spain). The article reminds us that 'el pequeño ruiseñor entusiasma al público cada vez que canta' (the singing nightin-gale enthuses the public every time he sings) and shows a scene of Joselito singing to a rapt cast and crew during a break in filming. If Sélica Torcal was responsible for dubbing Joselito's voice in that first film, his singing voice was clearly his own and posters featured a song-list prominently displayed.[42] But if Torcal's voice added a sense of the uncanny, this sense was merely reinforced by Joselito's voice, as a recent publication by Tatjana Pavlović makes clear. Pavlović begins with an evocative description of the 'errant voice' of boy soprano Joselito. The film opens with pan-shots of valleys, rivers and mountains before coming to rest on the figure of a woman carrying a suitcase. She is soon overpowered by an 'eerily magical voice singing *Ave María*' (Pavlović, 2011: 111). This errant voice is soon attached to a small boy in the church tower. Pavlović shows how Joselito's voice comes to reflect his 'inner self' and a search for origins as Joselito is an orphan, his disgraced mother having fallen pregnant as the result of an adulterous union with a flamenco singer. Joselito is told merely that his mother is the Holy Virgin. The film shares many elements with the pious *Marcelino, pan y vino*: the orphan who is searching for his mother; a prayer to an icon which will be heard; the framing of a sick child as well as aesthetically religious surroundings. But *El pequeño ruiseñor* might also be said to share elements with folkloric musicals of the era, such as Luis Lucia's *Un caballero andaluz* (An Andalusian Gentleman, 1954) (starring Jaime Blanch). The priest of *Un caballero andaluz* has become a stock character; both films include star turns of singing and dancing; both have scenes of bull-running which wounds a child protagonist; both feature blood transfusions to bring the sickly child back to life. Pavlović sees the religious elements of the Joselito films therefore as part of a 'passional culture' (Mitchell, 1990) (she notes, for example, that Joselito's songs represent his mother's passion for her flamenco singing lover, despite attempts to pin her down to the image of the Virgin). Heredero concludes that 'no se trata, como plantea Seguin, de la España que deriva del nacional-catolicismo, sino precisamente de la España que sale de él, que empieza a quitarse de encima – muy lentamente – la beatificación inquisitorial y que busca el despegue ofrecido por el liberalismo económico' (it's not a case, as Seguin has it, of a Spain derived from National Catholicism but rather, precisely that of the Spain that is emerging from it, that is beginning, very slowly, to shake it off) (Heredero, 1993: 232). Pavlović concurs, suggesting that 'the presence of flamenco in Joselito's opus is therefore not a question of entertainment, but an articulation of the passage from the traditional to secularised society' [and citing Vattimo, 1992] "not one that has simply left the religious elements behind but one that continues to live them as traces"' (Pavlović, 2011: 123). This, moreover, is what the spectrality of Joselito's voice represents, now merely the trace of an old version of Spain (*la España profunda*) but not a blueprint for its future.

Notes

1 In an interview for *Ya* in 1989, Sánchez-Silva explained that the story was not written in a style meant for children – rather, the adults were to read the story and re-tell it to their children. In fact, parents simply bought the book for their children (Medialdea, 1989: n.p.).

2 For the fascinating story of how Vajda escaped Nazi persecution see Camporesi (2007a).

3 After opening at the Coliseum cinema in Madrid, it was awarded the Sindicato Nacional del Espectáculo prize of half a million pesetas and stayed in cinemas for 105 days. Chamartín, responsible for production, sold distributions rights to seventeen countries, including France, Great Britain, Germany, Syria, Greece,

Egypt, the USA, Canada, Uruguay and Switzerland. The film was particularly popular in Poland and Japan.

4 In a blog entry from 2007, the poster asks whether the story of Marcelino is 'real'. See http://catholicforum.fisheaters.com/index.php?topic=1608361.0 (accessed 23.09.2012).

5 For example, the centrality of the infant Jesus which was the model for many of the boys of the *cine religioso*, or the phrase, 'Let the children come and do not hinder them, for the Kingdom of Heaven belongs to such as these' which Prout (2005) sees as relevant to *Marcelino, pan y vino*.

6 When the film opened in Buenos Aires, Francisco Madrid accused Rossellini of plagiarism of Ramón María del Valle-Inclán's *Flor de santidad* (Flowers of Holiness, 1901/4) (Madrid, 1948: 6).

7 It was remade as a TV movie, *The Small Miracle* in 1973, and stars Vittorio de Sica as the priest. The film still enjoys distribution through religious outlets.

8 Vajda was awarded the Isabel la Católica prize in 1952 and was naturalised as a Spaniard in 1954. Camporesi (2007a) draws our attention to an interview conducted by Ann-Marie Jolivet with Sánchez-Silva. Jolivet, whose text notes only that Vajda's own religious beliefs were less than clear, transcribes an interview she conducted with José María Sánchez-Silva who noted that his religion was unclear (Jolivet, 2004: 246). He goes on to explain that Vajda asked Sánchez-Silva to remove a line from the script (and that Sánchez-Silva removed it from all later editions of the published book): 'es que a la pregunta que le hace Cristo al niño: ¿sabes quién me hizo esto?; refiriéndose a sus heridas, el pequeño contestaba, 'sí, los judíos' que se cambió por 'los hombres malos' (to the question that Christ asks of the child, 'do you know who did this to me?' referring to his wounds, the child answered, 'yes, the Jews' which was changed to 'the bad men') (Jolivet, 2004: 246). In a small way, then, Vajda made a small contribution towards reversing the unthinking anti-semitism of Francoist Spain. The film's cinematographer was Enrique Guerner, born Heinrich Gärtner, an Austrian Jewish cinematographer who brought strains of Expressionism to Spanish cinema (Kinder, 1993: 482).

9 Was cinema, as the writer of one pamphlet handed out during screenings had it, a dark space where seductions of the five senses could take place, and against which one had to place a filter (the filter of one's own intelligence, to be gained by learning about film and its effects) (Anon, 1960)? Writing in *Film Ideal* in 1956, José María García Escudero appears to concur with this view, but then it becomes clear that he is writing in response to a message from Pope Pío XII to the effect that in cinema, the aim is to 'convertir un rayo de luz en un rayo de Dios' (convert a ray of light into a ray of divine love). Cinema, then, can have an evangelising function. Interpreting the Pope's words 'for Catholics', García Escudero informs the reader that this means, 'educar, producir': making more good-quality films, not more religious films, and simultaneously educating the viewer into how to read films (García Escudero, 1956: 16). In the text it is a subtle distinction, but with far-reaching consequences. It also helps us to set out the discourse of the time, from those who saw cinema as a negative influence, to those who saw the power of cinema to teach the word of God, to those, like García Escudero, who wanted good cinema to get made regardless of its perceived moral effects. Where the anonymous writer in 1960 saw the cinema as a place to activate the senses for a religious motive, Sobchack writes that, 'at the movies or elsewhere, as lived

bodies we are always grounded in the radical materialism of bodily immanence, in the "here" and "now" of our sensual existence'. She contrasts this with the ability of cinema in particular for transcendence – 'for a unique exteriority of being – an ex-stasis – that locates us "elsewhere" and "otherwise" even as it is grounded in and tethered to our lived body's "here" and "now"' (Sobchack, 2008: 197). Comparing the church to cinema, and pertinent to our discussion of *Marcelino, pan y vino*, she will go on to examine films which portray God as 'an apprehended figural gap in visual representation' (Sobchack, 2008: 202).

10 The crucifix was later checked for a 'mechanism' which made it open and close its eyes.

11 Marina Warner (2000) traces some of these monsters in a Spanish tradition (for example in Goya) in *No Go, The Bogeyman*. Miguel de Unamuno (1998) discusses the 'coco' as does García Lorca (1991). Vajda would go on to portray a child killer in the Swiss/Spanish co-production, *El cebo* (The Bait), which I have discussed elsewhere (Wright, 2008).

12 This photocomposition, marked 'anonymous' and printed in *España nueva*, Barcelona, June 1938, is reproduced in Llorente Hernández (2002–3: 56).

13 Paul Willemen (1994) notes the Catholic discourse which is used for some classical film theory. I return to this point in the discussion of Ana Torrent in Chapter 3.

14 Further destroying the illusion that Marcelino had glimpsed Christ, Calvo later noted that, 'Yo no tenia mucha idea de quien era Marcelino porque las escenas de la pelicua se filmaban salteadas, aprovechando el tiempo que se permanecia en cada escenario, asi que yo no tenia una idea global del argumento que se contaba' (I didn't have much idea about who Marcelino was because the scenes weren't filmed in sequence to take advantage of the time we had in each set, so I didn't have a global sense of the argument) (Aizpún, 1989: n.p.).

15 Yarza (2004) quotes Phillip Lacoue-Labarth and Jean Luc Nancy on Nazism's defining trait to be its ability to use the mobilising power of myth to transform fantasy into political reality (Lacoue-Labarth and Nancy, 1990: 304).

16 See Pinto (2004) on the school textbook, *Así quiero ser el niño del Nuevo Estado* (This is How I Want to Be: The Child of the New State).

17 See Palacios Lis (2003) on Francoism's indoctrination of mothers of shame and guilt. Shaviro discusses Nazi cinema as an exercise in the 'mobilization of cinematic affect' (Shaviro, 2010: 153n).

18 Celebrities were, in fact, photographed with orphans, a publicity strategy which would be parodied in Berlanga's *Plácido* (1961).

19 Cuteness performs the desexualisation of the child's body, redefining that body from an object of lust (either sexual or economic) to an object of disinterested affection. Thus it sublimates adults' erotic feelings towards children (Merish, 1996: 188). Merish relates the definition of cute to vaudeville 'freak-shows' and shows how it began by association with those who are physically or ethnically 'other' before being associated with childhood: 'haunted by its own freakishness, the cute ineluctably points to other possibilities of embodiment, other forms of subjectivity and desire' (Merish, 1996: 201).

20 Yarza (2004) begins his examination of Francoist kitsch with a discussion of the ways that films of the Transition used camp to interrogate this aesthetic. In the scene of the crying father, clear retrospective resonances of Pedro Almodóvar's reworking of the Madonna and Child visual paradigms are to be found.

21	Juan José, the child star discovered by Iquino (alongside 'Morucha', a girl of eleven who had won prizes for her dancing), with *Las travesuras de Morucha* (Morucha's Mischief) in 1962, later had more success in Caracas. Juan José had enjoyed success as a singing star on radio.

22	Pilarín Sanclemente took on supporting roles in *El Lazarillo de Tormes* (as the blind girl) and later as the boarding-school friend of Marisol in *Ha llegado un angel*. By 1962 at the age of eleven she had made twenty films (Anon, 1962a).

23	ONIEVA, A.J., Metodología y organización escolar, Magisterio Español, Madrid, 1961, p.314, quoted in (Amich Elías, 2005: 225). 'Se impone una vuelta a la sana tradición que veía en la mujer la hija, la esposa y la madre y no la "intelectual" pedantesca' (A return was imposed to the healthy tradition which saw women as daughters, wives and mothers and not pedantic "intellectuals").

24	See Young-Bruehl (2002).

25	In 1961 Jaime Blanch and Pepe Moratalla, now turning twenty, reported the difficulties they were experiencing in finding work as adult actors. Pepe Moratalla reports that, 'a mí, se me encasilló como niño golfo y siempre hice de niño golfo. Cuando crecí, como ya no era niño, quedé inservible y los directores no supieron utilizarme para otras cosas (they type-cast me as tearaway and I always played the tearaway. When I grew, as I was no longer a child, I was unusable and the directors didn't know how to use me for other things). He notes wryly that, 'nunca tuve padres en las películas que hice y los que tuve eran borrachos o estaban en la cárcel. ¡Todo un drama! (I never had parents in the films I made and those I did have were drunk or in prison. What a drama!) and concludes that, 'el aumento de edad, el crecimiento, el cambio de estatura, son los principales enemigos de los actores infantiles' (ageing, growing up, are the principal enemies of child stars) (Morales, 1961: 22–23).

26	This sense of capturing Pablito Calvo as a fleeting image would only increase as Pablito Calvo got older. In 1963 an article advertising an Argentinian film, *Barcos de papel* (Paper Boats), starring Calvo, reported that, 'ha quedado incorporado al sentimiento y al alma de todo el mundo en la encarnación de aquella angelical criatura. Aunque ha crecido bastante, todavía su carita dulce, su expresión inefable siguen siendo casi iguales [...] Quizás con *Barcos de papel* ha llegado Pablito, es decir, Marcelino, al límite de su representación infantil. Ahora, como ha ocurrido com Marisol, tendrá que dar el paso a su personalidad de adolescente' (his embodiment of that angelical creature has become incorporated into everyone's sentiment and soul. Although he has grown quite a lot, his sweet little face and ineffable expression are the same as ever. Perhaps with *Paper Boats* Pablito, or rather, Marcelino, has reached the limit of child acting. Now, as has happened with Marisol, he will have to move into adolescent roles) (Anon, 1963b). By the 1980s Calvo was selling properties on the Costas (Aizpún, 1989).

27	Rumours circulate that the Franco family were shareholders in the Galerías Preciados although these are impossible to corroborate (Toboso, 2000: 168). Certainly José Fernández supported the Franco regime publicly, sent out gifts to El Pardo (Cabrera and del Rey, 2007: 109) and Carmen Polo shopped often at the store. *Operacion plus ultra* (Operation Beyond, Pedro Lazaga, 1966), meanwhile, depicts a trip to *El Corte Inglés*.

28	Sally Faulkner (2006) has noticed the 'ludic references to the Spanish Civil War' in the *La gran familia* cycle, which she claims have yet to be incorporated into our understanding of the war and its representations on screen during the Franco era.

29 Amich Elías shows how child labour was still very much in evidence in a clandestine way during the 1950s in spite of social taboos on children working (Amich Elías, 2005).

30 My thanks to José Luis Ortiz and Valeria Camporesi for examples of child dubbing.

31 María Dolores Gispert (who dubbed *Pipicalzaslargas* [Pippi Longstocking] from Swedish into Spanish) notes that dubbing artists often may not understand the source language and so rely in part on facial gestures to relay mood, emotion and tone. From a private interview, 01.02.2011.

32 In the case of a film dubbed from a foreign language, the dubbing process involves a pre-run in which 'ajustes' (adjustments) are made to the translated text to make it fit with the cadences and linguistic patterns of the target language.

33 For example, in an article from 1952, Fernando Fernán Gómez, present at a debate on dubbing, in response to the suggestion that 'gracias a las películas dobladas la gente de los pueblos aprende el castellano más correctamente' (thanks to dubbed films people from the villages can learn Castilian correctly), replied, 'pero si éstas llevaran letreritos aprenderían a leer' (Grandes aplausos) (but if the films have subtitles they can learn to read (Great applause)) (Anon, 1952).

34 For a fascinating account of the child's voice in contemporary animated films, see Holliday (2012).

35 The castrato in *Farinelli: Il Castrato* (Corbiau, 1994) was produced in the studio by twinning a male countertenor with a female soprano and by using well-known old recordings, with the effect that, for one scholar, 'I simply cannot fathom the body that produced those sounds' (which she finds comes to stand for the lack embodied in the castrato himself) (Bergeron, 1996: 174).

36 Kinder sees pederastic overtones in this scene: 'though the spectacle is somewhat de-sexualised by being presented to the gaze of an innocent child, the context creates pederastic overtones' as 'Marcelino and Jesus are united in an erotic exchange' (Kinder, 1993: 244).

37 The negative connotations of dubbing pervade. See Nornes (2007).

38 I am grateful to Valeria Camporesi for suggesting I look at this concept.

39 Basilio Martín Patino's *Canciones para después de una guerra* (1971) is an extraordinary patchwork of the songs and images of memory and a perfect example of the way that sound can affect image. It ends with an image of the child Juan Carlos, looking out at the screen, as Patino notes, 'mirándonos a todos con no menos cara de perplejidad' (looking at us all in confusion) (Patino, n.d).

40 The figure is estimated to be in excess of 30,000. Childless couples were particularly singled out for parenthood of these 'orphans'.

41 Richards (2005) records that it is estimated that between 3,000 to 5,000 children were exiled in the Soviet Union (compared to 17,500 in France, 5,130 in Belgium and 4,000 in Britain). 'It was claimed by the Francoist authorities that the most robust children were selected for the Soviet Union, though there is no evidence of such a selection process' (Richards, 2005: 126). Whilst the Repatriation Delegation had considerable success in the early years of the regime for bringing children back to Spain from abroad (by 1949 it was estimated

that some 20,000 children had returned from exile), nevertheless fewer were recorded as returned from the Soviet Union in the 1940s: 'those who did return were considered negatively as "sovietised" and there were fears that they would turn out to be dangerous "sexual libertines" or "communist agents". According to the official discourse, they would need "physical and moral disinfection" on arrival in Spain' (Richards, 2005: 128).

42 From a private interview with Torcal (01.02.2011). Torcal notes that this fact appears to have been entirely suppressed/forgotten. Joselito provided his own singing voice and went on to dub his own dialogue in later films. Torcal tells an anecdote of Joselito watching her dub, sitting at the side of the studio, and remarking '¿por qué me pones esa voz de rata?' (why have you given me that voice of a little rat?).

2

Coming of age with Marisol

In Salvador Dalí's vivid montage *Shirley Temple, The Youngest, Most Sacred Monster of the Cinema in Her Time* (1939), the child star Shirley Temple is a scarlet fur-coated sphinx who lies spent in a parched landscape amidst the discarded bones of her victims. 'Shirley! At Last in Technicolor!' is encased in a gilt frame beneath her (*The Little Princess*, her first Technicolor film came out that year). If the painting displays Dalí's antipathy for Hollywood, it almost certainly also expresses his rage at the widely reported libel case brought by Temple and 20th Century Fox against Graham Greene, concerning a review he wrote of Temple's *Wee Willie Winkie* (1937). For Greene, Temple, 'wore trousers with the mature suggestiveness of a Dietrich: her neat and well-developed rump twisted in the tap dance; her eyes had a sidelong searching coquetry'. Temple's admirers, meanwhile, are:

> middle aged men and clergymen – [who] respond to her dubious coquetry, to the sight of her desirable little body. In *Wee Willie Winkie*, wearing short kilts she is a complete totsy ... her swaggering stride made her antique audience gasp with excited anticipation ... watch the way she measures a man with agile studio eyes, with dimpled depravity. Adult emotions of love and grief glissade across the mask of childhood, a childhood skin deep. (Taylor, 1972: 276–277)

Greene was forced to retract the review and his magazine *Night and Day* filed for bankruptcy. Dalí's painting is a parody of adult investments in the child. Temple is a monstrous hybrid, a vampiric incarnation of the meeting point between the desires of her creators in the cinema industry and her public. There's nothing left of the child but the cut-out black and white photo of Temple's head, reminiscent of the cuttings collected by fans, whilst the scarlet body of a sphinx is the undisguisable manifestation of the monstrous desire of Temple's male admirers.

In an article on Marisol, the blonde, blue-eyed singing child sensation of the 1960s, Peter Evans muses that 'had Greene seen any of the earliest Marisol films he might have written a piece about her of the sort that landed him in the law courts' (Evans, 2004: 133).[1] Film producer Manuel Goyanes saw the young Josefa ('Pepa') Flores González (b. 1948) – de un barrio de 'chupa y tira' (from a dirt poor neighbourhood)[2] – perform in a televised exhibition of the Coros y Danzas de Educación y Descanso (the poor relation of the state endorsed Coros y Danzas of the Falangist Sección Femenina). Goyanes moved Flores with her mother from their home in Malaga to live with his family in Madrid to start making films under the stage-name Marisol. The transformations Goyanes wrought on his young star were recapitulated in the 'Pygmalion theme' (Triana-Toribio, 2003: 88) which was the subject of most of her films (Evans, 2004). Marisol was the darling of the Franco regime. She was the incarnation of *simpatía*, the smiling orphan who, like a Spanish *Pollyanna*, brought together feuding family members or danced her way through brightly coloured (with Eastmancolor) fantasy worlds.[3] In the late 1960s she innocently sipped pink champagne with Francoist Dalí on his Mae West Lips sofa as part of a publicity tour for one of her musical extravaganzas. But in 1976 after the end of the dictatorship she sensationally posed nude in the magazine *Interviú*. A series of confessional articles as told to male journalists revealed the parties she was asked to attend as a child, naked, for the pleasure of Francoist dignitaries (Umbral, 1991: 17) and the sexual assault made on her by a photographer (Morales, 1979a; 1979b). Francisco Umbral, one of the journalists she related these confessionals to, cast her as Lolita to his Humbert – 'a las doce era una adorable criatura y a las catorce una lamentable anciana' (at twelve she was an adorable creature and at fourteen she was a lamentable old woman) (Umbral, 1991: 17). More recently, an unauthorised made-for-TV bio-pic, shown on Antena 3 in 2009 and based on the biography by Javier Barreiro (1999), *Marisol, la película*, focused on the public and private lives of Marisol: with the by-line 'el coraje de una mujer con una infancia arrebatada' (the courage of a woman with a stolen childhood) whilst a television programme asked, '¿Por qué Pepa Flores mató a Marisol?' (Why did Pepa Flores Kill Marisol?).[4]

In 1965 a series of shots, reproducing the effect of the photo-booth, showed off Marisol's new short haircut in publicity produced for her film, *Cabriola* (Prancer, Mel Ferrer, 1965). In them, Marisol pulls different faces, pouting and grimacing by turns. If they recall the early attempts by Etienne-Jules Marey to transcribe the body's language onto film, they are, through their gaps (they do not capture every nuance of movement as Marey's chronophotography attempted to do), haunted by those lost moments of movement in between those traced indexically on film. Opportunities for Marisol to hide from the camera's gaze were in fact few and far between. Alongside the film per year produced since her first feature *Un rayo de luz* in 1960, Marisol embarked on exhausting publicity tours and posed for photos at 'impromptu' meetings with photographers. Merchandising was launched on a grand scale with story-boards packaged like comics which told the plots of her films, cut-out Marisols to dress, a Marisol doll created in her image (a version of the upmarket Mariquita Pérez), sticker albums, records and a dedicated magazine named for her. Her biography, *Simpatía*, serialised in pamphlets for the consumption of young readers, related her rags-to-riches back-story (Anon, 1962a). The breadth of coverage of

Marisol through the films and their publicity afforded intimacy and a sense
of plenitude, and of capturing Marisol in 'real-time'. Lost in the gaps were
the realities of gruelling schedules, a surrendering of all aspects of her life
to the Goyanes star-making machine (including the changing of her name,
dyeing of her hair, cosmetic surgery on her nose in 1964 and modification of
her Andalusian accent) and an anxiety to capture more of Marisol's imprint
on film, with an intensification of the scrutiny of her body.[5] Marisol embodies not just the trace of the body on screen, but those elements which are not
traced indexically but which nevertheless form part of cultural memory.[6]

Laura Mulvey's notion of a 'delayed cinema' from her book *Death, 24x
a second*, observes how being able to use the pause and rewind functions
using today's technologies puts us in control of our subject and allows us
to get close to our icons. Time, for Mulvey, is often viewed in terms of its
'archivability' (Mulvey, 2005). The body's filmic traces, film's contingency
and the paradoxes of the capturing of the ostensibly ephemeral nature
of film performance make Marisol's body into an archive, what Doane
describes as 'the sense of a present moment laden with historicity at the same
time [as encouraging] a belief in our access to pure presence, instantaneity'
(Doane, 2002: 104). Viewing Marisol's films in the present may afford the
sense that the series of exposés in the 1970s were no more than the 'literal
realisation of the erotic subtexts' present in her films (Crumbaugh, 2009:
111). Commentators writing from the vantage point of the 1970s and 1980s
also saw in Marisol's naked body the opportunity to reflect on Spain's difficult transition to democracy, framing the passage of history through her
apparent shift from docility to rebellion. But the release of Marisol's 'body
of work' on DVD since the early 2000s (by Divisa Red), bears testament to
the renewed interest in Marisol since the turn of the century.[7] The bio-pic
Marisol, la película (Manuel Palacios) draws Marisol's films into an engagement with her personal history. The TV programme 'Por qué Pepa Flores
mató a Marisol?' used a confessional format with 'testimonies' from those
closest to Marisol and 'material inédito' (unpublished material) whilst it
lamented the lack of access it had to the star herself: '¿Por qué hay un código
de silencio en torno a Marisol? ¿Qué oculta Pepa Flores tras él? ¿Qué quiere
olvidar? ¿De qué huye? ¿Por qué Pepa Flores no quiere recordar a Marisol?'
(Why is there a code of silence around Marisol? What is Pepa Flores hiding?
What does she want to forget? What is she running away from? Why
doesn't Pepa Flores want to remember Marisol?) (Anon, 2008a). Whilst the
release on DVD of Marisol's films gives rise to questions of whether demand
for Francoist material has to do with nostalgia for the Franco regime or critique, it seems difficult to imagine how Marisol's films can be approached
without an awareness of the revelatory and confessional culture that has
grown up around her image. In the sense that this time-lag has to do with
a 'culture's understanding of itself', we might turn to Thomas Elsaesser
who turns to temporalities to address trauma in film. An earlier latency
period where the shock has been so severe that it impact has left no trace

(Elsaesser, 2001) is gradually replaced by what Susannah Radstone calls 'the beginnings of remembrance' and later understanding (Radstone, 2000). This corresponds to Marisol's filmic output, in particular, the unknowing perpetual-present of her early films, but also the beginnings of remembrance in her later films and the traumatic reawakening which now inflects all of her films. In the shifting temporalities between then and now, we can start to understand the 'patriarchally inflicted gaps, absences and traceless traces' (Elsaesser, 2001: 194) of Marisol's body of work.

Marisol and the *Pygmalion* effect

Marisol's first film, *Un rayo de luz* (A Ray of Light, Luis Lucia, 1960), fetishises transformations. Marisol's father has died and her mother, a singer and dancer of flamenco in dingy bars, has been disenfranchised by the upper-class Italian family of her dead husband. Originally from working-class Malaga, Marisol's blonde hair fitted perfectly with the image of the *niña bien*, allowing her to cross class boundaries in her films. Triana-Toribio comments on Marisol's ambiguous 'Nordic' appearance, very different from the traditional dark looks of, for example, the Spanish gypsy. 'Her blondeness was shorthand for "contemporary", "affluent" and 'cosmopolitan"' (Triana-Toribio, 2003: 88). When we first meet Marisol, she is dressed in blue gingham – what Dyer, in relation to Judy Garland, calls the marker of ordinariness (1986: 176). She looks bored as she sings for her music lesson. But her extraordinary voice is revelatory, powerful and transforming. Along with her natural charm, it astounds her grandfather (Julio Sanjuán) who will grow to love his sweet, gifted granddaughter, embracing a wayward daughter-in-law and gathering them both into the family fold. Here, as elsewhere in her films, stepping into the limelight is aligned with becoming a woman. In *Un rayo de luz*, her extraordinary voice is seen as being at odds with her childlike appearance. In the school dormitory Marisol is confirmed as the innocent child, fair-haired, surrounded in a huddle by girls in pink nightdresses. As the other girls move aside and the camera moves in to frame her at the centre, a game of scale is presented by the little girl with the extraordinary voice. But later in the film, when her uncle gives her a beautiful pale blue satin flamenco dress (the scene is shot to create the revelation of the dress, Cinderella-style), Marisol will dress up and perform for him like a tiny woman, hair pulled back into a chignon, waist neatly nipped. Her micromovements and tiny outstretched arms betray a fascination with the display of the miniature – Marisol is like a tiny living doll. In fact, a Marisol doll was manufactured as a marketing ploy in the 1960s. 'Una muñeca de cine, Marisol tiene su muñeca, también se llama Marisol' (A doll of the cinema, Marisol has her doll, it's called Marisol, too) was how the doll was advertised in 1961. The Marisol dolls formed part of the Mariquita Pérez collection. These were dolls for wealthy little girls, or aspirational objects for the less well-off. *Mariquita Pérez S.A.* was founded by Leonor Coello, who had been given a doll her mother won in a raffle in 1938. The doll was naked and Leonor's mother had made a dress for it that was identical to one of Leonor's. Coello founded the company in the new regime with a rich friend of hers (María Pilar Luca de Tena) she had met at school. Marketing included the institution of *Los jueves con Mariquita* (Thursdays with Mariquita), which featured catwalk shows where little girls and their dolls, both dressed identically, could compete for a prize. Leonor Coello paid to have her dolls dressed in the outfits worn by Marisol on screen, including *Ha llegado un angel* (An Angel Has Appeared, 1961, Luis Lucia), although she drew the line at *Marisol, rumbo a Río* (Marisol, Destination Rio, Fernando Palacios, 1963), commenting, 'nada de trajes vulgares. Sólo calidad y buen diseño' (no vulgar costumes. Just quality and fine design) (Yubero and Conde, 1996: 156). With the opening of Spain to tourism, Leonor Coello launched a doll called the *Mariví*, smaller than Mariquita and dressed in regional dress to respond to the tourist demand for local souvenirs of good quality (Yubero and Conde, 1996: 30).

Marisol was the real commodity.[8] She was manufactured and moulded, a figure of desire designed to encourage consumerism in young films and their mothers. Through an inter-subjective relationship with Marisol, female spectators were also intended to understand, in spatial terms, what it meant to become female. Thus in *Un rayo de luz*, we witness the move from the young child's view of the world as '"being a master of the universe". This is the existential space of the young world-making child – and (in our culture, also the "presumed (and assumed) existential space of the adult man")' (Sobchack, 2004: 32). In the film, Marisol dresses up in armour, complete with painted-on moustache, and travels over the countryside on foot. However, this 'master of the universe' space 'is very rarely the space of the adult woman'. Women, then, 'are the objects of gazes that locate and invite their bodies to live as merely material "things" immanently positioned in space rather than as conscious subjects with the capacity to transcend their immanence and posit space' (Sobchack, 2004: 32). Sobchack cites de Beauvoir's reference to the doll which represents both the whole body and a passive object. When she dresses up for her male relations, in this scene which is haunted by the 'little woman' Marisol will become, Marisol's spatial possibilities become restricted whilst her movements are controlled through the dance. Iris Young, musing on why girls throw differently from boys, with far more restricted bodily movement, concludes that 'the woman herself often actively takes up her body as a mere thing (Young, 2005: 155) whilst Weiss concludes that 'many women mediate their own relationship with their bodies by seeing their bodies as they are seen by others and worrying about what they and these (largely invisible) others are seeing as they are acting' (Weiss, 1999: 47). In this scene the sense is of the little girl who tries on her mother's clothes – but here Marisol does not teeter about on high heels but is perfectly poised as she twirls around her grandfather. With the controlled micromovements of flamenco, her tiny arms outstretched,

Marisol creates the space around her into a stage for display. Fighting back glycerine tears, and aided by the record on the LP player (it is not clear whether the lip-synch is a function of the dubbing of the film or whether Marisol is miming to a singer of the likes of Sara Montiel, Marisol dances a choreographed homage before the portrait of her dead father which adorns the sitting room wall, the mobile, fluid camera moves around her in circular movements, suggesting the freedom of space within limits. She dances under the adoring gaze of her female teacher and the female housekeeper, but these women are edited from the frame so that the camera circles Marisol, her uncle and grandfather, the latter for whom she appears to dance solely (and also reveals the local boys watching from the doorway). Underlining her role as 'little woman', it is the doubling of Marisol with her mother in this scene, who is working as a folkloric dancer and singer, that will later allow Marisol's mother to be gathered back into the fold (she will marry Marisol's uncle). Marisol mimetically and inter-subjectively takes on the gestures of adult femininity in her repertoire of embodiment.

Marisol's developing body – 'la niña ya crecidita' (the girl all grown-up) – is the main subject of her body of work. She is perpetually 'becoming a woman'. Linda Ruth Williams has noted that it is important that the child stays the same: the child is a transforming creature, she says, who needs to remain unchanged him or herself.[9] The child star's perfect youthfulness is under attack as they perpetually grow older, sometimes even visibly between the onset of the filming of a motion picture and its completion. Sameness, she says, is central to a child's image. Perhaps it is for this reason that when the child star grows up he or she loses their appeal. The child star is often depicted as going off the rails as revelations come out about pushy parents or chaotic lifestyles: they are construed as the products of the inevitable corruption of innocence. In the sense that the name 'Marisol' represented her brand, Marisol represented the sense of sameness and continuity that Linda Ruth Williams refers to, an anchor for the changes brought about in Spanish society in the 1960s, but Marisol was, at the same time, perpetually in motion and her body (the very embodiment of change) was under constant scrutiny.

Presumably sensing that an adult Marisol signified the 'death' of their commodity, Marisol's image-makers at first attempted to retain her childishness. Press cuttings of the time confirm the cultural obsession with Marisol's growing body. An article on the occasion of her birthday in February 1961 notes that she is turning eleven (although her birth-date in 1948 would suggest otherwise): 'el aplauso universal que ya recibe no le hace perder su infantil ilusión' (the universal praise she is already receiving has not made her lose her childish illusions) (Anon, 1961a: n.p.). Another compares Marisol to Shirley Temple noting that Temple is growing up: '¿cuántos años tendrá? Pocos para una mujer y demasiados para una niña. Shirley Temple nos resulta ya irremisiblemente veterana con respecto a la niña Marisol' (how old must she be? Too young to be a woman and too old to be a girl. Shirley Temple now seems to us to be a veteran in comparison to the girl Marisol) (Anon, 1961b: n.p.). An article of 1961 from *Primer Plano* claims that her recent tour of South America 'has not changed her' (Anon, 1961d: n.p.). It notes that she has grown a few centimetres but, 'no es el cuerpo lo que aquí cuenta, sino el espíritu' (it's not her body that counts here but her spirit) (Anon, 1961c: n.p), and in the photo to accompany the caption, 'Marisol, ocho centímetros más' (Marisol, eight centimetres taller), Marisol is still carrying an enormous toy chimpanzee and a doll given to her in Puerto Rico, Brazil or Argentina. Marisol is a child-woman, with the body of a woman and the 'spirit' of a child (Anon, 1961d). A year later, in February 1962, *Radiocinema* was reporting that she was turning thirteen, but 'la fama no la ha hecho perder sus encantos infantiles' (fame has not made her lose her childlike charms) (Anon, 1962c). In 1963 we are told that she 'crece normalmente como cualquier muchachita de su edad' (is growing normally like any girl of her age) (Fiestas, 1963: n.p.). Anxiety and ambivalence over a child's progress into puberty translated into the (libidinised) scrutiny of her growing body. 'Debe de ser terrible' (It must be terrible) wrote Manuel Vicent in *Retratos de la transición* in 1981, 'que a una niña le apunten las tetitas en la rebeca bajo la mirada espesa de un país entero, estar consciente de que treinta millones de contribuyentes miden cada mañana en su memoria el crecimiento de tu culo, sentir que los avatares de tu cuerpo forman parte de la opinión pública' (for a girl's breasts to start to show under her cardigan in front of the thick glare of an entire country, to be conscious that thirty million viewers are engraving on their memory the growth of your bottom each morning, to feel that the changes of your body form part of public opinion) (Vicent, 1981: 144). As Pavlović notes, even as Vicent denounces Marisol's exploitation, he fails to acknowledge his own libidinal involvements in writing about Marisol's body (Pavlović, 2011: 128). By December 1962 'la deliciosa niña de la película' (the delicious girl from the film) is now 'convertida en una maravillosa mujercita' (converted into a marvellous little woman) (Anon, 1962b), and in January 1963 we are told that 'Marisol al finalizar el año 62 se encuentra en plena evolución física. Es ya una mujercita encantadora' (Marisol is in full physical development at the end of '62. She is now an enchanting little woman) (Jordan, 1963: 36). This obsession with Marisol's physical evolution continued throughout her career, thus in 1969 the advertisement for 'Carola de día, Carola de noche' (Carola by Day, Carola by Night) announces, 'Marisol ya no es una niña … ni siquiera una adolescente ¡Es una hermosa mujer!' (Marisol is no longer a girl … not even an adolescent. She's a beautiful woman!) and as if to mimic the advertisements for the Marisol doll, '¡Y como tal actúa, habla, piensa y ama!' (And as such she acts, speaks, thinks and loves!) (Anon, 1969) and as we shall see, Marisol's past as the child star haunted and inflected her later work as an adult actress.

Marisol inspired others to imitate the success she had enjoyed.[10] Pili y Mili (Aurora and Pilar Bayona Sarriá), were apparently created as the Spanish

'Kessler Twins' (Farnegaes, 1962), although Disney had also had success with a cloned Hayley Mills (playing twins Sharon and Susie) in *The Parent Trap* (David Swift, 1961). They debuted with *Como dos gotas de agua* (Like Two Peas in a Pod, Amadori) in 1963 – after a brief, successful appearance to test the water on TV they were contracted by Benito Perojo for a four-year exclusive contract (Anon, 1963a) – and Goyanes responded with *Marisol, rumbo a Río* with Marisol playing twins in 1963. The title track, 'Tengo permiso de papá' (I've got Daddy's permission), was thought to be an embedded reference to censorship laws, with 'Daddy' as Franco himself. A coquettish Pili sings melancholically in an upper-class drawing room before unleashing a head-bashing 1960s jazz number and sitting on the laps of the men present. But Pili's performance is a carefully choreographed set designed to frame her as a self-assured, smoking, flirtatious young woman. Here, and in the other films (they stopped making films in 1970 when Aurora emigrated to Mexico to get married) Pili and Mili always have each other, which goes a long way to disperse their vulnerability. Rocío Durcal, launched by Luis Sanz, meanwhile, often photographed together with Marisol (the brunette to Marisol's blonde) was far older (eighteen when she filmed *Canción de juventud* (Song for Youth) in 1962 although advertised as sixteen) and far more self-assured.[11] Her films, whilst fun, centred on her dreams – such as the kitschy *La novicia soñadora* (The Dreaming Novice, Luis Lucia, 1971) – and paved the way for the successful singing career that would follow on from her films. She was as prolific as Marisol, but was presented as being like a calmer, older sister. In *Cristina Guzmán* (César Luis Amadori, 1968) she plays Cristina, a teacher of English with a child who (in shades of Hitchcock's *Vertigo*) is contracted to play Mara, the estranged wife of Javier Rivas, because of their similarity. Durcal plays both roles, the good-girl Cristina and the wayward, smoking, nasty Mara but it is Cristina who clearly triumphs at the end of the film.[12] Durcal's slogan was 'más bonita que ninguna' (prettier than all the rest) and she had an 'aire amable' (nice manner) which made her the idol 'de la juventud sin rebeldías turbadoras' (of young people who weren't into edgy rebellion) (Rollan, 1969: 13). Leonardo Martin, the co-scriptwriter on *Canción de juventud*, brought Luis Lucia (the producer of most of Marisol's films) a young Ana Belén to make *Zampo y yo* (Zampo and Me), in which Fernando Rey plays a clown named Zampo to Belén's singing and dancing orphan. But the film was not successful (although Belén, who went to drama school, would go on to a successful acting career as a young woman, her passage from Francoist child star facilitated by eroticism and her militancy in the Spanish Communist Party) (Aguilar, 2012: 13–28). Estrellita, meanwhile, seems like a carbon-copy of Marisol: in 1961 to announce her first film *Han robado una estrella* (A Star has been Stolen, Javier Setó), a film similar to *Tómbola* but which features a set from Estrellita as Charlie Chaplin, a press piece describes her 'desparpajo' (wit) and 'simpatía' (charm).[13] But these imitations of Marisol serve merely to reinforce the sense of Marisol's ubiquity and influence.

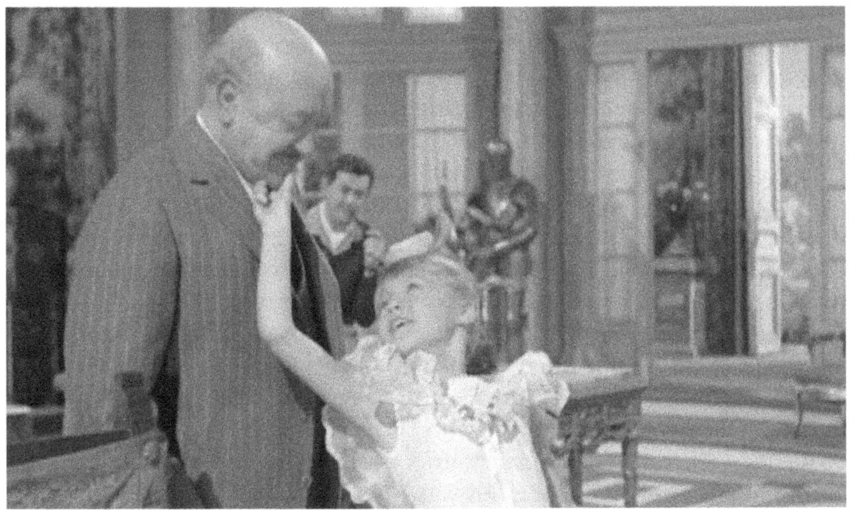

5 Marisol grasps her grandfather (Julian Sanjuan) in a 'chin chuck'
in *Un rayo de luz* (Luis Lucia, 1960).

Arguably too chaotic and tension-ridden to be part of a concerted
Francoist cultural ideological agenda (Pavlović, 2011), Marisol's films nevertheless might be seen to embody 'un nuevo tipo de sujeto/súbdito' (a new
kind of subject) as part of a banal and 'apresurada "educación sentimental"
neoliberal' (hurried neoliberal 'sentimental education') (Vilarós, 2005: 51).
In *Un rayo de luz*, a small gesture seems to skewer Marisol's position as
'sujeto/súbdito' (subject/subordinate). During her flamenco turn, a close-up
of her grandfather's face reveals his delight in his granddaughter before she
reaches up behind her and grasps her grandfather's face in a chin chuck.

A reversal of the typical caressing of the cute child, the chin chuck here
serves to underscore the way that Marisol transgresses her childish role
(there is something flirtatious about the chin chuck). But the image is also
strikingly echoed in a photograph of General Franco the following year in
January 1961. Franco had been involved in a hunting accident when a car-
tridge blew up injuring his left hand. In a staged photo opportunity, Franco
was captured as he left hospital extending his right hand to his grandson
(who has been pushed out into Franco's path by an unknown arm) whom
he grasps in a chin chuck (his other hand, encased in plaster, sticks out
monstrously from his overcoat) (Anon, 1962e). Photo opportunities with
children were, of course, common at the time but Gil Pecharromán notes
that this particular photo-call caused anxiety amongst the nation: 'pese a
la relativa nimiedad del incidente, su impacto en la población y entre la
clase política fue grande. Una de las derivaciones del carisma de Franco era
la creencia popular en su salud de hierro, por lo que la brusca hospitali-
zación conmocionó a muchos de sus partidiarios' (in spite of the relative
insignificance of the incident, it had far-reaching impact on the general

public and amongst the political classes. One of the derivations of Franco's charisma was the popular belief in his iron constitution and this brusque hospitalisation perturbed many of his followers) and 'la conciencia de la vulnerabilidad del general, que ya contaba 69 años, convenció a muchos de que el tema de la sucesión de la Jefatura del Estado no podía seguir pendiente por mucho tiempo' (the awareness of the vulnerability of the general, who was now 69 years old, convinced many that the question of the succession of Head of State could not be left hanging for much longer) (Gil Pecharromán, 1990: 18). Taking up the position of adoring granddaughter (furthermore, the visual similarity between actor Julio Sanjuán and Franco are striking but the similarity is to a Franco of a few years earlier),[14] Marisol's youth is contrasted with Franco's ageing, providing a shot in the arm to a regime that was ageing and which needed to galvanise the support of the younger generation (those who had had little or no direct experience of the war). If Marisol's commentators became obsessed with her growing body and advancement in age, this was a phantom manifestation and a disavowal of the unspoken obsession with the ageing of the regime embodied by Franco himself, which Sally Faulkner (2005) has examined in her excellent article on Carlos Saura's *La caza* (The Hunt, 1964). Another publicity piece depicts Marisol on a fishing trip (the journalist notes that this seems to have been staged for the occasion) (A. R., 1962). In her meeting, greeting, travelling and caressing of children, Marisol seems to mimic Franco's public outings. Two bodies, one youthful, the other decrepit, drew inter-subjectively from one another: Franco's body drew life itself from the young child star, whilst Marisol was the docile embodiment of authoritarian rule.[15]

The girl/older man paradigm begun in *Un rayo de luz* may have been an attempt to manufacture Marisol as the 'Spanish Shirley Temple' (with all its attendant latent eroticism) and this provided the opportunity for a string of variations in Marisol's films on the theme of substitute paternalism, as Evans (2004) has noted. One of the first publicity images for *Un rayo de luz* has Marisol posing alongside Julio Sanjuán, playing her grandfather, her finger raised to her lips in the gesture for the keeping of secrets ('ssshhh!'). This paradigm was repeated in pro-filmic press material which depicted Marisol as being kissed, hugged or sitting on the laps of a range of older male figures, from her substitute father Manuel Goyanes, to film directors such as Luis Lucia, or photographers. In *Ha llegado un angel* a group of singing stars she meets on the train describe her as 'la novia de todos' (everyone's girlfriend) whilst in *Tómbola* she becomes the angelic nurse-figure to a group of crooks. Manuel Vicent noted that Marisol was 'esa criatura que todas las madres de la tecnocracia hubieran deseado tener como hija' (that child that all the mothers of the regime would have wished to have as a daughter) (Vicent, 1981: 144), but increasingly 'habíamos pasado de la niña graciosa a la adolescente que cualquier madre querría para su hijo como novia' (we had gone from the funny girl to the adolescent that any mother would choose as girlfriend/bride for her son) (Aguilar and Losada,

2008: 169). This was a subtle distinction but if Marisol was known as 'la novia de España' (the girlfriend/bride of Spain) (Aguilar and Losada, 2008: 169), her symbolic value was as an exchange commodity to be circulated between men to the delight of all. This circulation was mirrored in Marisol's off-screen persona as Goyanes married her off to his son Carlos in 1969: a marriage that would ultimately end in separation in 1972. In the sense that Marisol's films appear to enact a perpetual present, continually enacting the exchange of Marisol between men, we may be reminded that one definition of trauma is the enactment of a perpetual present, 'resilient in its persistence and timeless in its inhabitation of a subject who does not, and cannot know *it*' (Pollock, 2009: 40). Something traumatic has happened, but 'I do not know it – that it happened or what it was that happened, the *eventless event, unremembered*' (Pollock, 2009: 40). Marisol's endless repeating of her role as plaything to an older man begins to seem pathological, like a return to the scene of the crime, Marisol compulsively re-enacts her turn to an older male figure to experience love and affection.

Spain's resilient perpetual present

Marisol's films take place in 'un contexto idealizado sobre el cual la sociedad civil o el Estado no mantiene ningún tipo de compromiso o responsabilidad' (an idealised context over which neither civil society nor the state maintains any sort of commitment or responsibility) (Heredero, 1993: 230). They practise a form of cultural amnesia which has no memory of the war and the poverty of the immediate post-war years, operating in a perpetual present-cum-future encapsulated in Marisol's developing body. This is, as Pollock writes, an 'eventless event, unremembered', a 'perpetual present because it is not yet known: was never known, hence never forgotten, and thus not yet remembered' (Pollock, 2009: 40). Marisol's films are full of movement and flux, light and colour.

Released two years before Manuel Fraga Iribarne's famous slogan supported by a nationwide campaign celebrating 'Twenty Five Years of Peace' in 1964, *Tómbola* seems nevertheless to endorse Fraga's central message that Spain is a prosperous land (the bellic language supplemented by discourse emphasising the advantages of economic prosperity) and that the hard-won peace (construed as a result of the Francoist victory) is subject to constant vigilance from forces (both internal and external) which would remove the dictatorship. In *Tómbola*, Marisol lives in a world of wealth and privilege whose *mise-en-scène* presents us with exercise bikes, horse-riding and large rooms with chandeliers. When Marisol mistakenly believes that her friend María-Belén (Joelle Rivers) has been kidnapped during a horse-riding expedition at school, she enlists the aid of the army and police (who appear to be roaming the countryside ready to carry out important missions). Long shots capture the expanse of the Spanish countryside whilst tight shots of Marisol on top of a tank, arms outstretched like the figurehead of a ship, recall the theatrical displays of military force which formed part of the parades of the '25 años' celebrations. María-Belén is from an unspecified African country and the imperialistic connotations of the deployment of Spanish military might are clear – even if, in this case, the military might is shown to be a misplaced force as María-Belén has not in fact been kidnapped. María-Belén (the daughter of a diplomat) has received refuge in Spain, and is Marisol's best friend (they are often dressed identically) but the racist implications are confirmed in a scene where María-Belén remarks to Marisol, 'estoy empezando a pensar que sería estupendo ser tan rubia como tú y tener los ojos azules como los tuyos' (I'm beginning to think that it would be marvellous to be as blonde as you and to have blue eyes like yours). Marisol's love for her friend is therefore rather like Sara Ahmed's description of love as one which 'return[s] the idealised image of whiteness back to oneself' (Ahmed, 2004: 129). The 25 años celebrations were sombre affairs designed to endorse the regime's stability with military marches providing the spectacle of pride in military might. *Tómbola* meanwhile, seems tongue-in-cheek: the army is roaming all over the countryside looking for minor crises to solve. But this good-natured mocking of the celebrations of peace also served to reinforce the notion of a stable country with strong defences.

Tómbola is a variation on Aesop's 'The Boy Who Cried Wolf' with Marisol at pains to get anyone to believe that she has witnessed a robbery. Marisol is the girl-spy – with resonances of the vigilant child-informer endorsed during early Francoism (from the comic *Flechas y Plelayos*, for example). Owing to her observational skills (she first sees that some clergymen have inappropriate shoes) she is the sole witness to the robbery of a painting during a school visit to an art gallery but no one believes her – her teacher even places her hand over her mouth to gag her. When Marisol appears on television in an attempt to recover the painting – the 'Madonna de las Rosas' (Madonna of the Roses) – she is lured into a trap by the crooks and kidnapped by them – one of the crooks used to work on stage as a ventriloquist with a dummy called 'Marieta' and he fools Marisol, posing as 'Marujita', the daughter of one of the crooks. You can't even trust what you hear, it seems, but must search for the truth in an environment of fakery. But if Marujita is a fake, Marisol is the real treasure (the painting and Marisol are elided as 'national treasures'). Earlier in the film Marisol and María-Belén discuss the presence of unknown forces which 'could be the enemy in disguise'. When María-Belén asks her which enemy she is referring to, Marisol replies, 'Vaya pregunta, de este enemigo de siempre' (What a question, the same old enemy as always). Constant vigilance is required to protect a nation which, like a child 'at risk', is subject to the perpetual danger of attempts to disrupt its peace and stability. When she is kidnapped, Marisol becomes the 'little woman', caring for the thieves when they are sick and cooking and cleaning for them. In this sense she coincides perfectly with the narrative of the 'little woman' which was peddled for girls by reading matter of Francoism. Thus, *La niña instruida* (The Educated Girl), a schoolbook for girls (my edition is 1945) explains how to keep house, do the cleaning as well as sections on nursing and cooking (with illustrations of the digestive system) (Ascarza, 1945). Luis Otero's semi-nostalgic *Mi mamá me mima* (My Mother Spoils Me – chosen for its alliterative effect) collects a series of examples of the indoctrination of little girls as mothers and nurses. One page of a schoolbook *El nuevo camarada* (The New Comrade) cites 'una buena hija' (a good daughter) as a child who looks after her sick mother and her little brother (Otero, 1999: 143).

In *Tómbola*, Marisol will invoke the Virgin Mary and Jesus in her quest to recover the painting, and enlists the support of the local priest, but as Pavlović notes, 'even when Marisol's films "promote" Christian values they are abstracted and embedded in entertainment' (2011: 127). In fact the religious references appear anachronistic. Thus the transformations of the film (the crooks' repentance) are secular: wrought out of Marisol's 'simpatía' and the prosaic product of the thieves having served time in prison and the film's ending, a spirited rendition of the theme-tune, *Tómbola*, reminds us that 'life is a lottery' in this land of opportunity as Marisol's face is superimposed on a whirling wheel of 'light and colour'.

As a perpetually 'becoming-woman', Marisol embodies the flux and change heralding the new economic developments of the 1960s (the *Plan de estabilización* and the *Plan de desarrollo*). Marisol burst onto Spain's cinema screens in the 1960s, a singing, dancing riot of energy which coloured (with Eastmancolor) cinematic dreamscapes, all sites of transition: TV studios, mansions, billboarded streets, airplane steps and airport escalators. Marisol's films represent a secular optimism: where Joselito (the 'singing nightingale' and Marisol's musical predecessor) was 'ridden by melancholic longing', Marisol occupied a space of future possibilities: she confronted life with ebullient wit, *desparpajo* (self-assurance) and *simpatía* (Pavlović, 2011: 126). The implicit narrative encapsulated in Marisol's persona was the move towards modernity. Traditional rural values of family and hard work may have contributed to making Marisol's star persona, but in the sense that her films take place in largely urban milieus, she implicitly represented Spain's move from 'backwardness' towards modernity, underscored by capitalism. For Teresa Vilarós (2005), Marisol is a biopolitical tool. Her characters, meanwhile, are comfortable in any social class (Pavlović, 2011: 126), symbolising fluidity and the possibilities of social climbing in the new Spain of economic growth. In *Ha llegado un ángel*, Marisol's transformations see her arranging for her cousin to obtain a job with 'El Señor Seat' (Mr Seat), whilst her flamenco performance on television will transform the economic fortunes for herself and her new family. Marisol's films repeatedly enact the moment when Marisol steps out onto the stage: a before and after exposure which dramatises her ordinariness and extraordinariness at one at the same time. Performing therefore becomes linked with economic opportunity: *La nueva Cenicienta* (The New Cinderella, George Sherman, 1964) for example, is a collage of stages for Marisol to perform on – natural talent and hard work (with a little luck) will be valued in the new, modern Spain. In that film, Marisol has to decide between the American Robert Conrad (whose accent retains its foreignness) or the home-grown Antonio: in her finale she gets to dance with both. If *La nueva Cenicienta* was a home grown version of the American musical, then flamenco (and metonymically, Spain) is shown to be sophisticated (filmed on stylistic meta-stages), stylish and thoroughly modern. The film centres on the preparations being made for a live transmission of Eurovision transmitted across Europe from Madrid. Television is identified with modernisation and Americanisation (Camporesi, 2007b). But chaos ensues when Marisol lets the pet chimp, Miguel, loose on the TV station and the transmission has to be taken off-air. The chimpanzee (Miguel, just one of the artists, we are told) has featured in set pieces where Marisol sings and dances as she cleans for the men of the household. The chimp is the comedy sidekick, learning to be socialised (he breaks the plates handed to him to be dried). But where Marisol operates with decorum at all times as she negotiates her role as little woman between two men, the chimpanzee offers relief from the decorum. Thus, he might be seen as the double of Marisol, but here a rampaging toddler psyche, an expression of the repressed childishness of Marisol as she seemingly perpetually turns into a woman. Miguel's face looms on the TV screen before being taken off-air and he is led away just as Marisol is soothed by Antonio who explains that the transmission did not go out to the world and that she can apologise to those concerned for her transgression.

In 1964, recently appointed Minister for Information Fraga Iribarne launched his famous slogan 'España es diferente' (Spain is Different) which was a vast campaign to be featured on brochures, postcards and tacky souvenirs until it was replaced in 1979 (Crumbaugh, 2009: 67). Designed to attract foreigners to Spain, Justin Crumbaugh suggests that it also had an important impact on the domestic cultural imaginary, coinciding with the regime's push towards modernisation, the first integrated Plan de Desarrollo in 1964 and the propaganda associated with the 'Twenty Five Years of Peace'. 'Those opposed to the dictatorship immediately recognised the slogan's political underpinnings and quickly refigured "Spain is Different" as a code for the regime's hackneyed conceptions of national culture and clumsy entrance into the international marketplace' (Crumbaugh, 2009: 68). 'España es diferente' promoted the bullfight and flamenco as an example of Spain's 'difference' for foreigners in an attempt to entice them to the costas. Amidst the dizzying display of revolving stages in *La nueva Cenicienta*, suggesting change, the film indulges in set pieces where Marisol dances, firstly with Antonio 'el Bailarín' and then with Robert Conrad. These moments slow the action down and in the first of these, in which Marisol contemplates a billboard of Antonio before he comes down out of the picture to dance with her, transformation is fetishised. Flamenco, the homegrown indigenous talent, is paraded as spectacle in a way that suggests its transformations from *españolada* to dreamscape of endless possibility.

Teresa Vilarós (2005) reminds us that Marisol's films received financial support from the Ministry for Information and Tourism and she sees them as exercising an 'educación sentimental' on the nation to instruct them into the new consumerism which had previously been out of reach to the average Spaniard. Where earlier films had stressed flamenco as the essence of Spanishness, in *Búsqueme a esa chica* (Get that Girl for Me, Fernando Palacios/George Sherman, 1964) it becomes merely the cynical performance of Spanishness, to relieve foreign tourists of their cash. In *Búsqueme a esa chica* we find Marisol at the beach, singing flamenco for tourists. Marisol was, by now, being touted (alongside Teresa Gimpera and Angel Malla, the 'kid' in Westerns) as a possible contender for huge international fame (Anon, 1965).[16] Marisol and her father (José Bodalo) (who falsely pretends to be blind) are two tramps who sing and dance for tourists in Mallorca: we first see them performing a song and dance routine to get some money out of a group of foreign tourists outside a hotel. When her father has had a meal with the 500 pesetas they are given by a wealthy American businessman, the 'crisis de desarrollo' that he has humorously referred to is, as Deleyto has noted:

> to be taken as a metaphor for Spain in the 1960s. The film suggests that after the Civil War and the isolation that Spain underwent in the post-war years, this is only a temporary crisis which, with the contributions of foreign tourists, will soon disappear, allowing the country to reach the international status its spiritual superiority warrants. Marisol's films present a golden future in which foreign nations, once they have unwittingly bestowed their unfairly gained economic wealth on Spain, will come to envy that country and recognise the superiority of its ideological doctrine. (Deleyto, 1993: 243)

The film is deeply cynical about its selling points and although Marisol's later associations with the Duo Dinámico and pop ye-ye go some way to improving the image of flamenco propagated by that early sequence, the overriding image is one of the 'self-consciousness (even blatant cynicism) regarding the marketing of national culture', which Justin Crumbaugh finds 'was not at odds with Francoism but rather became one of its defining features' (2009: 69). This self-consciousness seems to infuse Marisol's later work. *Cabriola* (Prancer, 1965) sees Marisol (sporting a new, sophisticated short hair-cut) disguising herself as a boy to train with a famous *rejoneador* and then appear in the bullring. Notably this is worlds away from the cynicism of *Búsqueme a esa chica* although Marisol's performance does seem self-conscious (she has become rather like what critics of Dyer's work on the star suggest is the star with an embedded irony and she struggles to keep the material fresh, innocent and unhackneyed) – this is a carefully crafted image of 'Spanishness' for internal consumption whilst the inclusion of the American star suggested that Spain's (sophisticated) 'difference' might sell well abroad. Little wonder that Carlos Saura, in *Carmen*'s (1983) attempts to rescue flamenco from a history of cheap appropriations in the name of *franquismo*, should include an older, wiser Marisol, who now went by the name of Pepa Flores. Flores was in a relationship with Antonio Gades by that time: both had received an audience with Fidel Castro and declared their Communist affiliations. But the inclusion of Marisol in *Carmen*, even in her minor role as the hand-clapping support to Paco de Lucía's flamenco guitar, provides a fascinating intertextual support for transformations.

In 1968, Marisol made *Solos los dos* (Just the Two of Us) with the young matador Palomo Linares. The story was conceived as a 'fotonovela', a genre which had been made popular through the publications of Corín Tellado and which suited the unnatural acting style of both leads (this was Linares's second film). Sebastián Palomo Linares was known as 'el fenómeno de los fenómenos' (the phenomenon of all phenomena) and the film also brought together Jaime de Armiñán – known for TV shows such as 'Las doce caras de Juan' (The Twelve Faces of Juan) and 'Las fábulas' (The Fables) – and Juan y Junior (the latter would marry Rocío Durcal in 1970), who were famous for pop music of the day. Publicity surrounding the film focused on the separation of Marisol from Carlitos Goyanes and there were the inevitable rumours of a relationship with Linares. But in spite of this promising cocktail, the film was not an enormous success.

Marisol and Linares are would-be lovers, but they are separated by their different worlds – Marisol belongs to the elite circles of Andalusian society and Linares is a bullfighter. Whilst Linares hates Marisol's world, she is afflicted by a traumatic reaction to the bullfight and cannot bear to see him in the arena. An early scene of *Solos los dos* cross-cuts Linares in the bull-ring, seducing the bull with his cape (we hear his thoughts as he hopes that Marisol is watching him) with scenes of Marisol in a short, white tennis outfit, playing tennis with an unknown male in the hills above the bullring, indifferent to the shouts which reach them from the ring below. The self-consciousness of the editing may remind us of Pedro Almodóvar's *Matador* (1983) (*Solos los dos* seems like an overlooked intertext for Almodóvar's film where the bullfight is the central motif for the two leads and their mutual seductions and this dictates the formal construction of the film). In *Solos los dos*, the divisions of Marisol and Linares, played out in the editing of the scene, are continued throughout the film, which sees the pair involved in a car chase, horse-back riding, sailing, tennis-playing, skiing and bullfighting as they attempt to work out their differences. Marisol's mother (the excellent Margot Cottens, whose kitschy yellow suit and affectionate comic turn also remind us of later Almodóvar heroines) attends a bullfight and reports it live to her daughter (who grimaces at the thought of harm coming to Palomo) via a walkie-talkie. In a later scene at Palomo's house, Marisol sees a mounted head of a bull on the wall and is afflicted by the 'memory' of past bullfights in a montage of canted shots of the bull's head interspersed with close-ups of her shocked eyes and mouth and wring-ing hands. These 'memories' echo an earlier scene where Palomo simply imagines the upper-class members of a charity benefit disappear because he does not want to get to know them. But where Palomo can imagine the world as he wishes it to be, Marisol is afflicted by traumatic memories. In spite of its apparent 'banalidad', the film appears to articulate trauma. Palomo takes Marisol to an empty bullring to show her his art and the imagined bullfight materialises before our eyes before disappearing once more. Palomo launches a lethal 'estocada' (thrust) as Marisol winces.[17] Earlier, we have witnessed Palomo and Marisol, the modernity of their clothes clashing strikingly with their surroundings, walking through an olive grove studded with gnarled ancient olive trees whilst Marisol recites lines from Antonio Machado's poem 'Los olivos' (the olive trees) with the lines, '¡Viejos olivos sedientos/bajo el claro sol del día' (Thirsty old olive trees/under the clear sun). Ostensibly this reference to the poet gives rise to the observation from Marisol to the confidence-lacking Palomo that, 'en los toros hay poesía' (bullfighting can be poetic), the reference to Machado naturally also invokes his death on the run from the Francoists and his diffusion of the phrase 'las dos Españas' (the two Spains) (one that dies and one that yawns – comically turned by Almodóvar in *Matador* into the 'envidiosos' (envious) and the 'intolerantes' (intolerant) representative of the split nation) in the run-up to the Spanish Civil War. Even the path that Marisol and Palomo tread through the olive grove seems to split it in two, whilst their modern 'beat' (beatnik) clothes clash with the ancient trees suggesting a split between generations as well as ideological convictions. Returning to the scene in the empty bullring, as Marisol winces as the bull is stabbed, she and the bull become elided with wounded Spain. The camera focuses on her face: she looks exhausted with anxiety. The camera pans around the empty arena and we hear the cries of past crowds. Crowds in the bullfight are split into 'sol' and 'sombra' depending on whether they sit in the sun or the shade. Marisol's traumatic reaction to the sounds of the crowds and the sight of the wounded bull gesture to the triggering of previous traumas. Through the earlier reference to Machado these ghostly crowds become related to the theme of the 'two Spains' and gesture towards the traumas of war.

The self-conscious formal techniques of the film, the cross cutting and montage effects, are joined by a split screen in the scene where Marisol goes alone, on a skiing trip. Ostensibly to 'get her head together', the screen suggests her inability to reconcile her conflicting emotions as it splits into four as she sings a set piece. The song 'Dos unidos' (The Two of Us, United) at the end of the film tells us that an ethical reconciliation is possible, but through split screens and a dizzying blend of locales and moods the formal techniques of the film speak otherwise. As a move from the mute trauma of the perpetual present 'into the narrativity that institutes time' (Pollock, 2009: 40), the formal aspects of the film splice time and space incoherently, but now the perpetual present is fractured into multiple dimensions. We are left with the sense that Spain has not yet come to terms with the traumas of the past, in the face of a maelstrom of lights, sounds and colours.

Coming of age

In February 1969 Marisol turned twenty-one and although she renewed her contract with Goyanes for another five years, she now took on more adult roles, even if, in *Carola de día, Carola de noche*, she first appears in a Red Riding Hood cloak whilst being whistled at by a flirtatious Fernando Fernán Gómez and in spite of her much-publicised wedding to Carlos Goyanes in 1969 (which lasted just three years).[18] In 1972, representing Spain at the Festival de la OTI – similar to the Eurovision Song Contest and broadcast on TV to millions of viewers (Aguilar and Losada, 2008: 74) – her entry 'Niña' contained the words, 'Niña/que te ves desnuda al espejo/y ves que tu infancia se aleja' ('Girl/who sees herself naked in the mirror/and sees how her childhood gets further away'), which ran into trouble with the censors. With a widely-publicised separation from Goyanes in her private life, the press began to refer to Marisol's 'aire de melancolíaa que acentuaba aún más su belleza' (melancholic air which accentuated her beauty), whilst one of her songs featured the lines, '¿Por qué yo habré nacido distinta a los demás? ¿Por qué no me dejaban jugar, cantar y andar' (why was I born different from the rest? Why didn't they let me play and sing and walk?) (Aguilar and Losada, 2008: 235). After gaining her own TV show '360° en torno a Marisol' (360° Around Marisol) in which she sang, danced and interviewed herself, Marisol made *La corrupción de Chris Miller* (The Corruption of Chris Miller), directed by Juan Antonio Bardem in 1972. Jean Seberg took the starring role, and Malcolm McDowell (who was fresh from success in *The Clockwork Orange*) was touted to play Barney, the drifter, but that role eventually went to Barry Stokes, a British actor well known on British TV. Marisol is a woman who is haunted by the trauma of having been raped in a shower – a clear reference to Hitchcock's *Psycho* (Aguilar and Losada, 2008: 75) – and now lives with her stepmother (Jean Seberg) in the north of Spain. Whenever it rains, Chris (Marisol) suffers nightmares and attempts to stab her pillow with a knife, only to be pacified by her stepmother, who soothes her (we presume, the screen goes black) by making love to her. The film plays on the shock value of having Marisol, the child star, not only often dressed in translucent nightgowns but also as the object of lesbian desire: Ruth states early on that men are cruel and violent – she has been left by her husband (Marisol's father) and now wishes to take her revenge on him by 'corrupting' his daughter, Chris. But Chris has already been traumatised, by the shower-rape, and, it is suggested, possibly also by her father, a puppeteer. Thus, when Barney, the drifter invited into their home to do odd jobs, remarks that many children's songs and stories are erotic she concurs, remarking that her father told her that grandmother was having an affair with the wolf, but when the wolf seduced Red Riding Hood, grandmother killed them both. We have already witnessed a murder at the start of the film, when a man dressed as Charlie Chaplin murders a film star somewhere in Spain. Now, when Barney takes a lawnmower and the camera's gaze appears to cut off Chris's legs as she lies sunbathing topless, we associate him with the murder. In a further murder, a figure with cloak and reap slashes an innocent family to death in their home. But after further scenes of schlock gore as Chris (in one of her nightmares) and Ruth slash Barney to bits, they will later discover that the man they killed was an innocent hippy who had a necklace of pea pods in his pocket: the real culprit was their stable-hand who is led away by the police. They bury the hippy and are pleased when diggers arrive to place asphalt on top to create a road. Later, in a foreign swimming pool, the camera cross cuts between the scene of Chris and Ruth in their new idyll and the police back at home coming to investigate pea shoots which are coming up through the asphalt.

In *La chica del Molino Rojo* (The Girl of the Moulin Rouge, Juan Antonio Bardem, 1973) Marisol plays a cabaret dancer and virgin who is chosen as a honey-trap for a Don Juanesque Larry, but she ends up (predictably) choosing the older male figure whilst in *El poder del deseo* (The Power of Desire, 1975), again directed by Juan Antonio Bardem, Marisol is the object of obsession, a *femme fatale* who wears various different wigs and is shown in various states of undress. A sex scene on the sofa is intercut with scenes from the television showing fish being caught in a net as Justina (Marisol, in a Sadean reference) convinces Javier (Murray Head, who had played Judas in Lloyd Webber's *Jesus Christ Superstar*) to kill her uncle but even after stabbing her he will learn that he has been the victim of subterfuge. By now Marisol had entered into a relationship with Antonio Gades whilst famously Castro himself had blessed the union.

In 1976, Marisol appeared nude on the cover of *Interviú*. Symbolic of the *destape* following Franco's death these shots capitalised on Marisol's past as a child star by capturing Marisol in a similar pose to that of the little girl in John Everett Millais's *Cherry Ripe* (1879) in which genitals are suggested by the shape of the hands which covered them. But now Marisol represents allegorically, 'el bello camino hacia la democracia' (the beautiful path towards democracy) and as Morcillo has pointed out, 'many actresses would pose naked in front of the camera in the late 1970s and early 1980s. They became the allegorical incarnations of the nation in such a political juncture – a vulnerable naked woman, a vulnerable democratic Spain' (Morcillo, 2010: 271). The slow period of *apertura* from 1962–69 had seen an imbrication of eroticism with politics. As Vázquez Montalbán noted in *Cronica sentimental de España*, 'los españoles de los sesenta se acostumbraban a medir el grado de libertad por los centímetros de las faldas de las mujeres' (in the Sixties Spaniards grew accustomed to measuring the degree of freedom according to the centimetres of women's skirts) (Vázquez Montalbán, 1986: 190). By 1976, the culture of the *destape* freely linked nudity and eroticism with post-Francoism. In 1976, Francisco Umbral imagined Susana Estrada, symbol of the *destape*, walking completely naked up to the Palacio del Pardo to where Franco had just died (Marí, 2003: 242). *La trastienda* (The Backroom, Jorge Grau 1976), which featured the first completely naked woman on the Spanish screen, the infamous Maria José Cantudo, linked this greater exposure to the revelry of the crowd celebrating after the San Fermin running of the bulls (itself metonymically standing for the freedoms of a crowd celebrating the death of the dictator). Marisol was not the only ex-child star to make films with shock value: Durcal's lesbian relationship in *Me siento extraña* (I Feel Strange, Enrique Martí Maqueda, 1977) was also causing sensations. In underground cinema, and like a response to Umbral's dream of Estrada visiting El Pardo, Antoni Padrós's *Shirley Temple Story* (1976) conceived of Temple going to an emerald kingdom (with resonances of *The Wizard of Oz*) to ask why the part had gone to Judy Garland and not to her, and finding on her way an array of representatives of corrupt Francoism. With her delayed lip-synch and surreal musical numbers, Temple seems like the underside of early Marisol (Padrós has her sitting on the toilet and committing murder in his corruption of the sacred status of the child star).

Eduardo Haro Tecglen remembers the first nude women in theatre thus: 'me parecía una conquista de un cuerpo siempre cubierto, a veces maldito por los padres de la Iglesia; el síntoma claro de que Franco había muerto. La mujer recuperaba su cuerpo, su derecho a su ser' (it seemed to me to be a conquest of the endlessly covered body which had at times been damned by the fathers of the Church, the clear symptom that Franco had died. The woman got her body back and the right to her own identity) (see Mari, 2003: 246). Juan Luis Cebrián, founding director of *El País*, remarks ambivalently that Marisol 'me parece una actriz mediocre' (seems to me to be a mediocre actress) but nevertheless, 'Marisol ha sido una de las pocas mujeres-objeto, a nivel europeo que hemos podido enseñar' (Marisol has been one of the few object-women that we can show off on the European stage) but for actress María Luisa Seco in the same pages Marisol represents, 'una mujer que vive su vida, que hace lo que quiere; en una palabra, una mujer libre' (a woman who lives her life, who does whatever she wishes, in a word, a free woman) (Martín, 1976: 31). But in spite of the apparent act of rebellion, in fact the photographs had apparently been taken in 1970 to send to Bernardo Bertolucci regarding a film with Alain Delon and were now used without her permission (Evans, 2004). Francisco Umbral, in a later piece for *Interviú*, would remark that 'a mí, Marisol siempre me ha gustado eróticamente' (I've always liked Marisol erotically) and 'siempre me ha parecido muy atractiva porque es la Ninfa, es la mujer que siempre tendrá algo de niña, pero algo de niña con mucho encanto' (she's always been very attractive to me because she's a nymph, she's the woman who will always be childlike, but it's a charming child) (Umbral, 1976: 20). Looking back to an interview he did with her for *Mundo Hispánico* in 1963 he remarked then that,

> hay periodistas y fotógrafos que todavía besan a Marisol como a la niña que en realidad sigue siendo. A nuestro hombre del flash lo ha recibido con besos de sobrina. Uno piensa que todos los fotógrafos de prensa son un poco tíos de

Marisol, y les gusta sacar a la nena de paseo un jueves sí y otro también para hacerle bonitas fotos en el Retiro. (Umbral, 1963: 26)

(there are journalists and photographers who still kiss Marisol like the child she actually still is. Our cameraman received her with the kisses one gives to a niece. It's as if the press photographers are Marisol's uncles and they like to take the girl out for a walk on a Thursday now and again to take pretty photos in the Retiro.)

Umbral posits himself as 'un tio mas' (one of the uncles) and after remarking that 'todavia le quedan graciosos visos de criatura de Malaga a la gentil Marisol' (Marisol still has the funny attributes of the girl from Malaga) he notes that she 'tiene los ojos increiblemente azules y viste en esta tarde de sábado su primera falda estrecha' (has very blue eyes and on that Saturday afternoon she is dressed in her first tight skirt). On learning that she likes Westerns, they go to the cinema together where Marisol,

se indigna con el malo, cabalga discretamente en la butaca al compás del bueno. Luego se acuerda de que es ya una senorita actriz y se pone muy tiesecita en la butaca, con sus primero empaques de mujer y mas encanto natural que posible coquetería. (Umbral, 1963: 27)

(she gets cross with the baddie, she discretely rides the chair to the rhythm of the goodie. Then she remembers that she is an actress and a little lady and she sits very stiffly in the chair with her emerging femininity and more natural charm than coquetry.)

Later, in 1991, he would describe how at their first meeting, in 1963, he had a jacket with 'la oscura mancha de la gran ciudad, la huella sucia de haberse/ haberme frotado contra todas las esquinas', recalling that 'era invierno en Madrid y a Marisol aun no le apuntaban los pechos, que luego serían como dos jovenes y hermosas cosechas' (the dark stain of the big city, the dirty mark of having rubbed/been rubbed by every corner … It was winter in Madrid and Marisol's breasts still weren't showing – later they would be like two young and beautiful harvests) (Umbral, 1991: 17). But even as he cast Marisol as 'como la Lolita de Nabokov, a las doce era una adorable criatura y a los catorce una lamentable anciana' (like Nabokov's Lolita, at twelve she was an adorable creature and at fourteen a lamentable old woman) (he does not go quite so far as to admit his similarity to Humbert), he relates how Marisol told him then, 'Me llevaban a un chalet del Viso y alli acudia gente importante, gente del régimen, a verme desnuda, a mí y a otras ninas' (they took me to a chalet in El Viso and important people were there, people from the regime, to see me naked, me and other girls) (Umbral, 1991: 17). Umbral had cast himself similarly as the 'hombre de saco' (dirty old man) to 1970s child star Ana Torrent, as Smith (2000a: 36) has noted. For Smith, Umbral discloses 'the repressed eroticism of the spectator's response to child actors' as well as 'the way in which audiences trace the chronology of their own lives in the shifting appearance of performers on screen' thereby illuminating 'the historicity of our own libidinal response to cinema' (Smith, 2000a: 37). The repressed eroticism of the child-woman would be played out in Ana Torrent's case by the film *El nido* (Jaime de Armiñán, 1980) where she played a thirteen-year-old temptress (Goyita) to Hector Alterio's sixty-year-old retired widower, who will eventually commit suicide. Marisol's early eroticism was more carefully contrived; her exploitation by the films of the *destape* more manufactured and her rebellion centred equally on her body. Umbral disqualifies her Communism by suggesting that it relates merely to her relationship with Gades (Umbral, 1991: 19) whilst for Manuel Vicent:

> Pepa aún está conquistando cada día el derecho a ser persona. Hacerse roja en este país significa ser dos veces mayor de edad. Ella usa ahora ideologia. Asimilada como una forma de amor, para agredirla devoción de una beatería de la derecha que aún desearía darle la papilla y acostarla todas las noches en la cuna. (Vicent, 1981: 146)

> (Pepa is still aiming to achieve her right to be her own person. Becoming a red in this country means becoming twice ones age. She now uses ideology, assimilated as a form of love, to attack the devotion of a sanctimonious right who still want to give her baby food and put her to sleep in a cot every night.)

Umbral, angry that his project to 'contar la historia del franquismo al hilo de la historia de Marisol' (to tell the history of Francoism through the history of Marisol) had stalled, writes that 'Pepa Flores asesina a Marisol' (Pepa Flores kills Marisol) 'pero a la hora de contar detalles se me acojona' (but when it comes to giving details she freezes up) (Umbral, 1991: 19). Marisol the child-woman, for Umbral turns into the protective mother, protecting herself from further pain. 'El hilo de oro de la amistad entre ella y yo y, en los extremos, la primera entrevista de la foto y la ultima entrevista a la Pepa amarga, a la otra Flores, a la vieja mujer joven: No me fio de ti, Umbral' (the golden thread of the friendship between us and, at each end, the first interview of the photograph and the last interview of the bitter Pepa, the other Flores, the old young woman: I don't trust you, Umbral) (Umbral, 1991: 19).

It seemed as if the *cine con niño* really had come of age and grown up. Ana Mariscal's children in *El camino* (The Path, Ana Mariscal, 1963) were struggling with psychological conflicts whilst Manuel Summers, who depicted Francoist Spain through the eyes of children in *Del rosa al amarillo*, was now making *Adiós, cigüeña, adiós* (Goodbye, Stork, Goodbye, 1971) about children's sexuality and *El niño es nuestro* (It's Our Child, 1972) on the subject of teenage pregnancy. In 1977 Mercero made *La guerra de papá* featuring the child star Lolo García as the child (Quiquo) of a dysfunctional family still traumatised by the war in 1964.[19] In 1978, Mercero turned again to Lolo García to make *Tobi, el niño con alas*, a children's movie which opened in the cinemas before doing many rounds on television (and has gone down in the memories of generations of Spaniards who remember the eerie scene where Tobi is observed by scientists through a glass as he rotates on a white table before his wings begin to flex).[20]

Tobi, el niño con alas tells the story of Tobi, a four-year-old boy who suddenly grows wings. The film is a morality tale about the dangers of exploiting children for commercial gain. Horacio Valcárcel, scriptwriter for the film, explains that Mercero was looking for another film to make with Lolo García – both found it funny that a man from Comisiones Obreras (a trade union with Communist sympathies) should have a son who sprouts wings (assuming the religious implications of the child-angel). Francois Ozon's 2009 feature *Ricky*, which shares similarities with *Tobi*, is based on Rose Tremain's short story 'Moth', about a baby who grows wings and flies. Ozon's film conceives of the baby as a manifestation of the excitement a new baby brings swiftly followed by the divisiveness of a difficult baby. Ricky is tetchy, irritable, leaving his parents exhausted and when he develops a bruise on his back, we suspect that the baby may be the victim of abuse by the father (Sergi López), or the mother, or both. Mercero's film does not enter into the insinuations of child abuse except through the theme of exploitation. Like Paco in *Ricky*, Tobi's father senses that he can make money from his son's uniqueness and calls the press round before recruiting him to make some advertisements dressed as a cherub. When the evil agent (who foreshadows the grasping business women of the 1980s) enrols him as a freak show at the local fair, Tobi will climb to the top of the tallest tower, spread his wings and fly off towards the horizon never to be seen again.

An article entitled 'La era de los "niños prodigio" ha terminado' (the era of the 'child prodigies' is over) focused on a new brand of *cine con niño*, from Summers, Ibáñez and Mercero, quoting Ibáñez Serrador explaining how difficult it is to find child stars in a country without acting academies or drama schools (Santa Eulalia, 1978: 56). Elsewhere, Mercero was explaining that 'Lolo García me imita como un animal mimético' (Lolo García imitates me like a mimetic animal) and the article also noted that 'el productor de *La guerra de papa* ha ganado unos ciento cincuenta millones' (the producer of *Daddy's War* has earned some one hundred and fifty million pesetas) (Tello, 1978: 19). Repeatedly, Mercero is grilled by journalists as to his reasons for making a film with García, and his takings so far. In one article Mercero exclaimed, '¿quién me iba a decir que los ojos azules de un niño tiene más fuerza que el pubis la Cantudo?' (who would have thought that the blue eyes of a child would make more of an impact that Cantudo's pubis?) (Martínez, 1977: n.p.) in reference to the clash between the libidinous pleasures of the films of the *destape*, which depended on revelation for their effects, and Lolo García's unknowing nakedness throughout the film.

After some unsuccessful attempts to wear the clothes designed for him by his mother, Tobi runs away from the hospital where he is being investigated by scientists and skips naked through the night time deserted streets. He fools a drunk into thinking that he is a cherub come to life and then hides in the storeroom of a fashion house and pretends to be a shop-window mannequin. The child-mannequins are gesturing and Tobi adopts their pose but one points out the difference between him and them: his possession of a penis. Musing on Edward Weston's *Neil* series of 1925, a series of nude boy torsos which bear some similarity to the depiction of the angelic Tobi in this film, Anne Higonnet shows attitudes towards the nude child have changed over time. In 1925, critics saw in these works 'the pure calm flow the Greeks took as ideal', the way the 'sinuous shadows give life to delicate whites' (Higonnet, 1998: 134). But in 1980 when American artist Sherri Levine reshot six of them and exhibited her versions in a Manhattan gallery, there was more disquiet. Douglas Crimp would later remark in connection with Levine's shots that, 'the young men in my bedroom were perfectly able to read – in Weston's posing, framing and lighting, the young Neil so as to render his body as a classical sculpture – the long-established codes of homo-eroticism' (Higonnet, 1998: 137). In 1985 Sally Mann's 'Popsicle' imitated Weston's child nude torso but rather than the clean lines of Weston's sculpture, this body was smeared with some sort of fluid: 'what is that fluid in the boy's body, smeared sideways across his chest like dirt, splashed below his navel, trickling down his thighs, framing his penis? Is it blood? Is the child hurt? The mark demands to be scrutinised'. On scrutiny, 'it becomes clear that the child's body bears no wounds, and the fluid could be any liquid, as likely to be the "popsicle' drips of the picture's title as anything else'. Higonnet concludes, 'Mann's image certainly provokes fear' from her vantage point of the 1990s, 'but it is a fear of what we already have in our mind's eye. We the viewers are the ones who assume the worst, and while Mann's image allows the worst to be assumed, it also can dispel our fears' (Higonnet, 1998: 136–137). In *Tobi, el niño con alas*, Tobi's nakedness symbolises his innocence (running gags have the 'angel' sitting on the toilet, the profanation of the sacred or weeing into a policeman's hat) but it also comes to reference the desires he provokes in the greedy characters to exploit him. Lolo García's nakedness did not go entirely unnoticed by the Spanish press. *Tobi* had been chosen as the Spanish film for the International Year of the Child in 1979 but Mercero also attempted to cut a deal whereby García would be the mascot for the 1982 Football World Cup. *Interviú* featured a caricature of the child star, naked apart from football boots and with wings, but with an enormous penis which almost reached to the ground under the caption 'La tobita de Lolo' (Lolo's Penis). 'No cabe duda' (There's no doubt), we are told, 'de que Raimundo Saporta, director de relaciones publicas del Banco Exterior de España y presidente del Comite Organiador del Mundial '82 le gustan los niños' (that Raimundo Saporta, director of pubic relations for the Banco Exterior de España and president of the Organising Committee of the '82 World Cup likes children). 'Saporta estaba convencido que el angelical Lolo García, el niño del piruli magico, podia ser la mascota ideal para el Mundial de Futbol que se celebrará en España' (Saporta was convinced that the angelical Lolo García, the child with the magic penis, could be the ideal mascot for the Football World Cup to be held in Spain). But he was reminded, 'Don Raimundo, la idea de Lolo es magnífica, pero, ¿used sabe que dentro de cuatro años, la colita de Lolo, que ahora es tan bonita y mostrable en una revista, crecerá y será impublicable? Saporta sacudió la cabeza afirmativamente' (Don Raimundo, the idea of using Lolo is magnificent, but don't you realise that in four years' time, Lolo's penis, which is so beautiful now and printable in a magazine, will grow and be unpublishable? Saporta nodded his head in agreement) (Anon, 1979: 101).

Lolo García did not become the mascot for the World Cup and in fact he stopped making films, instead studying engineering and disappearing from the media. Marisol, for her part, became Pepa Flores. *Los días del pasado* (Days of the Past, Mario Camus, 1978) is a much more reflective meditation on the legacies of war and also stars Antonio Gades. Her final film is *Mariana Pineda* (Rafael Moreno Alba, 1984), a lush made-for-TV historical drama recreating the life of the near-mythical 'other' heroine from Malaga whose Republicanism brought her into conflict with Fernando VII at the end of the nineteenth century and whose mythologisation had been confirmed by the play by Federico García Lorca (Martin, 2003). The film opens to a close up of Marisol/Pepa Flores's face, zooming in on her lips, as she describes the political letter she is about to send. In the film Marisol/ Pepa Flores plays the passionate political woman although for Celia Martín, in a recent article, her personal Communist beliefs overshadow the film's overt message of political neutrality. Meanwhile, Marisol/Pepa Flores, who was still courted by the *revistas de corazón*, also appeared in *El País* when Maruja Torres launched a scathing attack on her Communist politics: 'para levantar el puño como el otro día lo hizo Marisol [...] hay que tener la fe desesperada del viejo militante que se resiste a ver morir su sueño o la fe pisoteada de la niña prodigio que nunca pudo crecer con una visión propia' (to raise one's fist as Marisol did the other day, you have to have the desperate faith of the old military man who refuses to see his dream die or the trampled on faith of a child prodigy who could never grow up with her own views) (Torres, 1983). Signing herself 'Josefa Flores', Marisol responded with the reply that Franco himself would have liked Torres's statement, but in describing herself as a 'niña progidio neurotizada' (neurotic child prodigy), Marisol achieves a distance from her image which affords her a position of strength (Flores, 1983). Rosa Montero defends 'Pepa' remarking that, 'se me antoja inquietante que a la Flores se la critique de esta guisa y que en cambio nadie diga, de los varios actores fachas que tenemos, que su interpretacion es mala porque al cruzar el escenario se le nota un asomo de paso de la oca o una desenvoltura decididamete falangista en el monólogo' (it worries me that they should criticise Flores in this way and that no-one should remark, meanwhile, on the fact that several right-wing actors act badly because when they cross the stage they notice a goose-step or a decidedly Falangist way of pronouncing the monologue) (Montero, 1984). Montero concludes, 'me extraña esta unanimidad en la virulencia, este frenesí en poner a la chica como un trapo, como si no se le perdonara el que, siendo nuestra niña prodigio como fue, se atreva a ser no nuestra, sino suya, rusófila, cubanista o lo que quiera' (I find the unanimity of virulence strange, this rushing to humiliate her, as if we cannot forgive that fact that our girl prodigy should now dare to be not ours, but her own, Russophile, Cubanist or whatever she pleases).

Marisol stopped making films after *Los días del pasado* and *Mariana Pineda*. Perhaps if she had made more films she would have been able to overcome the continual harking back to her youth, viewed later as the aetiosis for her later political radicalisation. José Aguilar notes that *Los días del pasado* is a very accomplished film which 'nos devuelve lo mejor de Marisol' (gives us back the best of Marisol). 'Ahora sí vemos lo que la malagueña puede hacer en la gran pantalla si es dirigida con talento' (Now we can see what the woman from Malaga can do on the big screen if she has good direction) (Aguilar, 2012: 188). But he cannot resist leaving on the commentary that, 'el recuerdo de su excitante cuerpo mojado sobre la arena de unas playas fascinantes en Brasil nos acompañará como un sueño inalcanzable en nuestros referentes eróticos. Contigo Pepa hicimos otra transición' (the memory of her exciting wet body on the sand in some fascinating beaches in Brazil will accompany us like an unreachable dream in our erotic lives. With you, Pepa, we made another sort of transition) (Aguilar, 2012: 188).[21]

Marisol retired from public life leaving endless speculation about her life, her private life and the ways she represents the feelings of the nation. In July 2012 a frenzy broke out in Malaga when it was revealed that she would be attending the launch of a new song by her daughter Cecilia Flores (her daughter with Gades). Paparazzi wanted a photograph of her on the arm of her daughter but had to make do with a dark image of Pepa Flores amongst other audience members. One article wryly notes that, 'los fotógrafos de los medios de comunicación locales buscaban la instántanea que haría que esta crónica pudiera pasar de ser de repercusión nacional o por contra se quede en una reseña de minúsculo eco local' (the photographers from the local media wanted the shot that would give this story national resonance rather than being just a review of minuscule local importance' (Marmol, 2012). On a more positive note, a tribute evening of Marisol's songs, at the Teatro Guerrero in Malaga in September 2012, was billed as follows:

> Hablar de la figura de Marisol da un vértigo increíble. Las dimensiones de su mito son desmesuradas. Existen libros y biografías, infinidad de páginas en internet, foros marisoleros, coleccionistas convulsos. Pepa Flores es musa gay, líder progre, ícono sixty, objeto de admiración de feministas y personaje profundamente admirado por su valiente trayectoria vital, acrecentada por su conocida negativa a aparecer en actos públicos.

> (To speak of Marisol makes one dizzy so great are the dimensions of her myth. There are books and biographies, an infinite number of Internet pages, Marisol forums, fervent collectors. Pepa Flores is a gay muse, a lefty, an icon of the sixties, admired by feminists and profoundly esteemed for the brave trajectory of her life, which increases due to her famous unwillingness to appear at public events.)

Marisol's greatest rebellion was to retire from the public eye leaving speculation, rumour and the archive of her filmic work. Marisol as archive and icon of cultural memory charts the coming of age of a nation who grew up with her, 'esa chiquilla que la derecha Española necesitaba para demostrar que el pueblo produce cosas sanas, graciosas e inocentes cuando este bien gobernado' (that girl that the Spanish Right needed to show that the people could produce healthy, funny and innocent things when they were governed well) (Vicent, 1981: 145). Later, her rebellion framed that of a nation coming to terms with its newly found independence whilst the stories of exploitation by her various creators remain indelibly traced in the capturing of her body on screen.

Marisol as 'recovered' memory

In her article on screening trauma, Susannah Radstone suggests that an initial period of 'we didn't know that then' might be replaced, over time, by the beginnings of remembrance and then understanding of the trauma that has taken place. Writing of the film *Forrest Gump* (Robert Zemeckis, 1994) she observes that the film 'constructs a visual literalisation of *nachträglichkeit*, that complex "afterwardsness" of remembrance represented by the phrase, "but we didn't know that then"' (Radstone, 2000: 98). She also muses as to whether 'I didn't know that then' might suggest victimhood and considers those critics who saw that film as the creation of a false, or prosthetic, memory of history. Ultimately, she is optimistic about the ways that film as prosthetic memory can aid in a realisation (awakening) and understanding of the past (Radstone, 2000).

In her article 'Narratives of Recovery: Repressed Memory as Cultural Memory', Marita Sturken considers the fact that many adults (mainly females) have recovered memories of child sexual abuse (although equally it has been suggested that many have had their memories 'implanted' due to their suggestibility). This compares with Marisol's films, with their structure of innocence followed by later realisation against recovered memory syndrome. This may help us to understand similar discussions about truth and falsity which arose around Marisol: Umbral insinuates her suggestibility when he appears to claim that her revelations might have to do with the bitterness of old age and a personal vendetta. But Marisol's statements about her exploitation by her 'mentors' were transposed as a 'law of the father' writ large against the Franco regime as (pro-filmically) she attended parties for Francoist dignitaries and (diegetically) she became the image of the Francoist child-woman. As Sturken writes, sexual abuse has much to reveal about the 'historical sense of ownership that fathers have felt over their daughters' bodies' (1999: 238). It is this sense of ownership that Marisol plays out as patriarchal structures are replicated internally in a *mise-en-abyme* of the 'family' structure. Viewing Marisol's films now in the light of revelations about her exploitation may allow us access to a part of Spanish history which might be reconsidered before taking its place in a revised cultural memory. The movement and colour of her early films may become suffused with a sense of melancholy, of our having 'arrived too late'. But viewing Marisol as a recovered memory allows us to acknowledge that 'all of these memories exist within a continuum of cultural memory' (Sturken, 1999: 233). 'These memories belong to all of us', writes Sturken (1999: 245). Acknowledgement of the abuses of the past is part of the process of recovery.

Notes

1 In fact Orson Welles reputedly referred to her as 'el animal cinematográfico más impresionante que había conocido' (the most extraordinary cinematic animal that he had ever met) (Aguilar, 2012: 173).

2 From the serialisation of her life for young girls in the publication, *Simpatía: la vida de Marisol contada por ella misma en 25 capítulos* (Anon, 1962b).

3 David Swift's Disney-produced *Pollyanna* (1960) starred the blonde Hayley Mills.

4 A bizarre conspiracy theory circulates on the Internet claiming that a child named Remedios Olaya made Marisol's first two films, *Un rayo de luz* and *Ha llegado un angel*, based on the testimony of Remedios Olaya: www.rememarisol.com/ (accessed 06.09.2012).

5 Several operations are reported in the press, such as the one to remove her tonsils in January 1962 (Quesada, 1962).

6 The seductiveness of Marisol's story lies partly in its gaps. In evoking 'cultural memory' I do not seek to establish the truth of, for example, Barreiro's biography, but rather to see that his revelations combine with our reading of the films to produce a work of 'cultural memory'.

7 Marisol as archive suggests that the release of her films might have to do with a nostalgia for collective archival memory, but as Derrida (1995) reminds us, the archive can be doubly inflected by loss: it is constructed as a response to a sense of loss (lost history, for example) but also anticipates the conditions of future loss. Nora is interested in what is lost in the process of archivisation, but also what exceeds the archive (1989: xxvii). Diana Taylor (2003: 36) counterposes the archive (of written documents) with the repertoire (which might capture the ephemeral aspects of cultural memory) in her analysis of theatrical performance. Marisol as archive seems to capture both the sense of storing the past but, when viewed from the present-day perspective, her films become a repository for cultural memory.

8 Castro de Paz and Cerdán note that even before grooming began on Marisol, the aim was to launch her simultaneously in the Latin American market as well as in Spain (Castro de Paz and Cerdán, 2005: 106) and within a year of the release of *Un rayo de luz* Suevia (the production company) had sold the film to France, Italy, Chile, Portugal, Brazil, Mexico and Israel. Once Cesáreo González signed a contract to keep working with Marisol, in 1961, he began to prepare Marisol's US tour, which would see her appearing on television on the *Ed Sullivan Show* where she performed the title hit from *Un rayo de luz*, 'Corre corre caballito' (Run, Little Horse, Run) (Castro de Paz and Cerdán, 2005: 108).

9 From a paper delivered at the 'Child Stars' symposium, University of Sunderland, September 2011.

10 Not all of them were successful. The radio-star Amparín Cano's break into cinema appears not to have met with much success, nor does that of TV star Maribel Martín, due to star in *Tres de la cruz roja* with Tony Leblanc. In 1963 *Primer Plano* was reporting the discovery of Antoñita by Rovira-Beleta – she had been dancing flamenco in a small Catalan village – she was deaf and had impaired speech (E. M., 1963). Chanette (Maria de la Ascencion) was another star of TV hoping to make it in cinema in 1962 (L. A., 1962). Conchita Goyanes, another star of TV, was to appear in *Canción de juventud* alongside Durcal in 1962 – Goyanes has worked consistently, appearing most recently in the TV series *Amor en tiempos revueltos* (Love in Troubled Times, 2009) as Sor Angustias (Lopez-Palacios, 1962). Maleni enjoyed reasonable success with *¿Chico o chica?* (Antonio del Amo) in 1962 (and then *Las gemelas*, 1963) which also starred the Mexican child star 'Pulgarcito' (Tom Thumb), Cesáreo Quezadas. 'Pulgarcito' also starred in the successful tale about a vagabond dog *La banda de los ocho* (Band of Eight, Tulio Demicheli, 1962). Singing, dancing star, 'Angelito' was launched with *Pachín* (Arturo Ruiz Castillo) in 1961.

11 Durcal was posited from the start as older than child stars and younger than adult actresses: 'el cine español tiene inédito todavía el éxito de una actriz, cuya juventud se distancia de aquellos y no se alcanza a estos' (Spanish cinema has yet to see the success of an actress whose youth exceeds that of [children] but does not yet reach adulthood) (Pío, 1962: n.p.).

12 The theme of female substitution recalls Hitchcock's *Psycho* (1960). The film also expresses the absurdity of attempting to translate flamenco for the US market. At the start of the film Cristina is helping a flamenco diva with her English: '¿Maria de la O?' 'Mary of the O', '¿carita de gitano?' 'gypsy face'.

13 As Pavlović notes, these were the words used to describe Marisol. Estrellita's story as she recounts it in 1962 is remarkably similar initially, at least, to Marisol's: she was dancing at a fair when she was spotted by Espartaco Santoni (although she learned to dance and sing at the Academia Adelita Domingo in Seville). After she made her second film her family moved with her to Madrid. The article also reports that she never misses a Marisol film although she hasn't had the opportunity to meet her yet. Hayley Mills is another favourite actress (Romo, 1962: 29).

14 Triana-Toribio (2003: 88) maintains that Sanjuán 'looked nothing like Franco', but she acknowledges that there was an association with the 'grandfather' dictator.

15 For the bodies of Francoism, see Pavlović (2003). Leo Steinberg studies the polysemy of the (erotic or sacred) 'chin chuck' in a genealogy traced from the eroticism or affection between lovers in New Kingdom Egypt or between Cupid and Psyche to its depiction in paintings of the Madonna and Child by, for example, Marco Zoppo, c. 1470 and Simone Martini, c. 1321–25 (Steinberg, 1984: 5).

16 Angel Malla was apparently due to start filming *Who Killed Johnny R?* (Sam Dobie, 1966) alongside Lex Barker: 'rara es la película del Oeste en la que no aparece' (rare is the Western that [Angel Malla] doesn't appear in), we are told. Gimpera, meanwhile, from the world of advertising, is about to make *Fata Morgana* with Vicente Aranda and 'tiene precisamente ese estilo internacional que el cine aprecia' (she has precisely that international style appreciated by cinema) (Anon, 1965).

17 The theme of the girlfriend of Palomo Linares who does not like the bullfight seems surprising for a cinema which was usually so in-line with Francoist endorsement of the traits of the 'españolada' but to some extent this is undercut by the hit song 'Yo no quiero ser torero' (I Don't Want to Be a Bullfighter) and Palomo's claim that he will always be a torero whatever Marisol says (but even in a film such as *Aprendiendo a morir* (Learning to Die, Pedro Lazaga, 1962), a semi-autobiographical film about El Cordobés, his sister is opposed to him becoming a bullfighter). There is equally an interesting number of oppositional torero films.

18 The publication *Miss* ran full coverage of the weddings of both Marisol and Rocío Durcal, which were hugely public affairs with the brides like identikit clones in white dresses with veils. Marisol, dressed in a 'maxiabrigo de color blanco' (white maxicoat) was also photographed at Durcal's wedding (Rollan, 1970).

19 There had been another curly-haired Lolo García, now forgotten, in the 1950s, who starred in *El milagro del Sacristán* (The Altar Boy's Miracle, José Maria Elorrieta, 1953). For an exploration of *La guerra de papá*, see Faulkner (2011).

20 Horacio Valcárcel, scriptwriter for the film, remembers that Mercero had briefed him to write a script that could replicate the success he had enjoyed with *La guerra de papá*. Mercero wanted a script about a 'niño con pijama rojo' (boy with red pyjamas) but Valcárcel came to him with an idea for a boy with wings, which he loved (personal communication with Horacio Valcárcel, 10.01.2011) Valcárcel's own film *Miguelín* had been presented at Cannes in 1965.

21 Admittedly Aguilar's book is on the actresses of the *destape*. But his comments are characteristic of the way that Marisol is continually haunted both by her past as a child, and by her later rebellion.

3

Memory and the child witness in 'art-house horror'

'Cinema can lay claim to the child, as the child lays claim to cinema', writes Vicky Lebeau, citing the sequence where Ana (Ana Torrent) and her sister Isabel (Isabel Tellería), two girls living in the post-war Spain of the 1940s, watch James Whale's *Frankenstein* (1931) in a makeshift cinema in Víctor Erice's *El espíritu de la colmena*: 'the sequence yields one of the most compelling images of children's *look* at the screen, or the look of the child caught up in the wonders, and horrors of the moving image' (Lebeau, 2008: 51). This is a pivotal moment in the film: after the screening Ana becomes obsessed by the monster and tries to summon its spirit. She will subsequently interpret her post-war world through the prism of her (monstrosity fuelled) imagination. The sequence has some similarities with the capturing of children's faces in the cinema audience in Truffaut's *Les quatre cents coups* (The 400 Blows, 1959), but here the camera dwells for longer on faces, whilst gestures (hands raised to faces, forgotten mid-gesture, for instance) register both the children's absorption and their anxiety at the scenes they are watching. Torrent's 'look', fetishised by the camera – as it will later be by critics who are entranced by her dark Goyaesque eyes (Smith, 2000a: 36)[1] – ushers in the notion of the child's gaze but as Joe Kelleher has written, the word 'gaze' will not *quite* do, [for] we need to speak of the child as looked at, looked for, as much as looking' (Kelleher, 1998: 42). The sequence bears eloquent testament to our ongoing fascination with the image of the child on screen: looked at, looked for and looking.

Chris Darke (2010: 156) notes how Ana has much in common with Lebeau's description of early cinema, which used the child to 'secure its appeals to verisimilitude, to the uncontrived, even haphazard' (Lebeau, 2008: 39). Ana Torrent has remarked in interview that during the filming of this sequence she was seeing Whale's *Frankenstein* for the first time – she was playing before the camera in a 'unique moment of innocence': her absorption in the images she is viewing is 'real', creating in turn a fascination amongst critics with the 'naturalness' or 'firstness' of her performance (Smith, 2000a: 35). Torrent's performance appears very different from the manufactured cinematic child of Spanish cinema of the 1950s and 1960s (her naturalistic whispers are worlds away from the dubbed voice of Pablito Calvo, for instance). For Darke, the sequence might be linked to a founding moment in cinema itself: the scene's aleatory nature encapsulates the 'epiphany of cinephilia' (Darke, 2010). Childhood's transience underscores the sense of capturing the ontological trace of a fleeting moment. Darke cites Erice's comments that the footage represent 'the best ... most important ... most essential'[2] moment he has captured on film and critic Uzal's affirmation that Ana's 'reactions touch us as if she was the first spectator and cinema was being reborn through her' (Uzal, 2007: 60, translation Darke, 2010: 155). The 'firstness' of Torrent's performance is significant: cinema through the child 'rubs off the real' (Lury, 2011),[3] but it also confirms the innocent, uncorrupted nature of the child's gaze. Childhood is presented as reassuringly separate from the world of adults and yet accessible to it. What captivates us about the child's gaze is the way that it stages the cherished ideal of childhood innocence which has repeatedly been expressed in visual terms since at least the mid-eighteenth century (Higonnet, 1998). The question of how far that innocence is intruded upon or sustained is a subtext here. As the quote from Uzal above reveals, this gaze represents seeing the world as if for the first time. Through the child protagonists, we look through the child and at the child, oscillating between innocence and knowingness, fascinated by the lure of the child on screen.

If *El espíritu de la colmena* presents an iconic example of the child on screen, then the child and cinema are also indelibly linked in this film with memory. In 1983 Marsha Kinder wrote of the potential of the child protagonist in films like *El espíritu de la colmena* to represent a generation of film directors – she cites José Luis Borau and Carlos Saura, but elsewhere Erice includes himself in this outlook (Latorre, 2006: 51) – who saw themselves as:

> emotionally and politically stunted children who were no longer young; who, because of the imposed role as 'silent witness' to a tragic war that had divided country, family and self, had never been innocent; and who, because of the oppressive domination of the previous generation, were obsessed with the past and might never be ready to take responsibility for changing the future. (Kinder, 1983: 58)

Critics' fascination with Torrent's 'dark gaze' might, therefore, have to do with an interest in the child as witness, particularly as innocent witness to war (Lury, 2010). Some scholars find that the child represents all children who grew up on the losing side under Francoism – Torrent is, for Kinder, 'the child actress who most vividly represents the children of Franco' (Kinder, 1983: 59).[4] But if the child makes an appeal through the memory of the film's director to a generation of 'Franco's kids', then it also is a potent enough figuration to appeal to our own. The child does not feature in Douwe Draaisma's *Metaphors of Memory* (although the honeycomb, landscapes and cinematography are cited), but one feels that it might merit inclusion (2000: 35, 72, 134). As Carolyn Steedman has shown, the child has come to represent the self in the cultural imagination – she begins with the notion that

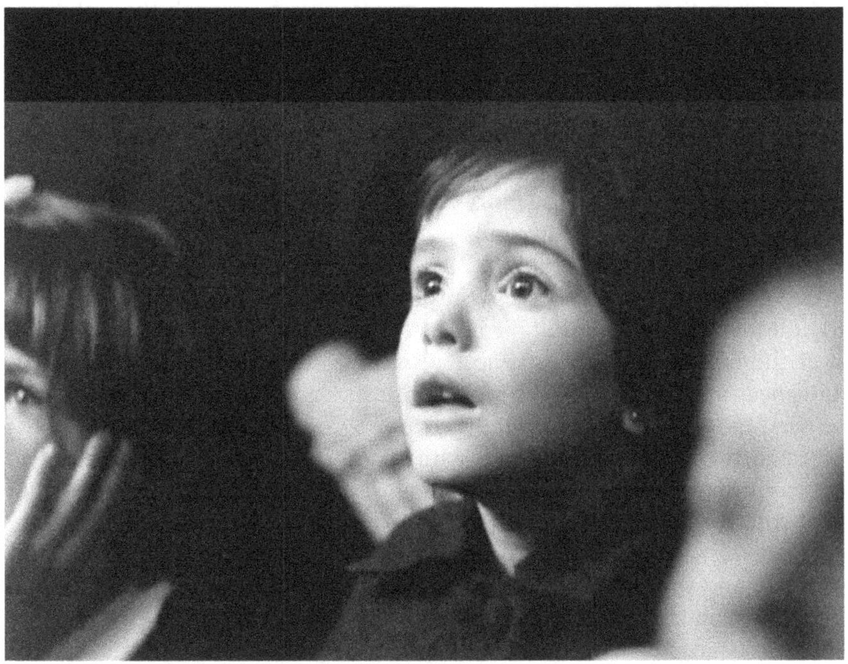

6 Ana Torrent's gaze in *El espíritu de la colmena* (Víctor Erice, 1973).

'children are the bloody fragments of another body, little parcels of flesh and bone split off from another' (interestingly she cites Frankenstein's monster as conceived by Mary Shelley as her illustration) (Steedman, 1995: ix), and shows how this idea morphed into Freudian psychoanalysis, in which 'childhood' was given another name, as 'the unconscious' (Steedman, 1995: 4). Psychoanalysis relies heavily on the notion of the self as inner child,[5] of one's psyche constructed through childhood and the 'talking cure' reliant on the relation of childhood memories in a potent imbrication of self, child and memory. Memory and the child seem implicated in each other to such an extent that one might ask whether adult representations of childhood that do not rely on memory are even possible. For Jacqueline Rose the child *always* represents adult investments in the child (Rose, 1992: 10), yet she notes that it becomes the 'universal social reference, which conceals historical divisions and difficulties' (Rose, 1992: 10). Thus, where Perriam notes that 'for those who lived through the war, and perhaps exile, and who saw *El espíritu de la colmena* in its early years of circulation, it must surely have been a reminder of their experience' (Perriam, 2008: 72), Smith (2000a: 28) shows how critics of the film on its release celebrated its evocation of a (shared) childhood whilst managing to erase or inscribe its possible political dimensions. This film makes a multiple appeal to memory through the child (that of its creators, of the vanquished, our own).[6]

For Chris Perriam, memory may provide a path through the pitfalls of abstraction and reference outlined by Smith in his essay on the film. Perriam shows how, in the years since the film's release, it has been subjected to a variety of different readings, from psychological studies stressing the film's politics (its background of post-war dictatorship) and the socialisation of children, to sexual politics (through Ana, her mother and sister) and latterly, trauma studies and memory-work (Perriam, 2008).[7] Drawing in part on Smith's discussion of the ruins in the film, a form of repressed memory expressed in visual terms (Smith, 2000a: 34), and Labanyi's (2000) seminal article on hauntology, Perriam writes of the ways the film invites the reader to 'follow in the footsteps of memory' through its various landscapes: moreover the film itself, with its continual returns through time from scholars, audiences and critics, and the way it forms part of Spanish heritage, might be seen as a dynamic memorial (Perriam, 2008: 72). Perriam's reading is inflected by the 'memory boom' with its raging debates over the need to confront the legacies of the past set against those who make accusations of the propagation of a false historical consciousness.

What does it mean, then, to claim that the film makes an appeal to our memory and who is reflected back in Ana's gaze? Are these Spaniards who lived through the war and its aftermath (and on which side)? Are they the children or grandchildren of those Spaniards who wish to gain a sense of their nation's past? Are they, alternatively, international audiences who gain access to Spanish history through the film and its guiding contextualisations by critics, scholars or the film's creators (the Criterion DVD provides a passionate reconstruction of the making of the film and reflections on its meaning) who locate its dramas and enigmas within the post-war setting? What does it mean to argue that these prosthetic memories, films which reconstruct the past to simulate first-hand experiences, might have a role to play in Spain's 'memory wars'? As Pam Cook has noted, prosthetic memories are laid open to:

> charges of lack of authenticity, of substituting a degraded popular version for the 'real' event, and to accusations that by presenting history as dramatic spectacle they obscure our understanding of social, political and cultural forces. The pessimistic view assumes that the images and stories of the past fed to us by the global media networks produce 'false' memories, or at least memory scenarios whose veracity, or relationship to the real, are impossible to determine. (Cook, 2005: 2)

'Yet', she reminds us, 'in the very act of addressing audiences as nostalgic spectators and encouraging them to become involved in re-presenting the past, the media invites exploration and interrogation of the limits of its engagement with history' (Cook, 2005: 2).[8] Prosthetic memories, irrespective of their 'authenticity' therefore might have an important contribution to make to collective memory or at least to the fostering of 'historical consciousness'.[9] But, in a sense, the question of cinema's ability to contribute to collective memory in Spain is not really in question. The law of 'historical memory' of 2007 pays testament to the increased 'historical consciousness' in Spain in which cinema's attempts to portray the Spanish Civil War as the return of the repressed have undoubtedly had a part to play. As Thomas Elsaesser suggests (of German film), cinema can give 'texture and voice to a "history from below" or "everyday history" – authenticating "lived experience" through the power of immediacy inherent in the moving image' (Elsaesser, 2001: 197). But where the child protagonist might be laid open to accusations of rendering the Spanish nation as passive victims of history, without even much understanding of the past (the direct access purportedly offered by the child's gaze is in fact a partial view which arguably reproduces the unrepresentability of trauma), cinema's 'capacity to "fake" such authenticity' also comes into play. As Elsaesser notes, this is the 'definitively "traumatic" status of the moving image in our culture, as a symptom without a case, as the event without a trace' (Elsaesser, 2001: 197).

Recent years have witnessed an increase in Spanish films featuring child protagonists which focus on memory, a response doubtless, to the 'memory boom' in Spain (Delgado, 2008). It may make sense to speak of a new *cine con niño*, a genre in itself. The child might be seen as a lingua franca which allows directors to present an attractive and comprehensible face to investigations of the Spanish past (both for Spanish audiences and internationally). The child ushers in a generational matrix and may be figured frequently as a metaphorical or literal orphan: whether orphaned by war (the loss of one or both parents and the ensuing loss of a link to the previous (Republican) generation), or embodied as a longing for or death-wish against the father-figure (General Franco and his agents) or, as Labanyi suggests (2005b), stressing the link between past and future generations. *El espíritu de la colmena* is the prime example of what has been dubbed the 'Francoist aesthetic' in which a desire to get past the censors of Francoist Spain led to an elliptical, allusive style as well as to a public sensitised to the reading of images. But *El espíritu de la colmena* is also paradigmatic in terms of its representation of traumatic memory. In her analysis of the controversies over films which attempt to represent the Nazi Holocaust (after Adorno's famous remarks regarding the impossibility of representation), Miriam Bratu Hansen has noted that Claude Lanzman's *Shoah* (1985) was lauded for the way it refused representation (compared with Spielberg's *Schindler's List* (1993) (Hansen, 1996),[10] how it engaged with memory embodied 'in a proper way, avoiding the delusions of a presence of that which is to be remembered' (Huyssen, 2000: 69). *El espíritu de la colmena* likewise embodies memory in a proper way, through its open-ended, densely allusive style, its post-traumatic landscape, and the way that the ravages of traumatic memory are played out over Ana's body.

In this chapter I continue with Kelleher's description of the dialectical relationship with the child as 'looked at, looked for and looking' to explore the child as spectacle, narrative and gaze. Heeding James Naremore's call to read performance in order to 'reveal buried, paradoxical assumptions about society and the self' (Naremore, 1988: 1), I will begin with a reconsideration of Ana Torrent's performance to explore the ways that the film establishes the dark-eyed child's gaze as visual motif. The child's gaze binds together resonances surrounding childhood innocence and its corruption. The child is a 'lugar de la memoria', representing what has traditionally escaped from history (the child is persistently seen as representing such a marginalised viewpoint on history, the female child perhaps doubly so).[11] Specifically, Ana is called upon to bear witness to the memory of the vanquished of the Spanish Civil War. I will then explore films of the post Franco era which appear, in different ways, to refer back to Ana's gaze as the acknowledgement of the burdens of history. Through the re-enactment of Ana's dark-eyed gaze, Torrent's performance is, at times, a spectral presence in these films. The films chosen derive from two different time periods: the death of General Franco in the mid-1970s and the 1990s to the present. *El espíritu de la colmena* is an art-house film which borrows from horror and I shall explore art-house films, horror films and those which develop the art-horror hybrid. A recurrent motif in films with recreated memories of the war and its aftermath is the child and the monster, or, in a metonymic twist, the monstrous child. Erice's establishment of the child and monster motif (which itself might be seen as a cinematic appropriation and recontextualisation of Vajda's 'horror' *Marcelino, pan y vino* concerning the child who visits a monster in an attic) begins a concatenation of more or less conscious intertextual references to children and monsters or to monstrous children in an intertextual dance through time. The monster may refer allegorically to the horror of war, or to the monstrosity of those who grew up in the context of war's brutalisation or its aftermath in a repressive regime.

However, if the child's meeting with the monster represents, allegorically at least, the child's encounter with the horrors of past Spanish history, then it also represents the encounter of a child with cinema. Through the child's gaze, Frankenstein's monster comes to represent the prosthetic nature of the historical past represented on screen. In a *mise-en-abyme* structure, the child is a witness to a prosthetic memory as the spectator views history on screen through the child. Film then, itself is a *lieu de memoire*. Naomi Greene has noted how films might 'lend themselves to the expression of sentiments that have yet to assume verbal form, or that resist clear articulation' (Greene, 1999: 5). Collectively these films seem to be stalked by the spectre of the missing child (a topic which, as we mentioned in the Introduction, has gained urgency in the news of late as stories of missing children under Francoism emerge in the mass media as the embodiment of a lost national historical memory. Beginning with *El espíritu de la colmena*, and reaching an urgency with *El laberinto del fauno*, they engage with the notion of the status of prosthetic memories and thus make a fascinating contribution to the question of collective memories in Spain's 'memory wars'. Smith cites Ana Torrent's assertion that 'audiences have internalised her memory of her as a child' (Smith, 2000a: 35). Through cinematic homage or citation, these films appear to present their own memory either of Torrent's performance, or else they rework themes presented by Erice's film. In this chapter, cinema's twinning with memory suggests not so much Anton Kaes's 'return of history as film' (Kaes, 1989) but rather cinema as a 'technological memory bank' in which memory itself is always already mediated (Kilbourn, 2010: 2). The 'eternal returns' of the cinematic child and its imbrication with memory suggest 'cinema's own past and ever-present present' (Kilbourn, 2010: 45) and a key question will be whether this has to do with what Elsaesser (2001) has termed an 'obsessiveness' with the past, or whether it is a 'working through'.

Performance and the child witness in *El espíritu de la colmena*

El espíritu de la colmena turns on two echoing sequences of performance (two 'emotional intensities' in a film which is a 'mosaic of emotional states')[12] from six year-old Ana Torrent. In the first of these, Luis Cuadrado's cinematography captures the faces of the children as they watch James Whale's *Frankenstein* in the scene already discussed. Chris Darke describes Torrent's performance in these terms:

> As Frankenstein holds a flower in his coarse hands and, imitating Maria, raises it to his nose to smell it, we see Ana's reaction. Suddenly, she sits up in her seat and leans forward, enraptured at the spectacle she is witnessing. Opening her mouth slightly, she seems to shape a word to herself and then leans back. The light of the screen shines in her eyes. But neutrally, we see what Frankenstein shows and Ana's reaction to it. Put more expressively – and with greater fidelity to the moment of Ana's reaction as captured by Erice – we don't see what she sees, but her seeing it. We watch Ana's face itself becoming a screen on which the external signs of an internal epiphany are being played out, a revelation the child will carry into the world beyond cinema. (Darke, 2010: 153)

Bela Balázs (2010) suggested that we pay attention to the micro-movements of the face to reveal latent meaning, and for Deleuze (1986) the close up of the face can tell its own story (the film is punctuated by such close-ups which tell their own story).[13] For Naremore, the face is 'usually taken as the ultimate guarantee of reality, the very seat of emotions that are meant to be truthful' (Naremore, 1988: 96) and the child's face, perhaps we might argue, even more so. Darke acknowledges the 'theologically informed discourse' of French post-war film criticism described by Willemen and which enable him to discuss Torrent's performance in terms of an 'epiphany' and a 'revelation' (Willemen, 1994: 237). The complex dialectic of looking is clear in this sequence: we watch the children as they watch. Ana's innocent look has been choreographed in spite of its 'naturalness': watching in this sequence becomes a performative act, framed by the camera but Ana's look also 'rubs off the real'. We might compare Ana's face here to that of Iciar

Bollaín's in Erice's *El sur* (The South, 1983) where the solitary tear which travels down Estrella's face is a performative (for Lury all tears retain a sense of the performative, however naturalistic) for the passing of time and for Estrella's loss of illusions.[14] With Ana, the changes of light and gesture, the 'signs of an internal epiphany played out' on Torrent's face, signal that something has taken place, this is gesture as the register of change at an affective level. Ana (both the character and the actor) has been changed by this moment of looking and we have witnessed that change. The sequence might be said, then, to dramatise witnessing even as it also performs the child's face as the site of truth.

With its landscapes of ruins and desolate plains, *El espíritu de la colmena* encapsulates a sense of 'belatedness' characteristic of the aftermath of a traumatic event (Perriam, 2008: 76). The honey-coloured tint employed by cinematographer Luis Cuadrado as a backdrop to scenes suggests, through the beehive motif, nurture yet entrapment (Evans, 1982) but also the cloying texture and colour of amber, as well as the redolence of sepia, as it pins its subjects to pastness. Ana's father is engaged in writing a 'poeticised memoire'; her mother pens endless letters to a mysterious absent figure: both are fixated by loss. Ana, their daughter, with her melancholic demeanour and dark eyes can be seen as an example of post-memory, a 'memorial candle' (Wardi, 1992) who carries the burden of trauma undergone by previous generations, a loss which 'seeps and winds like invisible psychic ink through individual lives, decades, and generations' (Hoffman, 2010b: 406). Her sister, Isabel, appears fixated with death as she smears blood over her lips as a rudimentary lipstick, leaps over bonfires, plays dead for her sister, lays her head on train-tracks and half-strangles a cat. If Marianne Hirsch (2008) is correct in her assertion that the family is the primary psychic space for the transmission of memory, then here, too, we find 'the sites of the primal scenes of socialization', or 'a certain psycho-pathology of the postwar family' (Santner, 1990: 35). As Ana has no first-hand knowledge, merely the inheritance of the transmission of a trauma, her melancholy is not derived from the loss of a particular object: rather, her worldview is filled with the phantoms and spectres, 'a world of fantasy and inner distorsion' (Hoffman, 2010b: 410). Post-memory, for Hirsch and Hoffman, describes the transmission of memory to later generations through stories told second hand. Ana, we presume, has been told nothing by her parents, and in this sense she may be closer to what Abraham and Torok describe in terms of 'cryptonomy', the intergenerational transmission of the trauma of another which is hidden in the gap in knowledge where trauma resides (Abraham and Torok, 1994). On this reading, Frankenstein's monster is the inscrutable crypt which haunts Ana's present. But perhaps we also retain traces of Hirsch's 'not memories', communicated in 'flashes of imagery' and 'broken refrains' transmitted through 'the language of the body' which are 'precisely the stuff of *postmemory*' (Hirsch, 2008: 109). The ellipses in the narrative give rise to a sense of 'broken refrains', stitched together rather like the eponymous monster built by Dr Frankenstein. Here, too, Ana absorbs the horrors of the past (the Spanish Civil War and the represssiveness of the Franco regime) rather like a fairy tale and this emerges in her fantasy as a monstrous spirit. Her relationship with this monster, intimate and potent, is played out over her body. During a screening of Whale's *Frankenstein*, Ana wonders, 'why did the monster kill the little girl? Why did he kill her?' Afterwards, the two girls lie in beds placed side by side. After saying their prayers and invoking the Holy Spirit, Isabel tells Ana, in whispers, that if she summons the spirit of the monster, it will appear to her.

Marianne Hirsch's (2008) discussions of 'postmemory' centre on maternal loss and a desire for reunion with the mother. Yeon-Soo Kim's (2005) excellent study of Carlos Saura's *Cría cuervos* shows how the transmission of memory is demonstrated through the evocation of the maternal through photographs, which 'project her emotional intimacy towards the mother' and the ghostly figure of the remembered mother (the actress Geraldine Chaplin). The film takes place within a large house and shows the fortunes of sisters whose parents have died and who are cared for by an aunt. *Cría cuervos* centres on two scenes of trauma, which correspond to two phases of Freud's thinking on trauma: the primal scene, here presented as 'false' trauma, where Ana (also played by Ana Torrent, fresh from filming with Erice), believes that she has poisoned her father (where in fact he has died of a heart-attack after vigorous, adulterous sex), and the real trauma of her mother's protracted illness and painful death. The film turns on the longing for maternal love as Ana summons her mother's spectral presence which returns through a traumatic remembering. Ana uses the prosthetic memories evoked by the pop song ¿Por qué te vas? (Why Are You Leaving?) (a pop song by Jeanette which was briefly popular in the 1970s in Europe and Latin America) with its prolongation of pleasurable longing and the memories inherited through photographs, to work through the trauma of her mother's death. But if her trauma centres on the loss of her mother, the film also explores some of the ambivalence surrounding the recent death of the patriarch. The title of the film comes from a Spanish proverb, 'raise ravens and they will pluck out your eyes', and the film partly deals with what will happen to Spaniards after the death of the patriarch. Ana's desire to kill her father arguably articulates the desire of many Spaniards who wished they could do away with the ailing dictator but felt powerless to do so. The scenes of Ana bending over the coffin with her dead father in uniform, refusing to kiss him, perform a cathartic function for a nation still reeling from the death of the dictator.[15]

In *El espíritu de la colmena*, whilst Ana appears more interested in photographs of her mother as an adolescent as she peruses an old family album (her mother with a statue of the Virgin Mary against a map of Spain; a dedication to 'mi querido misántropo' (my dear misanthrope) when set to the melancholic strains of her mother's piano playing, becomes mysterious and is just one more enigma of the film – to whom was this dedicated?) whilst her father appears distant, moustached and poised. But it is through cinema that we get a sense of Ana's desire to connect with her father. Through its density of reference, the film makes links between the monstrous spirit, her father (whose footsteps we hear creaking overhead in a sound-bridge as the two girls lie in bed and Isabel tells Ana how to call the spirit) and the fugitive in the woods. Castro de Paz suggests that *El espíritu de la colmena* might be viewed as maintaining a strong psychic link to Jomi García Ascot's hauntingly beautiful experimental film of 1962, *El balcón vacío* (The Empty Balcony) made whilst the writer was in exile in Mexico: 'el film de García Ascot es el "espíritu de la colmena" del exilio exterior, mientras que el de Erice podría constituir, en algún sentido, e incluso plásticamente, el "balcón vacío" de la trágica ausencia y el solitario silencio interior' (García Ascot's film is the *Spirit of the Beehive* of foreign exile, whilst Erice's film might constitute, in some senses, including aesthetically, the 'empty balcony' of the tragic absence and solitary interior silence) (Castro de Paz, 2004: 381). Where Gabriela, the protagonist, crouches in the empty house, head in hands, and cries out as the bombs fall around her, 'por qué siento este miedo?' (why do I feel this fear?), she seems very much like the inheritor of a war that is not her own, and that has instilled in her an inherited fear for which she cannot even trace an origin. Castro de Paz suggests that the 'padre-joven republicano detenido-preso' (father-young man detained Republican prisoner) is a link as dense as the one provided by Erice for Ana of the fugitive father-monster. But where Gabriela feels solidarity with the prisoner behind the window as a response to the generalised insults thrown at 'los rojos' (including her father), Ana will eventually falsely believe that her father killed the fugitive when he shows her that he has recovered the pocket-watch that she stole from him to give to the fugitive. Gabriela feels orphaned by the war, both in the sense that she lost her father (which causes her trauma, as witnessed in the final scenes as she visits – in her imagination at least, suggested by Gabriela's repeated passing of herself as a young girl as she climbs the stairs – the now empty old house of her childhood and attempts to summon her parents to her) and because she has lost the link to a whole generation – this is the experience of the exile, who knows about the past through her parents but can retain no direct link to the past. Ana, meanwhile, projects her trauma regarding the death of the fugitive onto her father. It is partly this mistaken belief about the death of the fugitive which leads Ana to summon the monster: 'why did the monster kill the little girl?' and 'why is he then killed?' – a haunting double-murder without explanation.

The second sequence of 'emotional intensity', an echo of the first screen-watching scene (these two scenes form the emotional core of the film), takes place when Ana summons Frankenstein's monster to meet her beside a woodland lake. One night, in an after-dark scenario filled with the sounds of night-time creatures, Ana goes to a pond in a re-creation of the scene of the child and the monster by the lake in Whale's film. Cinema is the appropriate medium for the summoning of ghosts, both in the sense that Erice (whose starting point for the film was a poster featuring a still of this scene from Whale's film which adorned his wall) creates a homage to Whale and Ana recalls her viewing of the film in the playing out of her fantasies. As Ana gazes into the water, her reflection is substituted by that of the prosthetic mask of Frankenstein's monster, whose strange artificiality underscores his corporeality. As she turns back to face him as he advances on her, the monster reaches out to touch her and the screen goes black. If Ana represents an inherited memory, then cinema is instrumental in the articulation of the horrors which now circulate in Ana's mind. Torrent looks terrified in this scene, her face trembles slightly with wide-eyed fear before her eyelids slowly close and the screen fades to black.

Ana's performance is markedly different in tone from the earlier sequence and what we are witnessing on some level is the exploitation of a young child star by her artistic directors. In the scene where Ana's mother, Teresa, combs her hair in front of the mirror Ana's half-smile at her mother's affectionate hugging and tickling may be timid delight at the change of tone from co-worker Teresa Gimpera who reports that Ana was 'un poco pesadita, la niña' (a bit difficult), did not want to sit for the scene and she had to pinch her bottom until tears almost came and they were able to film the sequence.[16] In the scene where Ana's father (with a wonderful economy of performance by Fernán Gómez) brings out his pocket-watch at the breakfast table and stops the children's giggles with an admonishing glance, Ana's answering look speaks of real fear and we, when viewing the scene in terms of its narrative sequence, interpret it to represent Ana's father's crushing disappointment at her behaviour. Erice has noted that he knew that Torrent was terrified when she was confronted with the monster in make-up.[17] Ana's gaze registers a change here, too, but unlike the earlier 'epiphany' of witnessing, here Ana's gaze speaks to the curtailing of childish fun, to fear and anxiety. In the context of the film's back-story, we come to interpret this change in mood as a sense that Ana has absorbed the post-war situation of trauma and repression in which she finds herself. She is receiving history as a burden.

In his essay, 'Notes on Gesture', Agamben (2007) describes how cinema's rise coincided with a sense of the fragmentation of the self, a loss of the whole unity of the body. Images have lost their aura, for Agamben, they are no longer whole, capturing gestures, but are stills from fractured film (Murray, 2010: 87). At the same time, he celebrates the ability of film to capture movement, citing Muybridge's split second photographs as a way to maintain the 'dynamis' of gesture and da Vinci's *Mona Lisa* and Velázquez's *Las Meninas* which should be seen 'not as timeless static forms, but as fragments of gestures or as frames of a lost film, solely within which they would gain their true meaning' (Agamben, 2007: 139). *El espíritu de la colmena* plays with stasis and movement: the freeze-frame where Isabel leaps over the fire shows how images are what Agamben would term 'fragments of a gesture, or [...] frames of a lost film' (Agamben, 2007: 139), a phrase which holds resonance also for the children's drawings at the start of the film which enact key scenes. At the same time, the film celebrates the way that cinema can run static images together to create life, just as Frankenstein's monster creaks to life from the assembly of body parts. Agamben maintains that gesture enacts nothing, 'there is neither production nor enactment' but 'undertaking and supporting' (Agamben, 2007: 140). He explains this further in the sense of carrying a burden. Agamben's main point is to celebrate cinema's ability to showcase the medium: gesture is the exhibition of a mediality: it is the process of making a means visible as such. This seems pertinent to Ana's gesture in the scene of the monster and the lake. The scene is clearly unreal, from the monster's prosthesis to the strange, night-time ambience: Torrent has remarked in interview that although she had seen some films before and knew that the situation with the monster was a fiction she nevertheless confused fiction and reality 'sabes que no es real, pero de alguna forma lo es' (you know it isn't real but somehow it is). Stanley Cavell's attitude to film is that it is not an unmediated realism, but rather 'holds reality before us' and 'reality is free to exhibit itself' (1979: 189). As Ana closes her eyes (in a gesture rather like Lacan's *petit mort* – ecstasy or agony – for Agamben gestures are mute), Ana seems to assume the burden of her prosthetic memories – she receives them as ontological realities (Cavell, 1979).

Just as Alison Landsberg maintains that memory might be inherited by watching film (interestingly she relates this to the inheritance of a trauma), so Ana 'sees through another's eyes' (Landsberg, 2004), symbolically endowing Don José with his prosthetic eyes and inheriting trauma through her viewing of Whale's *Frankenstein*. If she is a 'belated witness', providing a performative function as an *addressable you*, then, in a *mise-en-abyme* structure, we as spectators are witnesses to the witness (Levine, 2006: 4). Tyrus Miller (2003) has explored Ana's mimetic, dream-like projections with the monster of *El espíritu de la colmena* through Deleuzean film theory. Deleuze moves on from the passivity of the child to note his/her capacity for the 'intensification of sensory experience that compensates for the loss of active agency' (Miller, 2003: 230, referring to Deleuze, 2005). Comprehension of the event witnessed, then, may take many forms. And where Agamben in a different work stresses the impossibility of witness-ing,[18] the liminal, mute, affect-laden response of Ana as the inheritor of past traumas may be the most potent motif we have at our disposal for the question of how to address the Spanish past. Ana does not understand what she is witnessing, but her affect-driven response authenticates her experience. Van-Alphen (2002) suggests that as eyewitness accounts become rarer with the passing of time, the issue of the transmission of memory is a vital one. Ana's response puts faith in the transmission of memory and in the ability of the 'belated witness' to see events through another. In the context of Spain's 'memory-wars', Ana's affective response performs the important function of authenticating counter-memories, what Jonathan Ellis and Ana María

Sánchez-Arce elsewhere call the 'psychological' (rather than the historical) recovery of the traumas of the Spanish Civil War and the years of repressive regime in its aftermath (Ellis and Sánchez-Arce, 2011).

Vision is central to *El espíritu de la colmena*, as we see particularly in the biology class when Ana is called upon to add the eyes to the mannequin – 'Don José ahora puede ver' (Don José can see now), the teacher tells us as the camera focuses in on the mannequin's eyes, purportedly in a point-of-view shot from Ana: the redoubling of looks in which Ana's vision becomes fused with that of the monster (a scene which will be echoed in the lakeside scene where Ana's face fuses with that of the monster). Ana is, then, able to witness, but what has she seen? The scene from Whale's *Frankenstein* that Ana chooses to recreate, the scene of the little girl and the monster, was censored upon its release in 1931, but the cut version (cut to allay the fears of child protection bodies) conjured up scenes of child molestation in the discourses surrounding the film's release (Skal, 1993: 137). In much the same way, in the scene we watch from Erice's film, we see Ana move towards the monster before cutting to a scene of her lying unconscious as dawn breaks. The 'cut' scene has led some critics to surmise that the monster is a fantasy (or false memory) of seduction, or a hallucination provided by the trauma of seeing the film (or of eating poisonous mushrooms) but others posit that Ana may have been raped by a man in the woods and that this is the trauma that the film articulates.

Landsberg's theories stress the utopian potential of cinema – 'prosthetic memories enable individuals to have a personal connection to an event they did not live through [...] to make possible alliances across racial, class and other chasms of difference' (2004: 156) – but she has also been criticised for her use of the term 'sutured' which is seen to imply a passive implantation of memory which might be open to a darker interpretation (Burgoyne, 2009: 107). Ana's engagement with cinema has a similar ambiguity: has her inherited memory made her suggestible, leaving her susceptible to a cinematic seduction akin to Francoism's 'brainwashing' through propaganda? (Indeed, Kinder suggests that under the pressures of the war that divided the nation, 'an entire generation of impressionable children felt a mixture of love and fear for repressive patriarchs – a combination that generated distorted fantasies of heroic allegiance and rebellious patricide and that led them to identify with both the victim and the monster' (Kinder, 1993: 128). Alternatively, however, the film may retain some of Landsberg's utopianism, the sense that 'commodities and commodified images, are not capsules of meaning that spectators swallow whole, but rather the grounds upon which social meanings are negotiated, contested and sometimes constructed' (Landsberg, 2004: 149) as, after all, Ana's meeting with the monster is her own fantasy (Perriam (2008) points out the importance of viewing Ana as a girl entering puberty and the resonances which the monster carries over from the horror genre of adolescence and sexuality).

However, despite the doctor's words to Ana's mother that 'she will get over what she has seen', what remains is the spectre and horror of the missing child, not completely assuaged by the relief at the vision of her crumpled body lying in the marshland. Ana's face does not operate completely here as the site of truth. Ana is paradoxically burdened and yet inscrutable: pointing towards some dreadful but unnameable trauma. Like the latency of Ana's face, Spanish memory is full of secrets to be unearthed and discovered (both now and at the film's release). Ana's truth is the secrets that still remain to be discovered. As the two 'moments' of cinematic performance mirror one another, what we are witness to is the loss of childhood innocence: Ana has been changed by her experience and the innocent curiosity of the earlier sequence when Ana and her friends gaze at the cinema screen is now lost. Ana is no longer a child, she is now the *femme-enfant* so praised by the Surrealists.[19] A missing child (the earlier image of Ana, aleatory, innocent, poignant in its transience) stalks this film as a potent but repressed image of the loss of national historical memory.

The monstrous child

Saura's *Cría cuervos* won the Special Jury Prize at the Cannes Film Festival in 1976. But that year also saw the release of a film that was very different in tone but deals similarly with the cathartic release surrounding the death of the dictator. *¿Quién puede matar a un niño?* (Who Can Kill a Child, 1976) opens with a vision of horror: newsreel footage shows children mutilated and maimed in Auschwitz, Vietnam and Biafra. If this is the child as witness to history (statistics reel off the numbers of children killed) then this is the child as mute witness, the 'impossible' witness who has not survived to tell the tale (Agamben, 1999). This moment of horror is unmatchable, unbearable and presents a distortion of vision: how can the audience at this B-movie horror by Narciso Ibáñez 'Chicho' Serrador, well known for his television work, *Historias para no dormir* (Stories to Keep You Awake) and the film *La residencia* (The Dorm), settle back into standard 'genre' fare after such an opening: how can prosthetic horrors possibly match the horror of historical events?

The film will make further demands on the spectator – the central conceit of the plot is that children, out of revenge at their treatment by history, rise up and become monstrous murderers of adults. Tom and Evelyn, British holiday-makers to a Spanish island, find a locale devoid of adults with children rampaging and preparing their move to continue their destruction on the mainland. After establishing the notion that child-murder is a despicable act, the film proceeds to present the spectator with a pseudo-ethical conundrum: Tom must kill the monstrous children in order to save the world and the spectator is asked to side with the child murderer. Contemporary Spanish reviews of the film found the opening footage of the film perplexingly out of place – the notion that it was an attempt to elevate the material (an art-house horror, perhaps?) was met with scorn whilst the suggestion that it provided a revenge motive for the actions of the children was even a 'grosera manipulación' (vulgar manipulation) (Egido). But others noted the startling juxtaposition of the opening footage and the focus, with the shift to the present and 'la sugestiva presencia de unos niños bien alimentados de un país y unas playas de sol' (the suggestive presence of some well-fed children in a country filled with sunny beaches) (Cebollada, 1976).

The central conceit of the film suggests that children have been gripped by a hynotising force which has turned them into adult-murdering monsters. Tom remembers the idyllic childhood he spent on a Mediterranean island and is unaware of the corpse that washes up (reminiscent of *Jaws*) on one of the beaches. Almanzora turns out to be deserted apart from some local kids: the children have murdered all of the adults. Taking refuge in the cell of the police station, Tom is driven to shoot one of the children, and for a while the murderous kids recede. But Evelyn's unborn child kills her from within. Tom guns down several children in a standoff in the main square and makes it to the boat but the arriving policemen shoot him for, presumably, 'what kind of person would kill a child?' At the end of the film, we see the children plotting to travel to the mainland to continue with their killing spree.

Following the traditions of the genre, the film draws on primal fears which circulate metonymically. The film taps into (male and female) anxieties about female pregnancy: Tom and Evelyn are enjoying a holiday together now that their children are old enough to be left: we learn that Tom had had reservations about having a third child – discussions of the baby intrude into the space of the hotel bedroom on the mainland creating a split between the pair as they argue. Tom infantilises his pregnant wife; she suffers from heat exhaustion on an island where they have been warned by the hotel concierge on the mainland that there is no doctor; Evelyn is unable to run because of the baby which slows her down (the unborn baby is seen as parasitic on the mother). Anxieties about Evelyn's alienated, pregnant body (carrying a monstrous foetus representative possibly of fears about congenital abnormalities) combine with fears about a painful and possibly fatal birth (Evelyn is killed from within by her unborn baby).

Evelyn is conflated with maternity (she and Tom are turned away from the hotel on the mainland like a latter-day Mary and Joseph), programmed to protect her unborn child at all costs. We learn that Tom had considered abortion as an option. But if the autonomous foetus might be seen to advocate a pro-life stance then Tom's urging Evelyn to run for her life for the sake of their other two children might be seen as a pro-choice position as well as the rather regressive fear of congenital abnormalities).[20] Pregnancy may mean a risk to the mother's life or have an adverse effect on existing children. Tom and Evelyn discuss under what circumstances it might be permissible to kill a child, considering a scene from Fellini's *La Dolce Vita* (1960) in which the protagonist, Steiner, is moved to kill his children to protect them from the world. Child killing, then, in spite of the visions of terrorised innocents which open the film, might be viewed as the ethical position.

Two moments of child performance consolidate the justification for the killing of a child. In the first of these, Tom and Evelyn take refuge in a deserted *hostal* with one of the few surviving villagers. Suddenly, the daughter of the villager appears at the door. Filmed in close-up, tears falling down her face, she begs her father to accompany her because 'la tía Isabel está mal. La abuela está mal' (Auntie Isabel is in a bad way, Grandma is in a bad way). By this point we know that the children are murderers. If the villager accompanies his daughter he will meet certain death. The child's performance is wholly convincing: she grasps her father in tearful desperation. But our knowledge about these murderous children turns her crying into a performance. What is particularly horrific here is the sense of the masquerade of innocence hiding malevolence (a child who is false) and paradoxically, the simultaneous vacuity of the child. Thus, the children's stare is empty (posters for the film presented the children as glassy-eyed), without comprehension of events, without compassion, understanding or ethics. *¿Quién puede matar a un niño?* dwells on the limits of the image of the child. Stories of monstrous children are not new: Valentine conceives of the history of the child in terms of a contrast between angels and devils, a variation of Jenks's Apolline and Dionysian child (Jenks, 1996; Valentine, 1996). Ziolkowski (2001) writes of the Biblical tale of a pack of boys who set upon a holy man (the mockery of Elisha) which he sees as strikingly defying the traditional Judaeo-Christian and Romantic view of the child as a symbol of innocence. Whilst the theories of Philippe Aries have been subjected to various criticisms, he is credited (apart from his stunning revelation of the constructed nature of the child, the 'emergence of the multiple, variable child – a child which thereby enters the messy realm of history') as the 'inventor of childhood innocence' (Cook, 2004: 27). As Higonnet has written, 'whatever the exact timing or rapidity of change, an older concept of a child born in original Christian sin, correctible through rigid discipline, hard work, and corporal punishment, gave way to a concept of the child born innocent of adult faults, social evils and sexuality' (Higonnet, 1998: 26). The children of this film are the inheritors, moreover, of a horror tradition of demonised children (such as *Village of the Damned*, Rilla, 1960) which Schober has related to the Puritan tradition whereby children are vulnerable to corruption by a demonic force (Satan) (Schober, 2004). The children of *¿Quién puede matar a un niño?* have been corrupted by a demonic force which hypnotises them into killing adults. Thus their uncanny transgression relies on the initial establishment of pursuits which are generally related to childhood innocence: we see children playing with what we presume to be a *piñata* (as in a previous scene of children playing) but the camera takes us up along the rope they are pulling on to see that what they are jabbing with a farm implement is, in fact, a bloody corpse. The scene where some children are disrobing a corpse to look at her naked torso suggests, not a Freudian sense of the inherent sexuality of children, but childhood sexuality as an aberration. These are rampaging, evil monsters, beating one old man to death with a stick or charging disrespectfully through a church (Santa Eulalia, 1978) noted in interview that controlling the 250 children between the ages of seven and thirteen was his greatest challenge – the film captures the sense of anarchy). But just as they are subject to an unknown force, they exert power over the adults. When the villager's daughter appears crying, begging her father to accompany her because 'la tía Isabel está mal' (Aunt Isabel is in a bad way) – we know that he will meet his death if he goes with the child. Despite protestations from Tom, the villager replies, with a shrug, 'es mi hija' (she's my daughter) and follows the child outside where he meets his death at the hands of a crowd of children (we hear his shrieks and theirs). These children are knowing, sexual or evil but no one, it seems, can resist the lure of the child.

Later, Tom and Evelyn are holed up in a police cell as the children batter down the door in a long sequence of cross-cuts. Behind Evelyn we see that a young child has climbed up to the barred window and is pointing a gun at the back of her head. The child, framed by the window, eyes downcast, chubby face, draws on the image of the vulnerable, innocent child of our mnemonic heritage which comes together in Romantic and religious configurations (Higonnet, 1998). The child bears a resemblance to Joshua Reynolds's *The Age of Innocence* (1788), to countless cherubs in religious iconography and to countless versions of the *cine con niño* in the 1950s and 1960s in Spanish cinema. We might see the child as a 'pathos formula' as Warburg would have it (Michaud, 2004), a figure with an emotional charge unbroken throughout the ages. But through the scene with the villager, this image has been revealed to be an unreliable construct. The child is looking down, an image of humility and innocence, but as the camera pans down a gun is revealed: the child is getting ready to shoot Evelyn. Tom has to make a decision regarding his responsibilities to himself; as a father and husband; and to the island/nation. Can he turn against entrenched ideology and kill the child? Tom raises his pistol and shoots the child, who slumps, thick red blood oozing down the white-washed wall.

In one of the few scholarly treatments of the film, Steinberg (2006) suggests that we read the film against its historical contexts (the film was released on 21 April 1976, just five months after the death of Francisco Franco). Noting the similarity of the film's theme to the age-switching comedies – *Freaky Friday* (1976), *Viceversa* (1988), *Big* (1988) – alongside the aforementioned horrors about uncanny youth, Steinberg suggests that the film rather be placed within the body of Spanish Oedipal drama detailed by Marsha Kinder. For Steinberg, following the death of the dictator, the film:

> forms an allegory, albeit a vulgar one, on which its 'children' are the suffering, infantilised masses of Spain, loosed upon the world following the removal of the conservative, clerical Francoist state. Tom, the protagonist, is the subject

called upon to end the youthful insurrection, and to sustain the previous order (or replace it, if you prefer), which, precisely through the violent uprising of the masses/children, shows itself to have been not excessive but necessary. (Steinberg, 2006: 26)

The film is thus 'symptomatic of the anxiety surrounding what is to become of Franco's kids (and for this film we are all, in some sense, Franco's kids)' (Steinberg, 2006: 26). Steinberg's reading is persuasive: his suggestion that the absent body of the film is that of the dead despot is compatible with Eric Santner's (1990) suggestion that in the wake of the death of a dictator the nation attempts to find ways to mourn.

However, the film also articulates the cathartic release enjoyed by the breaking of taboos. In an intergenerational switching, I would therefore like to suggest that the taboo on killing a child stands in metonymically for the desire to kill General Franco. It was not just through the *cine con niño* of the 1950s and 1960s that the child became linked to Francoism. The Franco regime was, as we saw in Chapter 1, based on just such an ideology of 'reproductive futurism' (Edelman, 2004: 29) which proclaimed the cult of the child through its imagery, particularly that of the state-run aid programme for the children of the vanquished, the *Auxilio Social*. Even the Spanish beaches, sold to the foreign tourists through repackaged versions of the *españolada*, were presented to Spaniards through images of Franco himself holidaying with his grandchildren, complete with bucket, spade and blazer and cap (the dictator's off-duty uniform). What better image than the child to represent the power of Francoism. I suggest, then, that the taboo surrounding the killing of the child is directly linked to the taboo surrounding the death of General Franco and that playful innocence of childhood stands for Francoism's benign face masking horrific acts.

Steinberg links the opening sequence of newsreel to the state NO-DO of Francoism. But it is notable that Franco's state newsreel presented a mask to the world which never mentioned, for instance, the violence perpetrated by the regime on its children i.e. the embodiment of the proverb 'Cría cuervos'. The film places the spectator as an ethical decision-maker. The newsreel images at the start of the film return us to the notion of 'prosthetic cinema' and our role as the consumers of history on screen. Irrespective of whether we are horrified by the images or indifferent due to their familiarity, we are equally passive due to the enormity and familiarity of the atrocities which unfold (indeed to act to kill may, the suggestion is, align us with the perpetrators of atrocities) as well as their distance from us in time. The film therefore permits a cathartic release from the death of the child at the hands of Tom, metonymically standing in for the death of the dictator. López García (2008) has traced some of the different cultural works which reflected Spanish contemporary concerns with how to bring an end to the Franco regime or to imagine his death. Franco died peacefully in 1975 but this film imagines the killing of the dictator as a (missed) encounter.

Yet, the film also presents the problem (which is far more serious) of how to work to change a deeply entrenched ideology (here represented by the children and the police who come from the mainland and kill Tom). Rather than fear of an orphaned nation running amok, the film imagines an orphaned nation still under the power of its long-gone agents. In this film, the mnemonic heritage of the child as innocent victim is contested even as the child represents not just Spain's heritage, but also her uncertain future. Nothing can compete with the unbearable vision of horror presented at the start of the film in the form of the footage from the 'wounds' of history (arguably the film never recovers from its opening sequence) and the maimed children haunt the film. But the sinister, vacuous child, without ethics, who is unmoved by events, an uncomprehending witness, in other words, is another of its enduring images.

Childhood and nostalgia: *Secretos del corazón*

Child protagonists might be seen to provide the emotional and affective truth of a film. For Landsberg, this affective truth is more important than the 'authenticity' of the events depicted in a prosthetic memory. The 1990s in Spain saw the release of films which might be seen as presenting a glossy, nostalgic view of history. We have seen how Cook regards prosthetic memories, even those regarded as 'inauthentic', as providing the opportunity for spectators to engage in representations of history. But what is at stake in these representations? Are they reliant on specific contextualisations or references which allow spectators to engage in a 'proper' way? *Secretos del corazón* (Secrets of the Heart), directed by Montxo Armendáriz, was released in 1997. Set in the 1960s, it featured a child protagonist and made visual and thematic allusion to *El espíritu de la colmena*. But, like *La lengua de las mariposas* (Butterfly's Tongue, José Luis Cuerda), released two years later in 1999, which similarly delivered affective performances through its child protagonist, it raises questions concerning its use of nostalgia and its representation of 'history'.

Secretos del corazón, a film about a boy's rite of passage into adolescence, is set in Pamplona, Navarra, and a small town in the country in the 1960s. Javi (Andoni Erburu) and his brother attend a Catholic school in the city, where they stay with their aunts, María and Rosa, and travel to the rural village to their mother and uncle for holidays. Javi's coming of age twins his understanding about adult desire with his discovering of the secrets in the melodrama of his own family. The film adopts the child's point of view and Javi is persistently depicted as child-witness: peering out wide-eyed and uncomprehending through doors or from behind trees. In this sense, the film borrows heavily from the resonances of Ana Torrent's 'dark-eyed gaze': innocence, the threat of its corruption and the child as the witness to history. Where Ana was the *femme-enfant*, susceptible to fantasy, Javi is equally susceptible to the lies of his brother, to create a possibly sinister view of the world of adults. Whilst Javi's confusion over the word 'chingar' (to fuck) mobilises a sense of his naivety, we do not, from the start, know any more than him about the family secrets, nor the source of the noises emanating from the haunted house in the city or Javi's father's chair. In a key scene, the boy sits in his father's blood-spattered chair and listens to the ghostly moans. As the camera zooms in on his ear we become aware that the sounds relate, not to the groans of the dead, but to the moans of love-making. If we know more than Javi at this point, our superior knowledge is short-lived: Javi spies through the door and witnesses his uncle leaving his mother's room. Javi has become a latter-day Hamlet: his uncle has moved in with his mother whilst his father is a ghost whose spirit still occupies his chair.

Javi's older brother is the one who first tells Javi that he can communicate with his father through the chair. He relates this to the noises that Javi has heard in the haunted house in town and says that the noises in the house are the voices of dead people, screaming to be heard. This relates the film to the sense of Spanish history as engaged in an exploration of the unquiet dead. In Landsberg's theory of prosthetic memory, film can suture the spectator into a relationship with history. Through the child's point of view, *Secretos del corazón* potentially presents the spectator as engaged in a moment of history in which he/she may have had no part. But the child's point of view may also usher in a sense of nostalgia for the past. *Secretos del corazón* enjoys a nostalgia for the aesthetics of Francoism: the altar boys, the school play of 'Garbancito y el Mago Tragaflor' (Tom Thumb and the Magician Tragaflor); period music on the radio; the frowning upon of dancing to the 'Twist', cigarette cards depicting naked women (which coincides with a nostalgia for the artefacts of Francoism, a heritage mode seen in Spain in the late 1990s, with the production of reproductions of pamphlets of the *Sección Femenina* as a coffee-table book and Francoist films released in the *Clásico Español* series). Set against this is the subtle indictment of life under the regime depicted in the film: the violence taken out by the schoolchildren on a straw man, which seems like a random act in its unconnectedness; the rigid gender roles which keep Aunt Rosa in her place (if not María); the madness of Carlos, presumably a victim of war; and the impotence of Javi's grandfather whose ideas are assumed to be the rantings of an old man. Its unevenness might be compared to Imanol Uribe's *El viaje de Carol* (Carol's Journey, 2002) which, despite depicting the 'paseos', Civil Guard brutality and the killing of a child, nevertheless manages to dwell lovingly on period detail (the rebellion of the child protagonist is featured as her being told not to wear trousers which make her look like a *miliciana*) in a way which makes the film seem like nothing other than a holiday romance for the protagonist (notably at the end of the film Carol leaves war-torn Spain for a life with her beloved father in the United States). The difference in tone and treatment between this film and Agustí Villaronga's *El mar* (The Sea, 2000) is striking. In *El mar*, the witnessing of a 'paseo' leads the children who watch to murder and then to a life of the traumatic replaying of their crimes (in a hospital for tuberculosis viewed as a fitting metaphor for the corrosiveness of Spanish post-war society and which provides little relief from its theme of death, repressiveness and sexual obsessions). Writing of José Luis Cuerda's *La lengua de las mariposas* Smith notes its 'soft-focus nostalgia', its 'picturesque' settings which gloss over the poverty of Galicia which would have been rife in the region in the year before the opening of the Spanish Civil War and its creation of a 'Galician whimsy' (Smith, 2000b: 39–40). The main narrative strand of the film concentrates on the relationship between an asthmatic boy, Moncho (Manuel Lozano), and his teacher Don Gregorio (Fernando Fernán Gómez) and takes place in the year preceding the opening of the Spanish Civil War. Whilst, for the main part of the film, they enjoy an idyllic relationship of understanding and nurture, at the end of the film Moncho is called upon by his mother to shout abuse at the teacher as he is led off to certain death. Other critics found that the child actor (Manuel Lozano) provided a 'saccharine', overly 'cute' image which threatened any of the possibilities for serious engagement with the film.[21] The child ushers in the motif of education – the incarnation of Rousseau's *tabula rasa* (Don Gregorio is seen as a parallel to Antonio Machado) – whilst the benefits of a liberal upbringing endorsed by Francisco Giner de los Rios are confirmed, at least for Spanish audiences. Don Gregorio's opening up of the magical world of nature to Moncho provides an interesting parallel to the classroom teacher in *El espíritu de la colmena*, who encourages a mysticism around the dummy who she calls Don José. But in *La lengua de las mariposas*, simultaneously the motif of the 'end of childhood' and a return to a prelapsarian past (depicted as a rural idyll) might be seen as dwelling in too much nostalgia: as Stewart has written that nostalgia 'creates a longing that of necessity is inauthentic because it does not take part in lived experience ... nostalgia wears a distinctly utopian face, a face that turns towards a future-past, a past which has only "ideological reality"' (Stewart, 1993: 23). The film recreates scenes depicted in photographs in the opening sequences, but as Stewart writes, photographs 'can be transformed into narrative forms that deny the lived experience of the past' (Stewart, 1993: 23). Thus, if *El espíritu de la colmena* recalls Svetlana Boym's description of a reflective nostalgia, which stresses *algia* (longing) and does not attempt to search for a perfect completeness in the past but 'lingers on ruins, the patina of time and history, in the dreams of another place and another time' (Boym, 2001: 41), *La lengua de las mariposas* might have more in common with her 'restorative nostalgia', from *nostos* (home), the past as a 'value for the present', a kind of erasure of history through a return to a prelapsarian tradition or 'truth'. But if the child provides a focus for the nostalgia of the film, it is the child's face that also provides the site for ambiguity that might usher in more complex readings of the film. In the final scene of *La lengua de las mariposas*, Moncho, a five-year-old boy, watches as his teacher, Don Gregorio, is led off, presumably to his death, as we witness the change here from innocence to hatred as Moncho's face becomes contorted

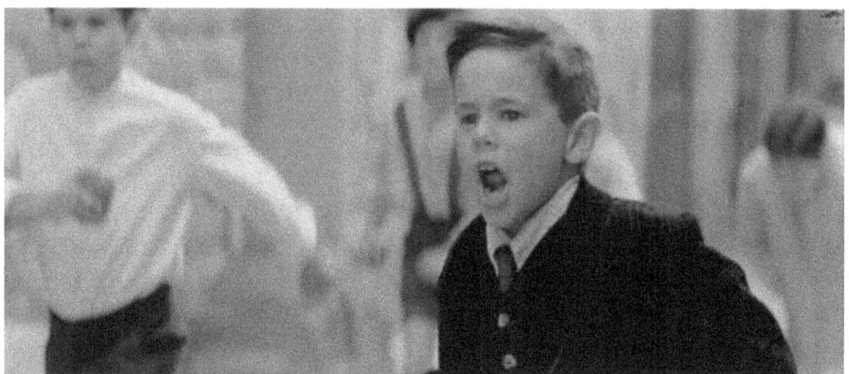

7 Moncho's gaze in *La lengua de las mariposas* (José Luis Cuerda, 1999).

into a vision of hate. After hesitating, wide-eyed and perplexed, Moncho runs after the cart, mimicking the others, 'rojo' 'ateo' (red, atheist) but then shouts the names of the Latin-based words that Don Gregorio has taught him for things they found together in nature: 'tilonorrinco' and 'proboscis'.

Has Moncho become a 'monster' in an evocation of the phrase 'cría cuervos' (raise ravens and they'll pluck out your eyes)? Or is his use of the Latin terms his defence, a code to suggest that he is not complicit in the abuse? This ambiguity lends depth to what otherwise becomes a scene which drowns in sentimentality lent by the swelling music, the still snap-shot of the boy on screen and the rather hackneyed theme of lost innocence. For Paul Grainge, nostalgia does not always necessary refer to loss, but might act as a signifier for nostalgia (Grainge, 2002), but the image of the boy's face contorted by hate seems to signify loss of a previous innocence. But Moncho seems to be far more, therefore, than what Sobchack (1996), writing of Forrest Gump in the film of the same name of 1994, explains as providing the sense that 'history happens' whether we comprehend it or not. We do retain that sense of Moncho as a victim of the events which engulf him, but also through the ambiguity of his comprehension of his response, the notion that he might act to resist the 'falsely constructed hatred' (Lough, 2007: 153) around him. Francis Lough's work on the film is the most nuanced to date: he carefully explains the references through Antonio Machado to the liberal view of education and the ways that these are only available as a reference point to those critics and viewers familiar with that aspect of Spanish history. For Lough, the film should not be read as a 'desire to return to or simply lament a lost utopia' but (particularly when seen to tap into anxieties in the late 1990s in Spain concerning the defence of democracy) can be seen to enact a 'more complex commentary on the corrupting violence in an oppressive social context' (Lough, 2007: 167).

Returning to *Secretos del corazón*, the past is presented in the film as full of secrets which presents us with the confusion of a child. The past is there to be investigated. Through intertextual citation, the film returns us to the past invoked by *El espíritu de la colmena*, *Cría cuervos* (and, interestingly, to *Marcelino, pan y vino*) and thus to memories of Spanishness. *Marcelino* is cited in a visual reference to the basement of Javi's uncle's house filled with cobwebs, where Javi is sent to fetch wine and which recalls the attic Marcelino visits where he meets up with the Christ statue. It is also evoked in the old chair which Javi sits in to try to call up the spirit of his father just as the Christ-figure materialises before Marcelino and sits in the chair in *Marcelino, pan y vino*. *El espíritu de la colmena* is evoked in the train which whistles through the city, carrying away the voices of the spirits the two boys hear in the haunted house, and in particular, in the scene where Javi and his brother lie side by side in bed and hear the creaking of footsteps in the darkness before Javi attempts to reach the spirit of his father. Here Torrent's performance is evoked as a spectral presence. These citations provide an example of appropriation and recontextualisation. Thus, just as the footsteps Ana hears are in fact those of her father, so here, Javi will discover that the murmurs he hears emanating from the chair are none other than his mother making love to his uncle. Marcelino's spirituality is replaced by a secular lesson in realism. But if Ana's witnessing of the primal scene points to her real trauma in *Cría cuervos*, here Javi is not traumatised by what he has discovered and his anger at his uncle is short-lived. Towards the end of the film, Javi discovers, through an overheard reference from his mother, that his uncle is his real father. It seems that the relationship between his mother and uncle was known about and disapproved of by everyone in the village. When they decide to marry, the villagers are pacified and Javi looks happy, until he sees his grandfather's friend loading a rifle, a reference to his father. He runs inside to ask his grandfather about his father's death and learns that he committed suicide: 'hay cosas que no tienen explicación' (there are things which have no explanation), his grandfather tells him. Thus Javi, through an investigation of the past, has discovered the less than prosaic truth: the voices in the haunted house were nothing other than his Aunt María, making love to her lover, Ricardo. As she runs off with him, Javi manages to cross the river, marking his passage into adolescence. Now Javi understands about adult desire but he has also resolved the mysteries of the past. As the final scenes of celebration show, Javi feels no anguish about his uncle's usurping of his father's place: indeed his uncle is his real father and the ghosts of the past have been extinguished. In Yeon-Soo Kim's (2005) reading of the film, she makes the case for Javi to be seen as a peripheral identity, seen as akin to Basqueness, which claims a political edge for this film made by a Basque film-maker. Citing Kinder's 'children of Franco' article, she points out that Javi is neither a murderous monster nor a poignant victim, and she points out that the film's failed Oedipal resistance (Javi's capitulation to the reality of his identity) might be seen to interrogate the post-Franco aesthetic. But although the film's narrative is driven by a desire to investigate the past in order to understand the mysteries in the present, its final message appears to be a rather conservative one. The intertextual references and the evocation of Torrent's 'dark-eyes' as motif invoke a sense of a Spanish heritage in order to suggest that it is time to heal and move on. This is not quite Jameson's 'historical amnesia', but it perhaps strays rather too close to a sense of narrative closure and the closing-off of history (Jameson, 1991: 68). In writing of *Shoah* versus *Schindler's List*, Miriam Hansen reminded us that, 'unless we take all aspects – omissions and distortions, displacements and possibilities – of public, mass-mediated culture seriously, we will remain caught in the "compulsive pas-de-deux" of (not just) intellectual history' (Hansen, 1996: 306). In 2001, Rob Stone remarked that in this film 'it is tempting to read golden-hued nostalgia for childhood, were it not for the chronology, which identifies Javi, who would be twenty-one at the time of the death of Franco, with the generation that came of age in the democracy' (Stone, 2001: 106). The film is, therefore, a celebration of the passing of the dictatorship. But from today's perspective, it seems difficult to see the film other than a conservative exhortation towards collective amnesia. Javi's clear-eyed gaze seems to register no loss of innocence. The past may hide some secrets but it is better to allow the dead to rest in peace and allow the living to get on with their lives in a spirit of reconciliation.

Ghostly children

Three films seem in different ways to celebrate Derrida's dictum that we should learn to live with the ghosts of the past: *El espinazo del diablo*; *El Orfanato* and *NO-DO* (The Haunting, Elio Quiroga, 2009). All three evoke the large haunted house of the gothic, and all three work productively with the theme of the double. All three also contain elements of the murder mystery which suggestively posits the past as a place which requires investigation. In *El Orfanato* and *NO-DO*, the gothic house comes to represent Spain itself, whilst scenes of tearing down walls to find the gruesome secrets hidden within stand as a metaphor for the need to uncover Spain's monstrous secrets of the past. These films present the theme of the ghostly child only to point to a partly repressed spectre of another missing child (who represents the missing child of Spanish history) (Delgado, 2008).

El espinazo del diablo twins the murder of a boy with the start of the Spanish Civil War. We open to the shuddering of a dying boy, Santi, as another, Javier, cradles the boy's bleeding head and then clasps his bloodied hands to his face in shock. Immediately the film cuts to the dropping of a bomb in an aerial shot over a landscape. As we will later learn, the bomb lodges, unexploded, in the Santa Lucia orphanage at the outbreak of the Spanish Civil War. As Anne Hardcastle has noted, the film's theme of a boy-ghost links it through hauntology to traumatic memory of the war (Hardcastle, 2005). The film is in part a recreation of Carlos Giménez's

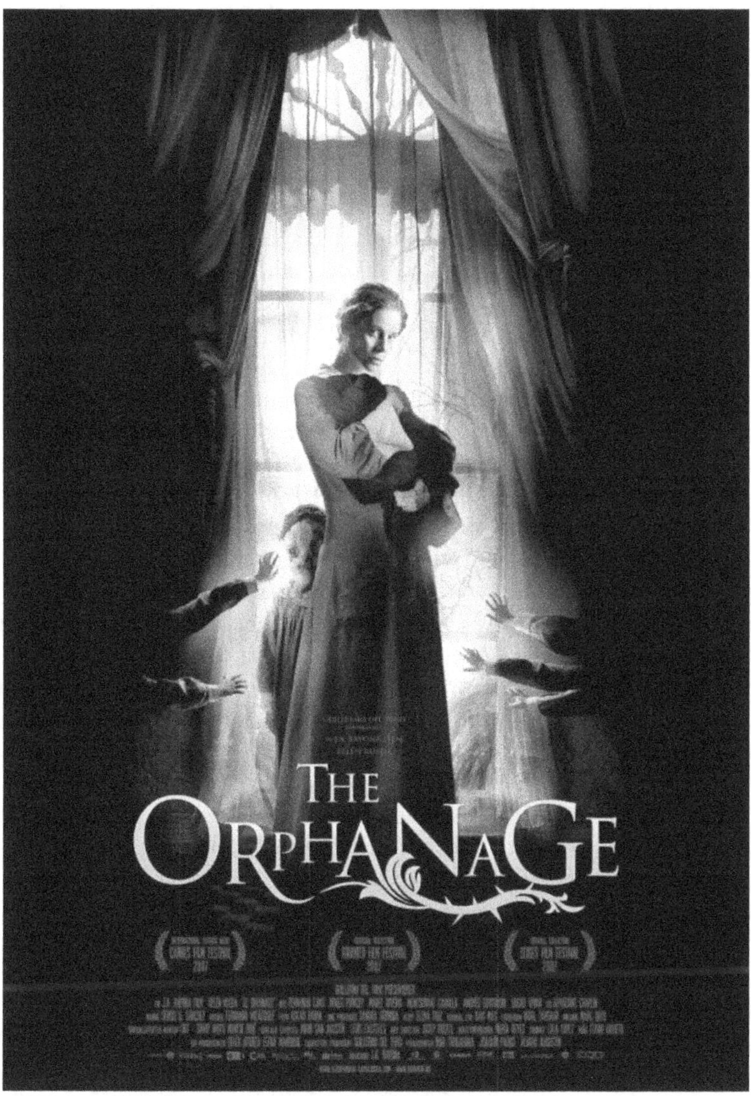

8 Poster for Bayona's *El orfanato* (2007).

comic-book series *Paracuellos* (2000) which tells the autobiographical account of a life in an orphanage run by the *Auxilio Social*, a state-run organisation which enjoyed huge media campaigns exalting the benign face of the dictatorship (Cenarro, 2009). The orphanage in *El espinazo del diablo* is, strictly speaking, a place run by 'rojos cuidando hijos de rojos' (reds taking care of the children of reds) but, as Lázaro-Reboll notes, during the course of the film:

as the war develops and the Nationalists approach the area, the space is transformed into and re-institutionalized as an official site of fascism, toeing the new ideology of *nacionalcatolicismo* (the Nationalist flag replaces the Republican, religious imagery takes the place of secular portraits, the crucifix on the wall as a sign of Catholic religiosity), bringing back to life the 'Historias de Auxilio Social'. (Lázaro-Reboll, 2007: 48)

In *El espinazo del diablo*, Carlos (Fernando Tielve) is left at the orphanage by his tutor. Carlos stares around at his new environment, eventually becoming a leader to his friends Galvez, whose flying goggles seem to parody the wide-eyed Carlos, and Buho (Owl), who rarely speaks, just observes. Part of the aesthetics of *Paracuellos* is, as Moreno-Nuño (2009) has noted, 'the feminine portraits of the keepers in *Paracuellos* show the perverting practice of motherhood, whose function was so acclaimed by *Auxilio Social*'. In *Paracuellos*, 'the zooms on the long sharp fingernails of the housekeepers exemplify metonymically the aggressivity that prevailed in the *Hogares*' (Moreno-Nuño, 2009: 181). In *El espinazo* this is recreated through the castrating scissors whose shadows runs menacingly across the wall of the dark kitchen when Carlos goes to fetch water and meets the ghost for the first time, whilst the aesthetic of black dresses and keys is recreated by the film through Carmen, the orphanage's director. Carmen treats Dr Casares cruelly – he drinks potions to cure his impotence, and is in love with Carmen. She prefers young and vigorous Jacinto (Eduardo Noriega), but Jacinto has been in the orphanage since boyhood, which turns her into a monstrously incestuous mother, a seductress whose monstrosity is enhanced by the calliper she wears on her leg, a familiar symbol of the Surrealists for the castrating female. The foetuses submerged in the liquid which Dr Casares drinks to cure his impotence suffer from spina bifida, but their spiny backbones refer, through their visual reminiscence of Man Ray's *Le Cadeau* (1921), to the mythical vagina dentata. Carmen lost her leg as a casualty of war (in the scene where the bomb explodes across the dusty plaza at the centre of the orphanage, sending shards of debris towards the screen, we are reminded of the capacity of war to create havoc in the civilian population, resulting in missing limbs in an echo (visual and thematic) of Picasso's *Guernica*, 1937). But as it is the place where Carmen hides the gold, her leg becomes a site of moral ambiguity (see Clarke (2004) for the associations of physical with moral deformity). Carmen is played sympathetically by Marisa Paredes, who brings warmth and humanity to this dehumanised role, but Carlos will not find a suitable mother-figure in Carmen.

If Carmen as a surrealist icon is a possible reference for this film, the partially submerged reference to Salvador Dalí's *The Metamorphosis of Narcissus* (1937) emerges as an interesting intertextual link.[22] In the opening scene, Javier crouches over the watery tomb where Santi enjoys a fitful deathly rest in a posture which appears to mimic the crouching figures in Dalí's painting. Dalí's luminous egg-head with the flower protruding from the top appears to be echoed in Santi's ghost whose translucently white head is followed by a trail of blood emerging from the top. Dalí's painting draws on the myth of Narcissus, the beautiful boy who is so entranced with his own reflection that he falls in love with it and stays at the pool-side until his death, to begin a series of mirrorings and opposites. Mirrorings are also a clear theme of Del Toro's film. The cloudy yellow of the tank also links Santi with the monstrousness of the foetuses in the jars in Dr Casares, which, as Dr Casares explains, were placed there because of superstition which saw their condition as monstrous (they are suffering from spina bifida). The opening of the film dwells on their monstrosity, although it must be noted that they exude a surreal beauty which takes the information that Dr Casares is drinking the liquid from the jars as a cure for impotence to reinforce their monstrousness. In an excellent article, Ann Davies (2011) links the seductive monstrosity of Jacinto, Carmen's lover, to the virile aspirations of the Spanish brand of Fascism. Citing Perriam's discussion of Eduardo Noriega's physical attractiveness – 'In terms of Noriega's career the film builds on the productive tension between extreme good looks and extreme bad conduct' (Perriam, 2003: 178) – she compares this form of masculinity with the monstrous, abject form embodied by Santi (the blood coming from his head is seen as a menstrual flow). Echoing the Narcissus theme, here it is the beautiful Jacinto who, out of self-absorption, will be motivated by greed, whilst Santi is condemned to entrapment in time and space. In fact the fear generated by Santi relies on the tension caused by fleeting shadows on walls, footsteps on wooden floors and shapes behind curtains. Once Carlos finally comes face to face with Santi he is revealed as a prosthetic memory in the sense that the special effects create of him a friendly ghost (just as Ana's Frankenstein was rather too prosthetic to cause fear by his image alone) (Hardcastle, 2005). True monstrosity lies in the film embodied by Jacinto, a product of Francoism, driven by greed. At the end of the film the boys spear him like the mammoth they have learned about in the classroom before tossing him into the watery grave.

As James Rose (2009) has noted, the film seems to play with notions of lightness and weight: the crucifix carried into the orphanage by Carlos, Galvez and Buho to signal the victor of the Nationalists, for instance, is heavy – 'Christ, for a dead guy he sure weighs a lot' – whilst Carmen's leg, filled with gold bars, is lugged around like a cross to be borne. Bur Carlos's gaze, recreated by the camera, is fluid and free. Towards the start of the film we saw the potential for the corruption of Carlos's innocent gaze as he realised that his tutor had tricked him into leaving him at the orphanage. But just as Javier chooses not to imitate his near namesake Jacinto (the visual echoes between them are clear: both smoke, both are in love with Conchita), Carlos chooses the right path.

In an excellent article, Lázaro-Reboll (2007) considers Hardcastle's interpretation of the film: that it helps to overcome the traumatic legacy of the

Civil War and 'unify potential subjects around the theme of the democratic, enlightened, modernised and finally influential Spanish nation' (Hardcastle, 2005: 127), troubling in its sense of closure. But returning to Dalí, what haunts his painting *The Metamorphosis of Narcissus* is the information that it may have been painted as a tribute to his dead brother, also named Salvador, who died of meningitis before Dalí's birth. The crouching figure by the pool may refer to another, lost figure (the egg with the flower is seen as a reference to the earlier Salvador Dalí's illness). In a similar way, Santi refers directly to the children lost or maimed by the violence of war ('many of you will die') but also may provide a hint to the other lost children of Francoism.

In an echo of *¿Quién puede matar a un niño?*, Elio Quiroga's genre horror *NO-DO* (2009) opens with footage from the Francoist state-newsreel. The premise is that Francoists filmed Marian apparitions, exorcisms and miracles and saved these in secret archives that were sent to the Vatican.[23] The film intersects directly with the documented apparitions of the Virgin Mary and Archangel St Michael in Garabandal, northern Spain from 1961 to 1965. The ecstasies of the four visionaries involved were captured on film and now circulate on YouTube.[24] The credits for *NO-DO* include reference to Tranche and Sánchez-Biosca's book and CD Rom which has collected excerpts of the state newsreel, but it is not clear that visions were, in fact, filmed by NO-DO. Also mentioned in the credits is a thesis from the University of Las Palmas, about the story of Samuel Ferren, the inventor of a type of film that could capture the supernatural world on film. But librarians at the university have been unable to locate the thesis nor is it included in the catalogue.[25] An elaborate hoax by Quiroga? At the moment it is hard to tell. *NO-DO* rests on the proposition that certain hidden newsreels contain the truth about the Franco regime.

In the film, several clergy are involved in the exorcisms in a house, which end in the murder of children and the cameraman, Senel Martín. Coming hot on the heels of *El orfanato*, the film operates on the same double-premise of the mother mourning a lost son and whereas *El orfanato* revels in the intertextual resonances provided by Geraldine Chaplin's appearance as a medium (the actress was the mother to Ana in *Cría cuervos*), here Ana Torrent herself appears as the female lead. Francesca (Ana Torrent) works as a paediatrician at a local hospital where she likes to baptise stillborns. Suffering from post-partum depression (a child of hers had died ten years previously) she is encouraged by her husband and friend, Jean, a psychiatrist, to take some time off: she and her husband and new baby, Pablo, move into the same house which had witnessed so much terror in the past.

At first, Francesca's husband believes that her problems stem from her post-partum depression. Unlike Pedro (Francesco Boira), the viewer can see the ghost of the daughter whom Francesca lost ten years earlier. Little wonder that Francesca should be nervous of losing her other child and the film plays on the anxieties of the new mother, checking to see if her baby has stopped breathing in the night. Eventually, Francesca is encouraged to use a baby monitor, but soon she begins to hear voices through the monitor, which add to her hysteria. But, in parallel, Blanca has woken from a coma lasting around forty years and provides a link to the past. Blanca was the wife of Senel Martín, the cameraman who devised the Ferren emulsion which could record supernatural life on film, and is now snooping around the outhouses mumbling about priests and miracles. But the house soon begins to reveal its secrets. Francesca finds a room full of votives – plaster limbs used to perform miracles. Far more than the ghoulish aesthetic of National Catholicism, the votives turn out to signal the violence performed by the Francoists in the name of religion. The ghosts, we will soon realise, exist in far more than Francesca's imagination.

In *NO-DO*, we can see that the digital can come close to the truth of Spain's past and current traumas even as the newsreel (whose black and white aesthetic we have learned to read as 'history')[26] is revealed as partial, framed or even wilfully misleading. In *Framed Time: Toward a Postfilmic Cinema* (2007), Garrett Stewart suggests that the digital ushers in a pre-occupation with viewing the passing of time on screen – where analogue animated the still to create the illusion of movement but at the same time provided an indexical trace to real bodies, the digital concentrates on the ability of time to appear to stand still for internal mutation whilst the connection between real bodies and the image may be severed in the erosion of the digital's photographic base. Stewart views this as potentially a political disengagement of the image in a Baudrillardean consciousness. But the severed prosthetic limbs hanging from the ceiling in a boarded-up room in the house are votives which bear more than a passing relationship to the real limb they represent in the working of miracles. If they also recall Landsberg's description of prosthetic cinema, which can be worn like a prosthesis and which covers a trauma, this seems a particularly apt image for this film for whom film's ability to capture history is rendered more truthful through its capturing of psychic contours of Spanish memory than through historical referents. In *NO-DO/The Haunting* the digital can reconnect with the political where the official capturing of Spanish historical reality is found to be inadequate in the face of the digitised materialisation of Spanish horrors on screen (Wright, 2013b).

However, the real 'lost child' is Ana Torrent herself. The film dwells on Torrent's mournful gaze, searching and bewildered, and when she finds herself watching in and through the lost film footage we are reminded of the scenes from *El espíritu de la colmena* where she faced the monster by the lake. Rather like Ana, Francesca speaks little, preferring to stare out with dark eyes which recall her earlier performance. The film borrows from Torrent's star persona – Torrent brings with her the sense that she was the child as the victim of history – but specifically it recreates the sense that she, far more than the ghostly girl-children which populate the film, is the missing child at its centre. In reviews of subsequent films in her career,

Torrent has been dogged by the memory of her first performance. Torrent is, as I argue elsewhere, a palimpsest which, 'like Freud's Mystic Writing Pad, promises the erasure of her past incarnations with every new character in each new film, but which simultaneously contains the trace of her first iconic performance as well as selected subsequent ones which are foregrounded or displaced in a series of polysemic intensities' (Wright, 2013b). In interview, Carlos Saura has noted that after her first films she 'lost her earlier magic', which may recall comments by Linda Ruth Williams that child stars are surrounded by death in that they are forever on the road to growing up, to a loss of their childlikeness.[27] Through Torrent's performance, the film draws on these intertextual links to draw out the theme of child-murder and loss. The film provides a happy ending for Francesca, who goes to live in an apartment on the outskirts of town to be reunited with her husband and son. But the haunting sense of the loss of childhood, enacted through its star, remains as a spectral presence.

El orfanato has been read by Maria Delgado as having a direct link to the question of children who disappeared under Francoism (Delgado, 2008). In its twisting plot, Laura (Beleú Rueda) moves into the house which was the orphanage of her youth, with her husband and child, Simón (Roger Príncep). Due to a tragic series of events, revealed to us gradually, she will lock the child in the basement where he will perish. But the house is also filled with the ghost of lost children who died many years previously. Tomás, who is so hideous that he wears a sinister mask over his head, had been led to his death by the other children of the orphanage. Benigna, the warden, we will learn, subsequently killed and incinerated the remains of the other children, out of revenge for the loss of her beloved Tomás. In the film's main narrative sequence, Laura has lost her beloved son, Simón, and she soon becomes aware that the ghosts of children are leading her to solve the mystery not just of his death, but of Tomás's and their own. They indulge in childish games, leaving her trails to follow in the house. The film plays with a series of mirrorings (not least of which is the correlation between Simón, the boy who is HIV positive, and Tomás, the boy with the physical disfigurement – both 'othered' by society) which see Laura as possibly the victim of a mental breakdown following the loss of her son or, as will be revealed, a woman who is so sensitive to the past lives of the house that she will go to join the dead (the parallels to Amenábar's *The Others* are clear here). Laura attempts to evoke her childhood 'haunts': the crockery she lays out on the table which recalls the childhood pastime of dollies' tea-parties, the game of 'Grandmother's Footsteps' which eventually summon the child ghosts (after a series of ghostly apparitions we see a hand reach up a tap her on the shoulder). The adult female playing at being a child creates an uncanny sense of 'time out of joint'. Laura is a 'present past', in a perpetual mourning for her lost son, and the aesthetic of the orphanage – gothic house, grey uniform, doors locked with keys – evokes the orphanages of the *Auxilio Social*. The incinerated bodies of the children she finds provide a link between Laura's own loss and the 'Spanish Holocaust' which here takes on the figure of a lost child.

A series of revelations in the Spanish press since *El espinazo del diablo* has added renewed vigour to the motif of the child as a representation of memory. In 2001, Jaime Camino's documentary *Los niños de Rusia* featured oral testimonies of the children of Republicans who were sent to the Soviet Union during the Spanish Civil War in the spring of 1937 and the traumatic fall-out from that event (Gutiérrez Albilla, 2011).[28] In a sense it might be seen as a riposte to Rafael Gil's *Murió hace quince años* (discussed in Chapter 1). With their common themes of implantation of ideologies, the two films, albeit from different eras and genres, make for an interesting counterpoint. In 2002, *Los niños perdidos del franquismo* was published, a book by Ricardo Belis, Ricardo Vinyes and Montse Armengou (and a documentary of 2005) which explained the common practice under Francoism of separating the children of incarcerated 'rojos' (often in prison under the flimsiest of evidence) and killing them or sending them away either to state-run orphanages or for adoption by Francoist families. The documentary is a series of talking heads interspersed with brief fictional shots of, for example, a psychiatrist sitting in a laboratory. Vallejo Nágera, chief psychiatrist of the state, believed that Marxism was a (curable) mental illness. After periods of neglect (mothers were separated from the children and were not allowed to embrace them), atrocious conditions of hygiene and starvation, the children mysteriously disappeared: they were told that they had been lost, were often given new names and were sent to new families. The documentary tells of horrors far worse than those of Spanish horror movies: rape and murder of the women matched by terrible violence against women and children. The revelations continue, with a hospital that arranged illegal adoptions discovered in 2010. The story of the Saturrarán prison where a hundred children were removed from their mothers at once forms the subject matter of a film by Mikel Rueda, *Izarren Argia* (not yet on general release but dated 2010). These revelations make us look anew at the child ghosts of the most recent Spanish film production: where the changing of the name of Ofelia's brother in *El laberinto del fauno* might be seen as a direct challenge to the historical realities where the names of Republican children were changed as part of a process to replace their identities. It also may remind us that whilst the newsreel at the start of *¿Quién puede matar a un niño?* might be viewed as a Francoist NO-DO, actual NO-DO footage (shown, for example, in *Los niños perdidos del franquismo*), was parading children as propaganda for its *Hogares del Auxilio Social*, whilst hiding grim realities of child violence. I wrote earlier of Elsaesser's distinction between obsessiveness about the past and working through. These revelations mean that the memory that these films evoke is still ever-present for spectators, performing revisionist exercise as the discoveries about Spain's past continue to appear in this overdetermined landscape of Spanish historical memory with enormous rapidity.

Prosthetic memories: *El laberinto del fauno*

In its repetitions of the child and monster theme, coupled with its development of a child's fantasy as a form of prosthetic memory, *El laberinto del fauno* appears to take up where *El espíritu de la colmena* leaves off. The film skilfully weaves together two parallel realities: Ofelia's worldview from the perspective of the Spain of the 1940s – living with a bed-ridden, pregnant mother and her cruel stepfather, Captain Vidal, whose mission is to hunt out the *maquis* hiding in the woods – and a brightly coloured fantasy in which she is Princess Moanna and must complete a series of tasks to return to her family in the underworld. Smith points out the clear visual echo where Ofelia (Ivana Baquero) adds the eyes to the statue which is reminiscent of the scene in *El espíritu de la colmena* where Ana adds eyes to Don José: 'Del Toro thus not only replays Spanish history in a Mexican mode he has perfected elsewhere; he also remakes Spanish cinema by transforming Erice's austere and minimalist drama with gorgeously crafted *mise-en-scène* and deliriously inventive camerawork' (Smith, 2007: 5). Smith also notes the curious symmetries and mismatches between the two parallel worlds: whilst Ofelia is clearly the inheritor of the role of 'witness to history' (indeed we open to her shuddering, dying body as the camera penetrates her eye, signalling her point of view) there are moments in the film that she could not possibly have witnessed and other elements which have no explanation (Smith, 2007: 8). When the camera's fluid movements retreat into Ofelia's eye, the sequence may remind us of Georg Simmel's discussions of the human face in which the 'eye penetrates, it withdraws, it circles a room, it wanders, it reaches as though behind the wanted object and pulls it toward itself' (Simmel, 1959: 281). We willingly enter what we perceive to be Ofelia's world. Ofelia seems to be living out Walter Benjamin's observation that children use colours as a 'basis from which to create the interrelated totality of the world of the imagination' (Benjamin, 1996: 50): children experience colour in such a way that it might interfere with the law.[29] With its overt references to fairy tales, in particular the tasks set for her by the faun, we may retain a sense that Ofelia may be attempting to use fairy tales to 'comprehend and take emotional control over the war-torn landscape of childhood' (Haase, 2000: 361). The film hints at the sense that Ofelia is writing her own story through fantasy, but the question of how much narrative control she can have to write her own future is a question mooted by the film.

Smith (2007), alongside other critics, has pointed out the way the two parallel worlds interact: both worlds are cruel violent places; Vidal's dining room shares similarities with that of the Pale Man (whilst the latter's pile of shoes belonging to dead children recalls the scenes of the Holocaust – a fitting alter ego for the instrument of Fascism). Ellis and Sánchez-Arce (2011), meanwhile, view the grotesque Pale Man as an incarnation not just of the insignia of the Falange (the arrows seem to be echoed in the hands with eyes) but also of the Catholic Church. Miles (2011) begins his article

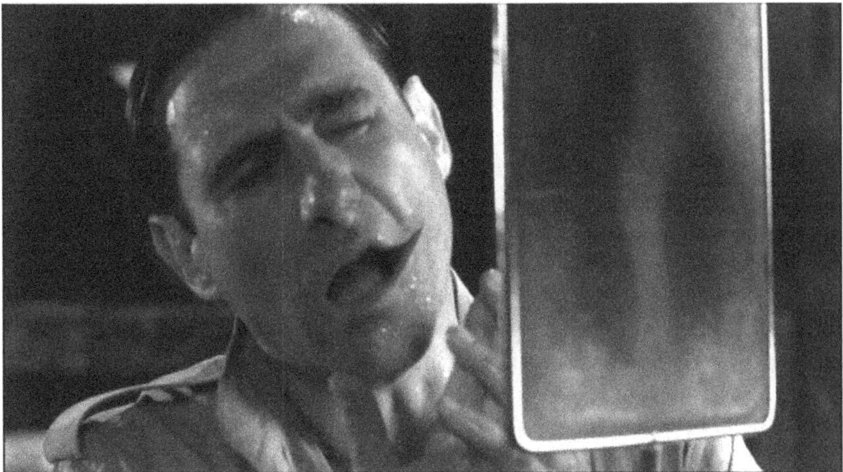

9 Capitán Vidal's slashed face in *El laberinto del fauno* (Guillermo del Toro, 2006).

with the parallels between the films by Erice and Del Toro with a reminder of the context of the later film: 2007 saw the tearing down of the monumentalism attached to Francoism in Spain, with statues torn down and squares renamed to remove traces of their past (we retain a sense of this notion in the fact that Vidal is desperate to continue his family name, which Ofelia and Mercedes rob him of when they claim that his son will not know anything of his father nor bear his name).[30] An interesting parallel is provided in the film where Mercedes stabs Vidal in the face, drawing a terrible gash through his mouth, literally defacing him. Vidal's face holds an extraordinary attraction/repulsion, which Wolfgang Kayser, writing of the grotesque, describes as 'the recognition of a resemblance to, or continuity between, the human form and other forms, such as animal or plant forms, or even other forms of pictorial representation' (Kayser, 1957: 185). Vidal's face is asymmetrical, like a clown's painted-on mouth, or the figure of the Joker from the *Batman* comic-strips.[31]

Mercedes's act of defacement parallels Vidal's smashing of the broken bottle into the face of the *maqui* prisoner earlier in the film. But Michael Taussig reminds us that defacement creates its own sacred power (Taussig, 1999) and Vidal, as a great comic-book villain, might be viewed as tapping into the fetishistic power of Fascism. Is the 'historical-realist' plane therefore seductively deceptive? Vidal retains an aesthetic derived from Hollywood movies featuring Nazi soldiers, suggesting, perhaps, a sense of resolution to the film (the vanquishing of Fascism) that works counter to attempts to recuperate historical memory (Davies, 2012). This, arguably, is Elsaesser's fear of a traumatised cinema: the moving image as 'the symptom without a cause, as the event without a trace' (Elsaesser, 2001: 197) wherein history is portrayed as a mélange of debris recycled from previous filmic realities, without true anchor in historical events.

However, Ellis and Sánchez-Arce (2011) argue that the power of this film is that both realities are revealed to be fictions; indeed Spaniards learned to live for many years with the mythologising of history put forward by the Franco regime and this film engages with the myths of history. They call this the 'psychological rather than the actual recovery of historical memory' and remark that 'cinematic "false" memories like those of del Toro would not hold up in a court of law. But they are narratives of what might have occurred at least as convincing as many of the myths propagated during Franco's dictatorship which were neither challenged during the Transition nor for the first thirty years of democracy in Spain' (Ellis and Sánchez-Arce, 2011: 174). But if Ofelia's worlds are revealed as fantasies, then so too is Ofelia herself, who is drawn from a host of intertextual references (from the *Wizard of Oz* to *Alice in Wonderland*) until she takes on an allegorical position at the centre of the drama. In the final images of the film, Ofelia lies shuddering in close-up, in an echo of the opening sequence of the film. If Vidal's face was subject to a defacement, then so too was Ofelia's in that opening sequence, an uncanny image which is obscene as it defiles the sense that children have to be protected from violence at all costs. Simmel's writing reveals his sense that the face is a mask, a productive model of the image. Ofelia, here, is revealed to us as a motif of the child's gaze. It is not, as A. Robin Hoffman maintains, that she collapses 'under the weight of polysemy' (2010a: 139). But rather, she represents history as a burden (throughout the film she is asked to take responsibility for her actions) and for the taking of responsibility for personal and collective futures. But if defacement reveals sacred power, then Ofelia's face retains a redemptive power. In echoing Ana in *El espíritu de la colmena*, Ofelia articulates the loss of Torrent's earlier image even as she also evokes the earlier image. Ofelia likewise represents the loss of national historical memory, but also reminds us of the redemptive power of prosthetic memories. The film may be contradictory, ambivalent and possibly deceptively seductive, but it also reminds us that, where historical accounts are missing, 'psychological' memories have a role to play in the recuperation of national memory.

The monstrous child revisited: *Pa negre*

Pa negre by Agustí Villaronga – famous for niche horror films such as *Tras el cristal* (In a Glass Cage, 1987) about an ex-Nazi child abuser, or *El niño de la luna* (Moonchild, 1989) with its controversial scenes of child sex – swept the boards at the Goyas in 2010 with this Catalan-language film based on a novel and some short stories by Emili Teixidor about a boy (Andreu), the son of those on the side of the vanquished, and his coming of age in 1940s Catalonia. In 2012 it was chosen as the Spanish entry at the Oscars (in favour of Almodóvar's *La piel que habito* (The Skin I Live In).[32]

It was not just the first time that a Catalan-language film had been selected for the Oscars but also the first time that a film in Catalan had won 'best picture' at the Goyas. Catalan critics mused on the regeneration of Catalan film-making that the success of this film implied, remarking that the film's blend of hyper-naturalism returned to an earlier period of Catalan film-making and away from the current trends towards minimalism.

Contemporary reviewers noted the well-worn trope of the innocent child as witness to the wounds of the post-war era yet they also noted that this film provided something different to the genre. In fact *Pa negre* evokes the 'tópicos' (clichés) even as it deconstructs them, refusing simplistic notions of memory and nostalgia. The film opens with a scene of violence: a hooded man slits the throat of a man leading his horse and cart through the woods and then smashes his skull with an enormous rock. The man's son watches, cowering, in the covered wagon, before he and the horse are tipped over the edge of the cliff. Andreu (Francesc Colomer) finds his friend Colet dying in the wood, after he utters the word 'Pitorliua'. As Andreu later explains to the Civil Guard officer as he makes a statement, Pitorliua is a Latinate name for a type of bird – it is also the name given to a ghost haunting the Baumes caves. But after this opening, separated by titles, the film intertwines several melodramatic plot-lines. When Andreu's father, Farriol, is warned by the local captain (Sergi López in a more nuanced reprisal of the role of Fascist captain from *El laberinto del fauno*) that he may be the victim of reprisals after the murder of Dionís Segura (we initially believe this must be a false accusation), he purportedly flees to France but in fact (as in *Los girasoles ciegos* (The Blind Sunflowers), José Luis Cuerda, 2008) takes up residence in his mother's house in the country, where Andreu has also been sent to live and go to school whilst his mother earns a living in a factory in town. When Andreu's father is captured, Florència, Andreu's mother, turns to offering sexual favours to the Captain in exchange for clemency for her husband. She will also turn to the rich Mrs Manubens, whose homosexual brother was tortured and murdered in the caves of Baumes (giving rise to the myth of the ghost in the cave). At first this seems to be an innocent coming of age movie: Andreu is told by his father that he must always keep his ideals, no matter what others may say about them; he spies a young man by the lake and befriends him; he is given a lesson in sex from Núria, the young girl also living in the house. But 'chingar' (to fuck), unlike in *Secretos de corazón*, turns out to link Núria's predatory attentions from their teacher to Aunt Enriqueta's shaming affair with a member of the Civil Guard (revealed through the taunts by the girl who accuses them of being 'rojos'). Andreu's befriending of the boy by the lake is marred by taunts from Quirze who reveals that he is a consumptive, seen as a punishment for homosexual 'vice', promiscuity and masturbation. Andreu's father will, during the course of the film, be shown to be a child murderer, paid hitman and perpetrator of extreme violence. The powerful Mrs Manubens, it turns out, hired Farriol (whose butcher's business foundered when people stopped publicly supporting 'rojos') as a henchman, employing him not only to castrate and murder Marcel Saura, or Pitorliua, the lover of her brother, but then to kill his friend Dionís Segura, whom we saw murdered with his son at the start of the film.

The theme of the child and the monster is staged through cinematic rhymes. When Andreu first meets the boy in the woods, he is naked, bending down to look at his reflection in an echo of Caravaggio's *Narcissus* (Lomas brings out the homoerotic subtexts of Narcissus in the Dalínean and other variations). But he stretches up and appears to flap his shoulders like wings. In a later scene, with echoes of Marcelino's robbing of the food to take to the Christ-figure, Tisic stands at a grilled window whilst Andreu steals cakes from the friary for him. Always dressed in white, Tisic has an otherworldly quality to him, like an ethereal angel. He is connected thematically to the hope and freedom represented by Farriol's birds. But where Andreu kills Farriol's birds out of disillusionment at his father, he will again run to Tisic and ask him to run away with him (there are clear intimations of burgeoning love). Tisic explains that his wings will soon take him to Heaven, but when Andreu explains that his choices are to run away with Núria or to work in a factory, he urges Andreu (in echoes of the Icarus theme) to aim higher, reaching for his dreams. Another rhyme concerns Andreu and his father. After a ghost-story from *Abuela* (grandmother), Andreu lies in bed and hears creaking overhead in a recreation of Ana's hearing of her father's footsteps in *El espíritu de la colmena*. In this case we will discover that the creaking is indeed caused by Andreu's father moving overhead in the attic. Andreu will ascend the staircase much as Marcelino did but his father, although he sacrifices himself for his son (we discover finally that he made a pact not to inform on the Manubens if they promised to bring up Andreu as their own son) he is not a Christ-figure but rather a monster, perverted by the horror of the post-war years.

During the film, the components of the 'child and the Spanish Civil War' genre are dismantled. Andreu's father, associated with Republicanism, is shown to be a profiteer (rather than an ideologue corrupted by war) whilst his speeches to Andreu about morals are false rhetoric. The house gives a sense of anxiety: filmed often in hand-held sweeps which, as characters enter from side-doors, give the sense of porosity, invading the sacrosanct space of the family. When Andreu witnesses his mother and father making love, this is not the traumatic primal scene of *Cría cuervos*, but Andreu will receive his awakening as he spies his mother offering sexual favours to the Captain of the Civil Guard. The Republican teacher (immortalised by Fernán Gómez in *La lengua de las mariposas*) is here corrupted 'que conste que estoy a favor de los vencedores porque han sabido ganar' (I'm for the victors because they knew how to win) and he pays Andreu's cousin in return for sexual favours. The film borrows from other tropes, too: the wood as a shelter for refugees from the conflict (in this case those with tuberculosis, merged, in a way that is typical of Villaronga, with homosexuality) and as a magical place which might foster alternative realities. But the film does not entertain alternative realities for long – the suggestion that Andreu might find romantic freedom with Tisic is destroyed just as Andreu kills his beloved birds in an overdetermined symbolism of the loss of illusions.

The film's texture is a hyper-realism, glorious to look at, filmed in blue-black and yellow-tinted filters. Certain tableaus, such as the scene of Andreu's partially bombed house, look like a landscape painting and present the ravages of war with a decayed charm, mocking our pleasure in revisiting the aesthetics of post-war Spain and denying sense that the film is attempting to portray 'reality'. Andreu's dark-eyed look recalls the earlier child stars, but the hyper-real ambience makes Andreu into an archive of previous renditions of the child's gaze. Filmed in a 'nostalgia mode' (Grainge, 2002), *Pa negre* evokes the past but there is no clear lost object, merely the ghosts of other children's gazes, evoked almost in parodic form. This is the 'Forties' (Sprengler, 2011), but here the misty Gallic rural charm of *La lengua de las mariposas* has been replaced by a dingy, earthy brand of (magical) realism which seems to borrow from the world of the faun in *El laberinto del fauno*. This, the film suggests to us, is a 'prosthetic reality', displayed before our eyes, for indeed, how can any other account of historical memory be possible, particularly when the time-lag means that all of us will look through Andreu's eyes to see a prosthetic memory inserted by film.

In the final scenes of the film, Andreu, who has gone to live with the Manubens in order to escape from poverty and gain an education, is called out of his Francoist class to see a visitor, who turns out to be his mother. The aesthetics of the Francoist school are lovingly recreated in starchy uniforms, crosses and wooden desks – this is a glossy view of the past which reveals the seductive power of Francoist iconography. The conversation between them uses reverse angle close-ups but these serve merely to emphasise the gulf between them: Andreu's mother is teary and remorseful but Andreu is filmed with a steely gaze, clear-eyed, then narrowing his eyes, reflecting his hatred. Andreu's face is a mask: we get no sense of latency, no clue as to his thoughts. In a direct reference back to the title of *Cría cuervos*, Andreu is the monster. When Andreu's mother leaves, sent away by her steely-eyed son, we see how Andreu watches her through the glass that he mists by breathing on it, until he can make her disappear altogether. In an earlier scene, we had seen how Andreu summoned the ghosts of the past when he visits the cave and recreates the torture of Manuben's brother like the shadows on Plato's cave. In that earlier investigation into prosthetic memory, Andreu discovered the traumatic events which gave rise to the ghost – here, he actively turns his mother into a ghost – indeed he is now the more acceptable substitute for Mrs Manuben's homosexual brother and will take the Manuben name. If the reference to the whitewashing of history is clear (and recent documentation has uncovered accounts of children who were taken from the families deemed to be Communist and given to Francoist families to be brought up), then the

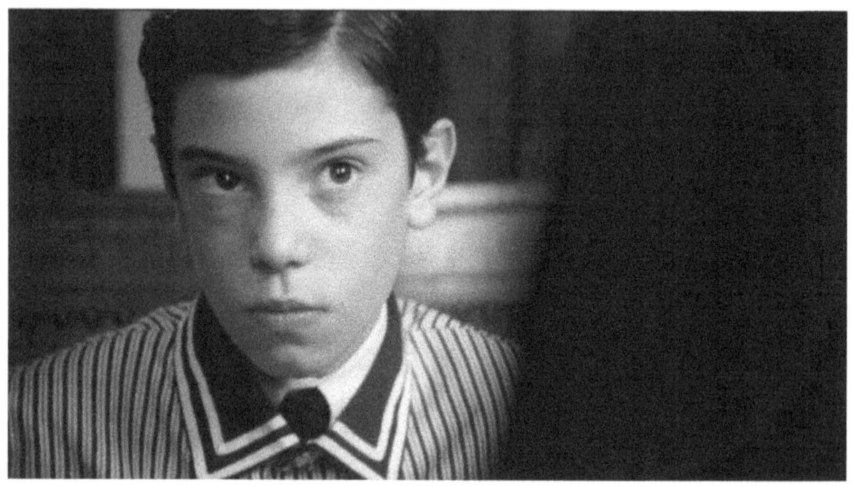

10 Andreu in the Francoist school in *Pa negre* (Agustí Villaronga, 2010).

scene also makes memory into a complicated and messy business. For Andreu has made a choice to join the Manubens and we have no hint that this is a mere performance hiding an alternative way of thinking (as in *La lengua de las mariposas*). Thus, how can an alternative historical memory be recuperated, when Francoist ideology obliterated its opposition so effectively? In *Los girasoles ciegos* Francoist education is also presented as a monstrosity: a priest who wishes to woo Lorenzo's mother and offers the chance for the child to join a seminary as a misguided pretext – Elena (Maribel Verdu) is in fact not a widow at all but her Communist husband is hiding in the attic of their house. Lorenzo (Roger Príncep) is thus continually under threat from his monstrous future, but despite the carefully described encroaching pressures, Lorenzo manages, in some sense, to escape the clutches of his monstrous future. His mother shields his gaze from his father's suicide (literally placing her arm across his face as Alberto (Javier Cámasa) leaps from the window) and, at the end of the film, we leave Lorenzo in a family dominated by females, far away from the clutches of the priest and his crushing education. But no such alternative space, even within an internal imaginary, is articulated in *Pa negre*. Rather, the film questions our desire to hang on to the trope of innocence which is incarnated in the child: in *Pa negre*, no one is innocent, not even its wide-eyed boy protagonist, burdened by history.

Notes

1 The absorbed gestures of children watching cinema were the focus of an article in 1936 about children and cinema (Romano, 1936. n.p.). Smith (2000a) notes Umbral's fascination with Torrent where, as in the case with Marisol, he casts a 'paedophilic' gaze on the child star.

2 *The Footprints of a Spirit* (*Les huellas de un espíritu*, Carlos F. Heredero, 2006),

television documentary feature included on Criterion Collection DVD edition of *The Spirit of the Beehive*.

3 My thanks to Karen Lury for sending me her paper prior to publication.

4 See also Lury's discussion of the cinematic child (including Torrent) as blank canvas for the projection of ideologies (Lury, 2010: 108).

5 For a discussion of the 'inner child' in American pop psychology see Ivy (1993).

6 Smith (2000a) deconstructs the auteurist approaches to this film. Erice's memories were supplemented with those of the producer and co-writer: Frankenstein's monster was a childhood obsession of the film's producer, Elias Querejeta; the school-room dummy was from the memories of co-scriptwriter Angel Fernández Santos.

7 See also Latorre (2006). In 2003 the film returned to the big screen in cinemas in Madrid and Barcelona. At the Goyas in 2010, Spanish prime minister José Luis Rodgríguez Zapatero included it in a list of Spanish cinema's greatest achievements. See also Arata (1983); Riley (1984); Camina (1973); Savater (1976); Martín-Márquez (1996).

8 Beyond the scope of this piece are the memories of audiences of this film – how far can film influence the memories we have of events, for example.

9 Sobchack describes 'historical consciousness' in terms of an increase interest in the portrayal of history on screen in late 1990s American culture (Sobchack, 1996).

10 Compare Wheeler (2009) who explores Godard's objections to *Schindler's List*.

11 Baackman (2004) (who advances the concept of the child's gaze as *lieu de mémoire* in German cinema), cites the work of Pierre Nora who writes that the *lieu de mémoire* is double: a site of excess closed on itself, concentrated in its own name, but also forever open to the full range of its significations.

12 As noted by Angel Fernández Santos in the Criterion DVD.

13 Chapter 1 explores the theories of Balázs and Deleuze on the face and the close-up in greater depth.

14 For excellent studies on the myth of the father in this film see Evans and Fiddian (1987) and Evans (1995–96).

15 See, for example, Medina Domínguez (2001).

16 Interview from the Criterion DVD extras.

17 From the Criterion DVD.

18 In *The Witness and the Archive*, Agamben (1999) distinguishes between the eyewitness who has lived through the traumatic event and the third party who might give testimony: but he explains that the *Muselmann*, the one who cannot speak, is, paradoxically, the true witness to the Holocaust.

19 Creed explores the potential of the *femme-enfant* for horror (Creed, 2005).

20 It may be worth noting that the pro-choice position is articulated by Tom, an Englishman and therefore not bound by Spanish law.

21 Andrew Pulver (2000) asks 'is there a secret law that says that in order to achieve significant international distribution a European film must point up a central relationship involving a cutie-pie kid and a wise old man?', whilst for Thomson (2000), Manuel Lozano, as the seven-year-old, is particularly powerful when he has to do more than just look anxious and cute (his cuteness loads the dice too much).

22 I have found no reference to the link between this film and the painting elsewhere, but its resonances (and other links to avant-garde art in the film) were

noted some years ago by Nandini Ramsaroop, a student of my undergraduate film class at Royal Holloway, and subsequent classes have found its possible connotations a fruitful line of inquiry.

23 Quiroga notes in interview that he has viewed footage of NO-DO) filming of the apparitions of Garabandel, a site for pilgrimage (Anon, 2009).

24 These films proliferate. See for example: www.youtube.com/watch?v=cNPD pl3kVeg&playnext=1&list=PL9C0E13BCDA190BC7&feature=results_main (accessed 03.08.2012).

25 The thesis is Rodolfo Ramos Castro, 'Mirando lo invisible: la leyenda de Samuel Ferren'. This website talks about 'No-Dos secretos filmados en Garabandal', http://no-do.blogspot.co.uk/2007/01/no-dos-secretos-filmados-en-garabandal. html (accessed 03.08.2012).

26 This may also be an implicit critique of the recent surge in nostalgia for the aesthetics (and politics) of the Franco regime. See also Cenarro (2008a) on 'Francoist nostalgia' affecting certain Spanish historians who she compares to those who deny the Nazi Holocaust. See also Paul Preston's comprehensive account of the 'Spanish Holocaust' (Preston, 2012).

27 Saura made these comments in an interview with Maria Delgado at the National Film Institute, London, for the BFI, summer 2011. Williams notes the associations of child stars with death in a paper given at the 'Child Stars and Performance' seminar, University of Sunderland, September 2011.

28 See also Devillard et al. (2001).

29 In 'A Child's View of Colour', Benjamin writes that children experience colour in such a way that it refuses to be subordinated to the tyranny of form – form, for Benjamin, is in league with the law (Benjamin, 1996).

30 See Richards (2005) on the theme of 'disappeared children' which included those taken from allegedly 'dangerous' parents as a 'strategy designed to sever the link with the past of families who were considered of dubious loyalty to the Francoist "New State"' (Richards, 2005: 124). Moreover, 'Hispanization' strategies included the renouncing of family names of the offspring of Republican prisoners in order to leave no trace of them ever having existed (Richards, 2005: 125) and, in the light of fears that exiled children had been renamed by 'foreigners' or were unaware of their real names, a law was formulated in December 1941 to 'physically and spiritually reintegrate children into the Fatherland'. Richards notes that, 'rapid inscription in civil registries, with the new name, following an application to the juvenile court (*Tribunal Tutelar*) would facilitate adoption as the process of repatriating Spanish children sent away to other countries during the worst period of the war gathered pace' (Richards, 2005: 125).

31 Interesting parallels are established with the disfigurement of faces as a motif in Alex de la Iglesia's grotesque tragic-comedy of the Spanish Civil War, *Balada triste de trompeta* (The Last Circus, 2010).

32 International commentators expressed surprise at the choice, but Smith notes how Almodóvar is often under-rated within Spain where the social-realist genre is regarded as providing more quality and a truer representation of 'Spanishness'. Similarly *Los lunes de sol* (Mondays in the sun, Fernando Leon de Avanoa, 2002) was picked in preference to *Hable con ella* (Talk to Her, 2002) (Smith, 2003).

4

Angels and devils: embodiment and adolescence in recent Spanish films

The proposition that the category '"youth" stands in for a crisis in the public sphere' (Smith, 2006: 75) seems to be borne out in Spain by the 'Generación Ni Ni' (The Neither-Nor Generation) who neither work nor study and who encapsulate the 'lost' generation unable to support themselves as a result of the current financial crisis. Whilst some find that this label casts them as the disaffected youth, others agree with the suggestion that it relieves them at least partially of the responsibility for their inability to find work or to fund study. But binaries of 'little devils' and 'little angels' have long haunted constructions of childhood (Jenks, 1996; Valentine, 1996; Jones, 2001). For Jenks, the Dionysian view of childhood casts the child's strangeness as corrupt and threatening, a strangeness to be disciplined away as child rearing and education bundles them into adulthood's order. Apollonian, romantically inflected views of childhood, meanwhile, see childhood as a state of naturalness, beauty and innocence, something to be protected and preserved for as long as possible from the inevitable fall into adulthood, or something which may be nurtured and carried into parts of adulthood (Jones 2001: 176). For Valentine (1996) it is adolescence itself that is demonised: adolescents are caught in a moral panic between the 'angels' that they were as children, vulnerable and needing the protection of adults, and the 'devils' that they are as adolescents, in need of discipline and containment. Spanish film, meanwhile, has produced its own contribution to these 'powerful symbolic centres of gravity' (Jones, 2001: 176). If angelic beings are present throughout the history of Spanish cinema, then it also has a strong tradition of the portrayal of delinquents and disaffected youth on screen.

The most obvious manifestation of the child as 'little angel' is, of course, Marcelino (along with the other children of the *cine religioso*). But arguably even the 'little devils' have angelic traits, or else use the innocent model as a counterpoint. Ronald Cueto's edited collection (1998), meanwhile, contains an excellent introduction to some of the films featuring disaffected youth from the 1950s, 1960s and 1970s. If the 1950s gave us *Surcos* (Furrows, Nieves Conde, 1951) about the black-market system flourshing in the post-war years of hunger, *Cerca de la ciudad* (Luis Lucia, 1952) dealing with juvenile delinquents who could be gathered into the fold, *Un cabal-*

lero andaluz (Luis Lucia, 1954) and *El Piyayo* (Lucia, 1955), alongside the emblematic *El Lazarillo de Tormes* (César Fernández Ardavín, 1959), it also led to Saura's masterpiece *Los golfos* (The Delinquents) of 1959 and his *Deprisa, deprisa* (Hurry, Hurry, 1980). Antonio Llorens traces the crime film with films such as *Los olvidados* (The Delinquents, Buñuel, 1950) and Iquino's *Camino cortado* (Closed Exit, 1955) and Rovira-Beleta's *Los atracadores* (The Robbers, 1962). Ana Mariscal's *Segundo López* (1953) followed the picaresque adventures of the eponymous López and a child around the streets of Madrid.[1] The 1960s brought *Young Sánchez* (Mario Camus, 1964) and *El último sábado* (The Last Saturday, Pedro Balañá, 1966). The 1970s yielded the *quinque* films, with their iconography of 'real-life delinquent actors, exciting cat-and-mouse car chases featuring stolen Seat 124s, corrupt police and the macarra slang of the period [...] as well as the explicit depictions of sex, drugs and violence which were typical of the destape'. This is adolescence as 'deviant and controlled, stylish and spectacular' (Whittaker, 2012: 99, 108).

Returning to the notion that youth is a synecdoche for crisis, this chapter will examine two films from the recent Spanish past. *El Bola* by Achero Mañas of 2000 is a sensitive portrayal of disaffected youth and child abuse. *Camino* by Javier Fesser of 2008 offers a scathing critique of the Catholic organisation Opus Dei. In the sense that both films offer up the image of the tortured teen body for our scrutiny, they might be said to represent what Mark Selzer (1997) in a US context has termed a 'wound culture'. Selzer writes of the 'pathological public sphere' featuring the 'shock of contact between bodies and technologies' (1997: 3). More specifically, he finds that in wound culture, 'the very notion of sociality is bound to the excitations of the torn and opened body, the torn and exposed individual as public spectacle' (1997: 3–4). Wound culture encodes 'a breakdown in the distinction between the individual and the mass, and between private and public registers. One discovers again and again the excitations in the opening of private and bodily and psychic interiors: the exhibition and witnessing, the endlessly reproducible display, of wounded bodies and wounded minds in public' (Selzer, 1997: 3). Pertinent to *Camino*, which features graphic scenes of operations, for Selzer the emergency TV drama is a prime example of 'wound culture' (1997: 26). *El Bola*, too, dwells on the beaten teen body as a bodily trauma and psychic interior pain (trauma binds the bodily to the psychic). In the sense that wound culture offers up a trauma to the spectator, this chapter will explore the traumatic legacies of endemic machismo and violence and National Catholicism on the Spain of the early twenty-first century.

For André Bazin films with children 'treat childhood precisely as if it were open to our understanding and empathy, they are made in the name of anthropomorphism' (Bazin, 1997: 121). This 'anthropomorphism' may remind us of Jacqueline Rose's assertions that childhood always has to do with adult investments in the child. But recent theories of children's geography, whilst acknowledging the difficulties of adult researchers' investments in the children they study, nevertheless posit that attempts to enter into children's spatial practices might profitably create the conditions for a more ethical consideration of childhood and adolescence. 'We have all been children, or at least biologically young', writes Jones, 'so perhaps uniquely in this concern for a form of otherness we have all been that way once and may still contain some form or traces of it' (Jones, 2001: 177). In *El Bola* we are returned to the powerlessness and vulnerability of childhood for ethical reasons. *Camino*, meanwhile, presents childhood imagination as a defence for local painful experience. Both films present childhood as the centre of multiple and often conflicting discourses. Constructions of the child oscillate, therefore, between viewing the child as other and entering the child's world. In the sense that these films open up the child to ethical considerations, the spectator becomes implicated in film form and in the 'shock of bodies and technologies'. This is the cinematic child as cyborg, betraying its mechanical origins and making its tortured teen body felt through the film. Touch emerges as a motif with interesting applications in both films.

Skin, embodiment, adolescence: *El Bola*

Achero Mañas's *El Bola* swept the boards at the 2000 Goyas winning best film, best original screenplay and best new actor for its star, Juan José Ballesta, described by one critic as 'el gran hallazgo de la película' (the great discovery of the film) (Heredero, 2000: 59). It might be located within Spanish concerns about domestic violence which overwhelmed the nation at the start of the new century, leading to the establishment of a centre for the study of violence (Centro Reina Sofía), setting in motion changes in law (the polemical *ley de género* of 2004 against 'gender-based violence') and propelled by a desire to eradicate the male bully. Notably, Rosa Montero maintains that this desire is not evidence of a Spanish tendency towards bullying – available statistics suggest that there are fewer wife-beaters in Spain than in other European countries (Montero, 2011). Duncan Wheeler has convincingly sets out the articulations in Spanish cinema of a long backstory of male dominance and female sexualisation which might provide the infrastructure for current cinematic, cultural and legal debates about domestic violence (Wheeler, 2012). In *El Bola*, however, the victim is not a wife, mother or girlfriend but a twelve-year-old boy, Pablo, nicknamed El Bola, who is regularly beaten by his tyrannical father. Belonging to the social realist mode, the film recreates the spaces of El Bola's world: the school, his father's shop, home, the fair, a friend's home, a brief interlude in the countryside, to the hospital and to the cemetery where his brother is buried. When a new boy arrives at school, El Bola befriends him and Alfredo's family offers a way out of his predicament. After a particularly savage beating, El Bola takes refuge at Alfredo's house. In the final scenes of the film, he addresses the camera, presumably explaining his case to a social worker.

The film opens to the cross-cutting between an approaching train and small feet scrambling over a wire fence and hands grasping a bottle in the split second before the train passes. A group of boys hangs out at the train tracks, on the outskirts of a residential part of town (Carabanchel in Madrid, the location of a famous prison) whose liminality reflects the in-between-ness of adolescence: temporally rushing between childhood and adulthood and spatially 'othered' by society.

Valentine (2004) has explored society's spatial 'othering' of adolescence where 'hanging around on street corners and larking about in public space becomes (deliberately and intentionally) a form of resistance to adult power' (2004: 83) and where 'young people are increasingly regarded as a polluting presence on the streets' (2004: 95). Spanish youths remain in the family home longer than their European counterparts (specifically this film treats the problems that ensue when the family becomes a space not of refuge but of violence) and in the 1990s 'student' was the profession most represented by young people in Spanish film (Fouz-Hernández, 2007: 222). Adolescence in Spain is a 'social issue' as it is elsewhere in the Western world: Spanish adolescents are noted for the *botellón* phenomenon where youths congregate in parks to drink and play loud music (muddying the reputation Spain enjoyed for moderate responses to alcohol). An experiment took place in 2009 in a space regularly used for *botellones* in La Coruña. Ostensibly to reveal how we demonise youth it applied the British-made Mosquitodevice©, a product which emits a noise inaudible to those over twenty-five but which is very irritating to those young enough to hear it. Spain appears, however, to have no plans to adopt another UK-devised strategy, the use of pink strobe lighting in areas where youths gather which acts as a deterrent by showing up that adolescent affliction of the skin, acne (literally showing young people in a bad light), and making it difficult to see veins whilst shooting up.

El Bola has been compared with François Truffaut's 1959 masterpiece *Les quatre cents coups* and is a moving exposition on the ways that society deals with adolescence. In the English promotion of *Les quatre cents coups*, the tag-line was, 'Angel-faces hell-bent on violence'. This is, as one film blogger has it, 'thoroughly absurd. There's nothing "hell-bent" about [the protagonist] Antoine. If anything, he comes across as a scared, but hopeful kid, who has repeatedly been given the short end of the stick' (Chazelle, 2010). Mañas's previous shorts depicted youths torturing animals for pleasure in *Cazadores* (Hunters, 1997), taking drugs for recreation in *Paraísos artificiales* (Artificial Paradises, 1998) and in *Metro* (Underground, 2005), scrapping, skipping school and glue-sniffing before playing a game of chicken with an underground train which will result in the death of one of the boys. If the adolescents of *El Bola* seem tame in their rebellion (Smith, 2003: 38) and less edgy than the youths of other teen movies of the period – such as *Barrio* (Neighbourhood, León de Aranoa, 1998), *Krámpack* (Dani and Nico, Cesc Gay, 2000) and *Historias del Kronen* (Stories from the Kronen, Armendáriz, 1995) – it may be because Mañas wanted to avoid the sense that Pablo's father might be in any way justified for his actions but also in order to steer a path through society's habitual demonising of adolescence.[2] If in doing so he runs the risk of turning his protagonists into angels – 'impeccably scrubbed and dressed, and impressively well-behaved in class' (Smith, 2003: 38) – that in itself speaks volumes about our attitudes towards adolescents and the culture of blame attached to the 'problem' of adolescence.

Adolescence is a time of hormonal changes, of bodily growth and of skin which erupts into the 'grumblings, heavings, ruptures, geysers, leakings, lesions and grudging detumescences' of *acne vulgaris* (Connor, 2002: n.p.). The adolescents of *El Bola* are not afflicted by problem skin in this way – in particularly its protagonist Juan José Ballesta appears, for example, in a list of 'los guapos del cine español' (the handsome faces of Spanish cinema) – and in the film his face has a luminosity which enhances the sense of his innocence.[3] The ways the skin can bear marks is a preoccupation of the film. Implicit is the question, where do adolescents fit and how can they be comfortable in their own skins? Skin makes itself felt in this film, as subject, but also extends into its possible modes of spectatorship.

When a female customer enters El Bola's father's shop at the start of the film she remarks that El Bola is lucky because he does not suffer from a bad back. El Bola and his father exchange glances. Later on in the film, we will see that El Bola's back is, in fact, covered in bruises following a beating from his father. These are the physical marks which betray the secret that all of El Bola's friends know about but no one can apparently do anything about. In parallel, skin is announced as a leitmotif through the theme of the tattoo. Alfredo (the new boy at school) takes El Bola to his father's tattoo parlour where they see the bare flesh, covered in tattoos, of the man being inscribed with the print of a dragon's head and skeleton (much is made of the revelation of the dragon's head. Alfredo's father says the skin is not ready yet but the customer urges him to allow El Bola to see it and he gazes at the raw, newly marked skin in fascination). Traditionally the preserve of sailors and the male working classes, in the nineteenth century tattoos became associated with the 'freak show' and by the 1950s they were still the badge of disreputable sub-groups. In the twenty-first century tattoos' attachment to celebrity culture exists alongside their reputation of 'tough' masculinity. Sanghera writes that 'tattoos are one physical indicator that can reveal an individual's threshold for pain. Thus the bigger the tattoo the tougher an individual is perceived' (for example the tattoo-armour of hyper-masculine hip-hop star 50 cent) (Sanghera, 2010: 348). Alfredo's father sports a skinhead and tattoos and when he goes to speak to El Bola's father to persuade him to let them take El Bola with them on a family outing, his wife urges him to cover up his tattoos. But here arguably we find rather the opposition between the tattoo as symbolic of artistic, liberal, alternative lifestyles embraced by Alfredo's father and the conservatively dressed working-class unreconstructed version of masculinity as embodied in El Bola's father.[4] The film dwells on the deceitfulness of appearances. Thus Alfredo's father turns out to be far more nurturing than his tough image might suppose, whilst El Bola's father, apparently a traditional family man, beats his son. But Connor notes that tattoos 'often play with the alternation of soft or hard, displaying image of reptiles' (as we have in *El Bola*), 'to suggest a kind of cicatrization, a toughening through the ordeal of exposure'. At the same time, 'the tattoo substitutes a surface for the actual surface of the skin: but it does so in a way that plays with the knowledge that the skin has been penetrated'. The tattoo flaunts the penetration of the body, presenting an 'ambivalent play between injury and self defence' (Connor, 2004: 63). Tattooing might, then, be regarded as playing with the notion of assault on the skin: at once involving a penetration of the skin and a protection against further penetration (through its propagation of a tough image). It is a reclaiming of one's body through visual markers. Connor suggests that the tattoo presents furthermore an 'imaginary stay' against ageing, as 'a means of cryogenic survival' (2004: 63), and this has an interesting correlation in the conversation between El Bola and Alfredo on death: Alfredo (the boy who will soon receive his own tattoo) says he intends never to die whereas El Bola is more pragmatic. But in the sense that the tattoo's marks mean that skin can 'never again recapture its infantile immaculacy and clarity', then it can present a rite of passage into adulthood. Alfredo's father tenderly gives his son his first tattoo. As the film's press-book notes, there is an obvious 'paralelismo entre un padre que es capaz de marcar a su hijo para toda su vida a través de una paliza y un padre que lo hace a través de un tatuaje' (parallelism between a father who is capable of marking his son for life through a beating and a father who does so with a tattoo). Tattooing presents a dualism therefore between caressing the skin out of tenderness, and beating it with violence.

El Bola carries a good-luck charm, a talisman – the tag-line for the film is 'un niño, un amuleto, un juego, un amigo, un secreto' (a boy, an amulet, a game, a friend, a secret) – a ball-bearing which lends him his nickname. He carries it always. In a scene on a fairground ride, Alfredo teases him about it, telling him not to drop it as they wait, suspended for the stomach-churning lunge to the ground. Towards the end of the film, an extreme close-up reveals how El Bola has placed his ball-bearing on the train track and it is crushed by the weight of the passing train. The crushing of the ball-bearing not only mimics what would have been the brutal consequences of arriving too late to rescue the bottle from the train track in the games of chicken that are played throughout the film (the smashing of bones and skin against the metallic force of the train – we learn that one child, 'el alto' (the tall boy), had been killed in an earlier game) but also suggests the ritual flagellation of flesh endured by El Bola during his father's beatings. El Bola's skin, like the ball-bearing, metaphorically spreads out, providing multiple opportunities for a cuffed ear or a blow to the back. In the scene of the film where we witness a beating (the other occasions are hidden from our view) El Bola crouches on the floor shielding his face and head from his father's blows, tucking his legs up inside his body to give his father fewer surfaces to strike whilst the camera circles in an attempt to get a view-point. This is a form of embodiment which, like Alphonso Lingis's savage versus civilised bodily dichotomy, spreads out like a surface of intensities. But whilst Lingis, in *Eros and Excesses* (1983), maps out the terrain of a libidinous body, a surface of erotogenic intensities, an inscription of pain and pleasure on the body, in *El Bola* we finds little account of libidinous pleasures: merely the pain of a fist or foot against flesh. Thus, a group of kids from El Bola's class looks at a picture of a half-naked cosmetically enhanced female pin-up – '¡qué tetas!' (great tits!) – but here we have none of the pleasures of searching out the possibilities of the body of other 'teen' films, nor the exploring of the body's orifices for masturbation in, for example, Cesc Gay's *Krámpack*. In the final lines of the film we will learn that El Bola's maltreatment by his father included cigarette burns, being spat on as well as being forced to take laxatives and to drink urine. This is a much more visceral lesson in the body's limits and surfaces than the lesson on the body's circulation and excretions that the class are engaged in upon his return to school after one beating (Fouz-Hernández, 2007). The wounded, beaten body extends through this film, making its presence felt.

In the sense that the skin which is extended through the film has an imaginary or psychic function, it may be useful to explore the theories of Didier Anzieu. Anzieu advances the theory of the 'skin ego' in which 'the ego is the projection on the psyche of the surface of the body' (1989: 63). Anzieu distinguished nine functions for the skin: supporting, containing, shielding, individuating, connecting, sexualising, recharging, signifying and assaulting/destroying. For him, the skin ego is the mental representation that the child forms on the basis of the surface of its body, which the child uses to picture itself as the vessel of mental contents. In other words, the main function of skin is to work as a container, to provide a sense of being contained. The primal scene connected with this psychic skin takes place, for Anzieu, through a skin-to-skin contact with the mother which allows for a fantasy of a skin common to mother and child. This dyadic fantasy allows the subject to understand attachment/separation – the pleasure of contact with the mother's body and the faculty of clinging are at the basis of both attachment and separation (Segal, 2009: 42) – and inside/outside. But a dearth of nurturing hands may lead to feeling like a kernel without a shell or what Ester Bick (2002) would term 'second skin formation' to provide an illusory sense of a protective, continuous skin. In the sense that El Bola's ball-bearing has a hard protective shell and it allows El Bola to enjoy some level of protection, we might see it as a second skin. Thus where Bick writes of the fear of spilling out of the self into boundless space if the second skin is not in place, El Bola clutches his ball-bearing whilst poised at the top of a fair-ground ride, in, perhaps, a bodily memory of containment (being held suspended in the air) imagining for a moment how he might hurtle through space, spilling out onto the ground, were he to let go.

El Bola's mother appears almost to have no identity of her own. From her reaction during a savage beating (she clutches at her husband, begging him to stop, before he thrusts her aside) we suspect that she was once a nurturing mother to El Bola. We do not know whether she has been the victim of a beating herself – it is her decision to finally get help for her son from a neighbour during a beating, which saves her son's life. But she also maintains the silence necessary for her husband to continue to act in the way he does. We witness no scenes of nurture from El Bola's mother. Rather than caring for her own son, his mother has taken over as caretaker to her husband's incontinent mother who wets herself at the dinner table (the care the grandmother receives here therefore seems partial when the situation could presumably have been prevented) and is brusquely led off by her daughter-in-law. In a beautifully lit scene reminiscent of a Vermeer painting, El Bola's mother washes the wrinkled, folded skin of her mother-in-law (whose body recalls now a painting by Francis Bacon with its uncompromising vision of the ageing body) as she stands up in the bath, supported by El Bola's arm. When the grandmother protests at the presence of her grandson she is chastised whilst El Bola, for his part, averts his gaze. This is a carnivalesque inversion of the mother–child dyad. El Bola, his mother and grandmother are locked together in an 'unnatural', shaming relationship of skin-on-skin. Furthermore, the sagging body illuminated against shades of brown might also recall Goya's *Saturn* (c. 1818–23) and act as a phantom memory of the monstrous father who devours his son.

Is El Bola a replacement child? His brother was killed in a car accident (was this before El Bola was born?) and annually the family adopts the sombre air necessary for a trip to the local cemetery. As they leave the house, the camera dwells on the empty rooms: the muted colours of the living room and the bedroom seem heavy with emptiness but a quick cut to a framed photograph of a blonde haired boy suggest his brooding presence. Now the heavy furniture and coarsely textured fabrics seem to have absorbed the melancholy of a family haunted by the death of a loved one. Anzieu's theories of the skin ego were based in part, on the observations of a replacement child: his mother, Marguerite Anzieu, a replacement for her sister, also named Marguerite, who fell into a fire at the age of five, entered into psychoanalysis with Jacques Lacan after she attacked an actress (Segal, 2009). El Bola, named Pablo, did not share a name with the dead brother, Pedro, but might he feel, like Marguerite, that he is 'inside the skin of another'? In fact the film does not answer these questions, and does not posit a theory of the replacement child as the real 'secret' alluded to in the tag-line to the film. In part this may be out of a desire on the part of Achero Mañas not to provide a justification for El Bola's father's maltreatment of him: this is not his father's story. But mainly it means that the film does not attempt to locate an aetiology for a neurosis: El Bola's problems are urgent and pressing and not to be traced back to a faulty relationship with caregivers as a baby.

We meet Alfredo's mother when El Bola visits Alfredo at his home.

Alfredo's little brother leads El Bola through the warmly modern and slightly untidy home (in stark opposition to the traditional dark Spanish pieces of furniture of El Bola's own home) to where Alfredo's mother sits on a sofa. Aguilar has noted that she 'sólo aparece en el ámbito familiar, ocupándose de las cuestiones nutricias y de intendencia de los hijos' (only appears in the family sphere, occupying herself with the nourishment and governance of her children) – she notes that this traditional role is surprising for a family depicted as supposedly 'progresista' (liberal) (Aguilar, 2004: 180). Warm, loving, she is locked in a loving embrace with her younger son, Juan, who clings to her rather like the rhesus monkeys studied by Bowlby and who influenced Anzieu for his work on the mother–child dyad. But as El Bola passes through the hallway, the camera takes in a poster on the wall partially obscured by ironing boards: rather like a parody of the Athena posters of a man and child from the 1980s, this depicts a large bearded man with a huge expanse of tattooed skin, sitting with a boy with a bandana. If in theoretical terms it is mothers who nurture their offspring through touch – even in the womb they are deemed to be touching each other's body to the point that '[in pregnancy] I feel my insides, strained and pressed, and increasingly feel the movement of a body inside me' (Young, 2005: 50) – here another model is proposed: fathers too can nurture their children through touch. This is a new paradigm for a father–child dyad, complete with folds of skin on skin.

In interview, Achero Mañas claimed that it was fatherhood that led him to get behind the camera (after a career as an actor). His third feature, *Todo lo que tú quieras* (Your Heart's Desire, 2010), is likewise attributed to the birth of a second daughter. In this melodrama Leo (Juan Diego Botto) is left to bring up his four year old daughter, Dafne (Lucía Fernández) alone after the death of his wife. Homophobic (as we learn when he goes to a cabaret show by an ageing transvestite (an excellent turn from José Luis Gómez), he will later befriend Álex and ask for lessons in cross-dressing so that he can fill his daughter's longing for her dead mother by performing as her every might. Whilst not entirely endorsing camp (there is little joy to be had in his nightly transvestism), the film nevertheless reveals the discrimination suffered by Leo as he goes out dressed as his late wife. Emotive scenes of a cross-dressed father and his daughter may recall Pedro Almodóvar's pre-op transsexual, Lola, who cradles his son in a reworking of a painting of the Madonna and Child in *Todo sobre mi madre* (All About My Mother, 1999). Mañas revealed in interview that his aim was to offer a vindication of the rights of men to share childcare and to share rights to custody of their children in law (Belinchón, 2010). Mañas, like Almodóvar, calls into question the traditional boundaries demarcating motherhood and fatherhood. But if transvestism is here presented as a loss of identity for Leo, at the end of the film he and his daughter accept his new role as a nurturing father (not a pseudo-mother). In *El Bola*, the mothers fade into the background as the Manichean vision of fatherhood is played out between the two differing

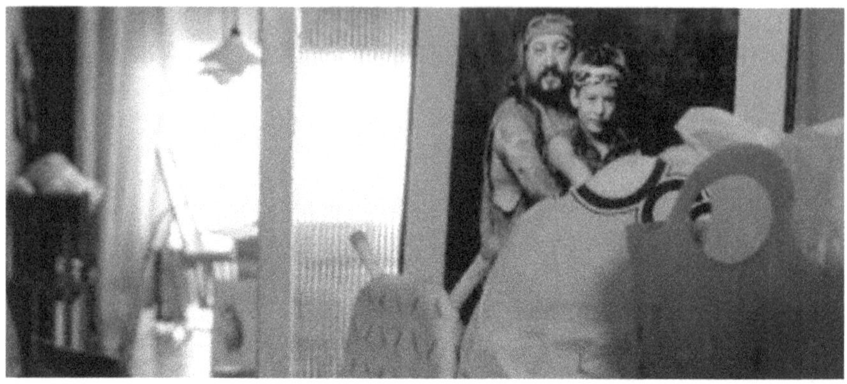

11 The poster on the wall in Achero Mañas's *El Bola* (2000).

approaches to the role of father (Smith, 2003). Alfredo's father (nurturing, tactile, with a friend dying of AIDS) tenderly tattoos his son's skin in a rite of passage into adulthood – the tattoo is never fully reversible as tattooed skin, even if the tattoo is removed surgically, will never regain the 'unmarked clarity of infancy' (Jablonski, 2006: 150). This is a view of tattooing in terms of its commemorative and protective properties as well as its ability to assign belonging (Jablonski, 2006). But as the press-book for the film makes clear, there is a correlation between this marking of the skin and the bruising and psychological scars inflicted on El Bola by his father. 'The fetishistic close-ups of the process suggest a new spilling of blood and marking of the skin strangely similar to El Bola's bruised and battered flesh' (Smith, 2003: 38). Towards the end of the film, after El Bola has run away and is found by Alfredo's father, Alfredo's father will gather up El Bola in a final father–child dyad which, like the poster image on the wall, reworks the traditional Madonna and Child iconography. But is this view of fatherhood quite so utopian as it first appears? Lingis (1983) draws a parallel between primitive scarification of the skin and bodies which are disciplined and punished (*pace* Foucault). Parents, school and the wider society are all institutions with the power to discipline and punish or nurture and support young people. But as Smith points out, 'perhaps the film is suggesting that even the best of parents leave marks on their children that are difficult to erase' (Smith, 2003: 38). Rather, perhaps, the film acknowledges that all fathers will leave their marks (even the absent ones) – but nurture provides a new paradigm for fathers' traditionally sidelined in theory and practice.

Spectatorship

Emma Wilson has written of cinema's capacity to return us to the 'lack of mastery' of the 'motor helplessness' that Deleuze has found to be so significant to the child in cinema. For Wilson:

emotions felt, remembered by an adult dispossessed, also recall a child's (more extensive) lack of control over its circumstances, its environment, even at times over its own body. The adult, overwhelmed by experience, by emotions of intensity of either negative or positive affect, in the very experience of being overwhelmed involuntarily returns to the child's state of helplessness (motor, emotional or political. (Wilson, 2005: 330)

El Bola returns us to the helplessness of childhood: the fear of violence comes to represent powerlessness at family and institutional level. But here it is not the emotions provoked that I want to examine, but affect in Massumi's (2002) sense of the bodily reaction to an event. In *El Bola* the film's body contains the 'physical imprint of the event' (a father's violence on his son's body) as 'a sense memory' (Bennett, 2005: 25) which it communicates to the spectator. In the course of his work on the skin ego, Anzieu describes a primal fear (which has to do with being torn from the comfortable dyad with the mother): 'the anxiety of seeing an object that moves tear out of the space in which it was located, take it with it, and encounter other objects into which it crashes, destroying their place' (Anzieu, 1993: 8). The opening scenes of *El Bola* involve just such an anxious scene: a train hurtling, unstoppable along a track whilst small boys throw themselves across its path. Whatever the truth of those near-mythical early film spectators who may or may not have ducked to avoid the oncoming train seemingly coming out of the screen at them during the silent film era, part of the anxiety of the opening scene of *El Bola* resides in the ability of the train to rush towards us. But this is also its thrill. Jennifer Barker, following Sobchack (2004) and Marks (1999), writes of the ability of film to touch us, in a sensual exchange between film and viewer that 'goes beyond the visual and aural, gets beneath the skin and reverberates in the body' (Barker, 2009, cover copy). Thus the tortured teen body makes itself felt in this film through a sense memory which combines with the mechanics of film to reverberate in the body of the spectator. This is El Bola as cyborg.

Kracauer insisted that film 'addresses its viewer as a "corporeal material being", it seizes the "human being with skin and hair"' (Hansen, 1993: 458). The opening scene of *El Bola* grips us in what Barker terms a 'muscular' engagement with film which she finds, 'dates back at least to the fabled panicking of spectators of early cinema described in decades' worth of historical accounts of the Lumière Brothers' *Arrival of a Train at a Station* (1895) and contained in contemporary action-adventure films labelled "thrill rides" and "roller coasters"' (Barker, 2009: 72).[5] Here, as in the scenes in the fairground in *El Bola* when the two boys spend the day on roller coasters, we are gripped by the movement of an object moving through space. Barker conceives of the film having a skin as the 'perceptive and expressive boundary between self and other' (2009: 29). The film plays with the notion of the train penetrating that skin, literally rushing out of the screen towards us. But as Barker notes, the touch enacted between film and viewer is a teasing one. 'While there is contact and intertwining, there is never a collapse or dissolution of the boundary between us' (2009: 29). Our enjoyment of this scene and the repeated scenes dodging oncoming trains derives, in a mimicking of the boys' game of chicken, from our ability to experience the thrill of the limit of touch (imagining ourselves crushed by the train) before swerving out of harm's way. But there is a sense in which, even in the shot which lunges us in a perpendicular tracking shot (from a camera attached to the front of the train) onto the fast receding tracks, we are never really at risk from the close proximity of skin and metal. The editing process, whilst creating chaos out of the collision of feet, hands and train, nevertheless works to keep children and train separate in the filmic space. In the scenes on the fairground roller coaster, we experience the twists and turns of the ride, but we are always anchored to a reassuring two-shot of the boys. I suggested earlier that the train might be seen as a trope to represent adolescence. We may be reminded, also, of its cinematic precedence in, for example, the scene where the two girls, Ana and her sister Isabel, press their ears to the track in Víctor Erice's *El espíritu de la colmena* as a game of death or desire to travel far beyond their present situation. In Almodóvar's *Todo sobre mi madre*, the train also initially allows the main character (Manuela) to escape (there the train is a feminine symbol linked to rebirth). González del Pozo (2008) finds in the repeated scenes of the train in *El Bola* a metaphor for El Bola's eventual liberation from his father. Thus the second time we visit the train we begin to see it in terms of a 'presencia acosadora y asfixiante' (asphyxiating and harassing presence) represented by El Bola's father. On the third outing, when Alfredo refuses to participate in the game with the train, El Bola will find the strength necessary to refuse the danger his life is put into by his father.

However, if we are cushioned against the contact of skin with a blunt instrument, in other ways the film shocks us into active engagement. Throughout the film we are shielded from the blows which El Bola's father metes out to his son. We know about them, but as we do not see them we become aligned with those characters who choose not to see what is going on: El Bola's school friends who know about the beatings but do nothing and his mother who chooses to look the other way, or the social worker who simply cannot do anything by law. In the final beating, we are suddenly thrust into a direct contact with the beating which may make us wince or even turn from the screen in its physicality. Alfredo's father is told that he cannot do anything in law other than to look away but he chooses, at the end of the film, to breach the law in an attempt to help El Bola. We, too, are asked, through modes of spectatorship, to take up an ethical relationship to the events portrayed on screen.

The final scene is an address as El Bola is presumably explaining his case to a social worker/police officer. The *mise-en-scène* does not reveal which and this is because, as Paul Begin explains, El Bola is 'in effect, giving his disposition to the spectator' (Begin, 2008: 272). Arguing for new reading of a technique usually regarded as 'anti-cinematic', Begin traces other such moments of actor addressing the spectator, or, as he puts it, 'victim meets voyeur' to suggest that this be read as a new mode of engagement with the spectator for the purpose of the social issue film. The final scene is mesmerising as we watch El Bola's angelic face tell of the abjection his father meted out to him: not just beatings but also cigarette burns and being forced to drink urine. These words are like blows which return El Bola and us to the original emotion of the event. Ballesta's performance in this scene seems completely uncontrived – the fact that we have not witnessed all of these acts gives the sense that they belong to a real child and are related to us now. Bazin (1997) argues that the child's face provides us with reassurance in the face of anxiety. This may be the case but here the child's face asks us to engage with a social problem. We might argue that the film touches us in new ways: mimesis argues for a meeting between viewer and the skin of the film which hopes for a new mode of social as well as cinematic engagement.

In the final scenes of the film, we witness El Bola's ball-bearing being crushed on the train tracks. If the ball-bearing represents a talisman, or even a 'second-skin' for El Bola, its destruction might be read negatively in terms of an annihilation of the self. But equally, the ball-bearing might be read as the 'impervious skin of memory that segregates itself from the present "me" ... everything that happened to this other "self" [...] cannot touch me now' (Bennett, 2005: 25).[6] The cross-cutting of these scenes with those of the cinematic address of the spectator suggest, rather, new ways for Pablo to engage with the world, new ways which rely on our willingness to make new spaces for adolescents within society. It also has to do with our willingness to see the marks and wounds endemic in the structures around us. Returning to Selzer's 'wound culture', El Bola's story traces the legacies of Francoist rule. Fouz-Hernández (2007) has noted that the film posits two families: the older, Francoist model and the new one in a modern Spain. Violence, the film suggests, is endemic, shrouded in secrecy and supported by structures of family and state. El Bola's father's rage has no clear cause and its only outlet is as a bullying patriarch at the head of his family whilst his machismo is damaging to both his wife and son. If family under this model is a failure then institutions are also failing. The police spend their time chasing teenage boys from the train tracks instead of tackling the real bullies; the law and social workers are subordinate to the model of the family. These are the legacies of the Francoist family, the film suggests, and reflection on those legacies and the possibilities for change are the aims of this film.

Martyrology in *Camino*

Javier Fesser's *Camino*, which swept the boards at the Goyas in 2009, was seen by critics as a radical change of tone and theme for Fesser, known for directing the box-office smash *La gran aventura de Mortadelo y Filemón* (Mortadelo and Filemon's Big Adventure) in 2003 based on the comic book series by Francisco Ibáñez Talavera. *Camino* is based on several real-life cases of cancer victims who were chosen, post-mortem, as candidates for beatification – Smith explains that mini videos featuring the home movies of several of these candidates are available to watch on Opus Dei's website (Smith, 2010: 12). Set in the present, the film follows the story of an eleven-year-old girl named Camino (Nerea Camacho) through the diagnosis and treatment of her cancer and death surrounded by her rigidly Catholic mother, other family members and members of the Catholic clergy. Camino's family belong to Opus Dei, the ultra secretive Catholic organisation founded by José Maria Escrivá Ballaguer and the film caused controversy in the Spanish press on its release over what was seen as a staunch critique of the organisation and its methods, whilst the family of Alexia González-Barros, a teenage cancer victim and martyr to whom the film is dedicated, wrote open letters to the film's director, Javier Fesser, in the Spanish press. The film revels in its polysemy: thus the martyrology discourse is imbricated with the young girl's (CGI-rich) Disneyesque fantasy life (also interspersed with out-takes from Disney's *Cinderella* feature from 1950) and her desire to play the lead in a production of *Cinderella* at the local youth centre.[7] In the opening scenes of the film, we see how on her death Camino expresses a desire to be with Jesus and to be admitted into 'la obra'. In a final twist at the end of the film we realise that 'Jesús' was 'Cuco' – the boy playing the lead in *Cinderella* – and that 'la obra' referred to 'the play' and not, in the double meaning of the word in Spanish, 'the work' (a reference to Opus Dei, or 'the work of God'). This 'double-voiced' conceit continues throughout the film: Camino (Path), whilst a common name in Spain, is also the name of Escrivá Ballaguer's founding text on Opus Dei.

After a shocking deathbed opening sequence which pitches the intensity from the outset at the heights of melodrama, the film reels back to the spaces of Camino's world. She attends a Catholic school, sings in assembly and, before seeing the doctor for the first time, runs to the statue of the Virgin Mary in the playground to ask for strength to overcome her fears. Camino's sister, Yeye, is now a *numeraria* in Opus Dei and Camino's mother hopes that Camino will join her there. Camino's mother is intransigent in her faith. When the family visits a second-hand bookstall, Camino sees Cuco/Jesús for the first time, riding on his scooter. He is looking at a children's picture book called *Mr Meebles tiene un problema* (Mr Meebles Has a Problem) by Jack Kent. When the boy moves away from the stall, Camino takes the book and tells her father that she would like to buy it but her mother wants her to buy a copy of Bernadette in the 'lives of the saints' series. In spite of her father's agreement that they can take home *Mr Meebles*, that evening we see Camino with the story of Bernadette as bedtime reading. In the book, Mr Meebles has a problem: he can only exist if children believe in him. This returns us to the theme of animation of the statue in *Marcelino, pan y vino* and its parallelism with the child who brings its toys to life through love. Through its use here it casts a retrospective alternative reading onto the earlier film: the implication is that the lives of saints, the story of the crucifixion and belief *per se* continues only in the sense that it can feed (vampirically) on the imaginations of the religious. Later in the film, Camino is attached to the hospital machines which are sustaining her physical body during the operations. The visual resemblances to Christ at the crucifixion are clear, with the contraption on Camino's head appearing like a crown of thorns. The contraption around her head also bears a resemblance to the robot Maria in Fritz Lang's *Metropolis* (1927). This is Camino as cyborg and begins a series of parallels suggesting that Camino is a construction of her creators (sustained by the 'hyper-real, theatrical performance' given by Camacho), and that her mother, by extension, is repeating a pre-programmed set of phrases inherited from Catholicism (Marshall, 2008).

When Camino persuades her mother to take her to a teen drama group at the local state-run cultural centre (the *Centro Cultural Camilo José Cela* – Cela's *La Colmena* will be later placed in the pile of books to be censored as part of Yeye's tasks at the Opus Dei), Camino will see Jesús again as the dancing teenage bodies move aside to reveal his entrance. Even though Camino sits primly on the settee, nothing like her foil Elena, who is also interested in Jesús, and who sits, chewing gum, the skirt of her school uniform riding up her legs, Camino's mother is far from keen on the theatre group. Later, at home, Camino dances to Shakira, arms out wide, face ecstatic, symbolic of her love for life and the happiness at her new-found love. But shortly afterwards she will suffer a devastating pain in her neck which pins her to the cabinet behind her. Camino is a cheerful girl full of life and energy. But soon both religion (channelled through her mother) and her illness conspire to present a nightmarish scenario which saps her of life.

Spectacles of suffering

In George Seaton's 1943 film, the box-office success *Bernadette's Song*, Jennifer Jones plays Bernadette, the peasant girl who reported to have seen visions of the Blessed Virgin Mary when she was out collecting wood. The film is a melodrama which sees Bernadette struggling against authorities and the Church to be believed. Towards the end of the film, Sister Vauzous, her teacher and mentor in the convent, looms before Bernadette and tells her that in order to be chosen by God one ought to have suffered and she has not suffered enough. In an extreme close-up Sister Vauzous tells Bernadette that she has suffered enormously in her life: her throat is parched from the continual praying, her eyes are tired from lack of sleep. As she turns to go, Bernadette says she would like to show her something on her leg. It turns out to be a tumour caused by TB on the leg. The doctor reports that Bernadette must have been suffering in silence for years. Sister Vauzous collapses in remorse and prays for herself and for Bernadette. Later, on her deathbed, Bernadette's face is surrounded by the bonnet which provides a visual halo around her features. As she dies, she sees a final vision of the

Blessed Virgin Mary (an ethereal statue in the corner of the room, unseen by any of the nuns gathered at her bedside). She cries out 'I love you!' and the Abbe Peyramale declares, 'Your life begins O Bernadette!' The sequence has obvious similarities with the story of Camino's death (Camino, of course, has also been given the story of Bernadette's life as bed-time reading). Camino's halo is, of course, the medical contraption round her neck, whilst her declaration of love, misinterpreted as a love of God, is in fact love for a boy. In terms of *Camino*'s play on words, we might be reminded that under Franco it was common for monologues about romantic love to be re-dubbed as declarations of love for God: hence the Spanish public were brought up on polysemy as a matter of course

In the press-book to accompany the film, Javier Fesser notes that:

> I came across the story of a teenager being considered for sainthood in Madrid, a process which began 20 years ago, in a book I was reading that gave a detailed account of her illness but, in fact, focused on the courage of this girl and her family in the face of suffering and death. That started everything off, because that tale sparked my curiosity and the need to find answers to things I was unable to understand: What does 'to offer' suffering mean? How can one accept that grief and despair are a signal of God's love? How can one die contentedly at the age of fourteen? How would I behave under similar circumstances?

The story of Alexia González-Barros has been published in several forms. In all of these versions it is a tale of suffering recounted for young readers. María Victoria Molins underlines Alexia's devout nature before her illness, on a visit to Rome she reportedly made her way towards the Pope and gave him a note – Molins's version has a photograph of the young Alexia with the Pope (Molins, 2008: 32) – and she took part in anti-abortion rallies and saw St Teresa of Calcutta on walkabout. Joan Cruz Carroll's potted version dwells on Alexia's suffering even more than does Molins: her wounds, soreness and unbearable pain are recounted in detail. It is 'almost reminiscent of a crucifixion', Carroll informs us (Carroll, 2006: 28).

In its recreation of Alexia's story, and its depiction of the diagnosis, operations and gradual decline of its protagonist, *Camino* offers a 143-minute assault on the spectator. Carlos Boyero, writing in *El País*, speaks of the film as 'un calvario' (a calvary) from which he desired release (Boyero, 2008). We see Camino's body hooked up to appliances, gaping wounds prised open with metal instruments, her bones filed, blood mopped. This is the 'shock of contact' between bodies and machines (Selzer, 1997: 3). In the fourteenth-century devotional text, *Meditations on the Life of Christ*, attributed to the pseudo-Bonaventure and apparently written for the instruction of a Franciscan nun, the body of Christ is an iconographical *mise-en-scène* designed to encourage the devotion of the spectator, in this case the Franciscan nun. Thus the text includes discussion of the look of the nails, of Christ's flesh and of the pain inflicted by them as well as a detailed description of the manner in which Christ was nailed to the cross. As Jill Bennett explains, the female devotee is asked to 'think', 'see', 'imagine' and 'consider', which operates 'in conjunction with the affective intensity of graphic descriptions of torture, pain and humiliation throughout the Passion scenes to place the devotee in direct confrontation with the image of Christ's suffering. The devotee is told to imagine herself present as "witness"' (Bennett, 2001: 5). This imagery, 'works through a kind of mnemonic of pain, inducing in the spectator a kind of affective response to the pathos and violence of the scene' and it does this, 'by operating on the "sense memory" or "emotional memory" of the subject, what "suits you" in effect means what relates to your experience, what resonates within your bodily memory' (Bennett, 2001: 5). *Camino* operates in a similar way. The first time we see the injection needle go into Camino's spine we wince as she does at the perforation of skin on screen. But later images of operations show us graphically the air pipe being inserted into the mouth and taped down, the metal forcing open a gash in the back of Camino's neck and surgical instruments not just being inserted, but hacking at bones. This works on our bodily memory as we feel the insertion of surgical instruments through what Sobchack (2004) would term 'the film's body' and into our own. There is a tactility in this relationship to the screen, but it must involve what Bennett elsewhere has termed the 'squirm', a turning away from the image on screen (Bennett, 2005: 42–43). Sobchack (1990) has written of the epic film that its length made the spectator feel that they too had experienced something epic. In *Camino*, the spectator feels that they have suffered with the film's protagonist and by the end of the film is hoping for a release from the physical suffering. But this 'squirm', arguably, prevents the spectator from an uncritical identification with the suffering of the protagonist. This might be compared to what Dominic LaCapra (2001) calls the 'empathic unsettlement' of certain images, in which we engage with critical distance. Camino's mother's exhortations to believe in God and even, at one point, her declaration that she is glad that her daughter is ill so that they can show their faith turns this suffering into an unbearable burden. Camino's father dies taking Camino a last piece of hope from the outside world after he visits the bakery where Jesús's mother works and Jesús asks him to take a message to Camino. By now the film has become a choking blend of hospital and religion.

Camino achieves release (and so does the spectator) through her imaginative flights of fantasy. It may be interesting to compare Camino's daydreams here with those of the protagonist of a 1963 film, Manuel Summers's masterpiece *Del rosa al amarillo*. The film relates two separate stories, the first of which concerns love in childhood, the other of love in old age, but it is the first which concerns us here. Guillermo (Pedro Díez del Corral), a pre-adolescent boy, is in love with Margarita (Cristina Galbó) and their relationship develops with the help of the go-between 'Ratona'. In the summer, Guillermo must head off for a Francoist summer camp for boys whilst Margarita goes to the beach. They exchange ardent love letters, but when the summer is over, Margarita tells Guillermo that she has a new eighteen-year-old boyfriend. The film recreates the spatial locales of Guillermo's world, from his upper-middle-class home, to the schoolroom and the military style camp. But it also concentrates on Guillermo's daydreams, head in hands as he sits in the classroom (the press-book is covered with doodles of love hearts). Writing on children's geographies, Chris Philo suggests that Bachelard's theories of 'reverie', 'not the dreams of sleeping for which other analyses are required, but the "daydreams" of wakefulness when we are in "relaxed time" and "function[ing] with inattention" to either the things around us or our more reflexive senses of self, biography and intentionality' might be a useful way for adult researchers to connect with their childhood selves for the purposes of research (Philo, 2003: 11). Guillermo's daydreams connect to this childhood space, where 'the imagination is restored to its proper, all-important place as the principle of direct stimulation of psychic becoming' (Bachelard, 1969: 8). As Susan Martin-Márquez notes in her excellent study, the film draws on modern cinema's new conceptualisation of time and space in order to recreate the spaces of childhood. She quotes Manuel Villegas López who observes that the film 'aquí ya maneja ese intercalado de escenas o simples imágenes, con las que pasa al otro lado de la realidad, al mundo de la imaginación, el ensueño, el deseo' (inserts scenes or simple images in order to cross over to the other side of reality, to the world of the imagination, reverie, desire) (Martin-Márquez, 1999: 58–59). Martin-Márquez shows how 'by providing access to this other side of reality, experimentation with image and sound in this film serves to represent the marginalized subjectivities of children' (1999: 59). Thus, the sound track can reveal mental states or 'the music indicates otherwise invisible bodily reactions, as when a progressively more rapidly alternating set of notes suggests that Guillermo's heart races as soon as he catches sight of Margarita' (1999: 59). We may be reminded that Antonio Mercero's 1963 experimental *Se necesita chico* (Boy Wanted) used the sounds of jazz to recreate a child's world in 1960s Spain.[8] But if *Se necesita chico* seems like experimentation with film form and the child's experience for its own sake, in *Del rosa al amarillo* the child's world is drawn for us to reveal the ideologies fed to children during the Franco regime. The film makes use of various intertexts from the 1940s, 1950s and 1960s such as the imagery of the religious Crusade and patriotic fervour of the comic *Guerrero del Antifaz* which Guillermo uses to punctuate his daydreams of Margarita. We first see him reading a passage from the comic:

> *Guerrero*: Dios os guarde, Ana María. Necesito hablaros de algunos asuntos de capital importancia para mí. No puedo ocultarlo por más tiempo. Os amo. No sé vivir sin vos.
> *Ana María*: Pero…
> *Guerrero*: No me interrumpáis, amor mío. Os adoro.
>
> (*Warrior*: May God protect you, Ana Maria. I need to speak to you about some matters of capital importance to me. I can't hide any longer. I love you. I don't know how to live without you.

Ana Maria: But...
Warrior: Don't interrupt me, my love. I adore you.)

Guillermo reveals a loveheart written on his skin, practises his lines in front of the mirror and repeats the conversation in his head when out on a walk. The overblown macho language is comic in tone, as are his anxieties over his lack of arm muscles (the camera dwells on the well-built sports teacher). But Guillermo's war martyr fantasy is more serious, a 'rapid montage sequence of thirty-three shots; these include a number of odd, almost surreal images that betray the boy's angst and confusion concerning nationalistic and other cultural discourses' (Martin-Márquez, 1999: 69) as he inserts himself into what appears to be archival footage from World War II, darting across the snowy ground before collapsing into a bloody heap. Rather lighter, however, is Guillermo's wilful misuse of a card given to him by his sister. The card reproduces a negative drawing of St Teresa with three small dots over the nose. Guillermo's sister bets him that if he stares at the dots and counts to eighty, he will see a floating image of the saint. The camera focuses on the empty ceiling with choral music on the soundtrack and Guillermo swears that he has seen the image. Later, in the summer camp, Guillermo will use the card as inspiration for a drawing of Margarita. As Martin-Márquez notes, 'by converting Margarita into a "miraculous" apparition, Guillermo engages in a form of *marianismo*, placing his beloved on a pedestal that elevates her to sainthood and beyond the expression or pursuit of her own desire' (1999: 63–64).[9]

In *Camino* the protagonist's reveries take the form of drug-induced hallucinations under sedation. During one long graphic operation sequence we cut to a close-up of Camino's face, gagged by tape to hold the breathing apparatus in place, her eyes suddenly shoot open and she appears, in a fantasy sequence, at the door of the operating theatre and then runs out into the corridors where she will chase a mouse and then ride on a scooter through the passageways. After crossing a door marked 'prohibido el paso' (do not enter), Camino finds herself in a marvellous coastal landscape (rather like Bachelard's hill slopes) where she can run freely along the beach. Her sister is there, but now recuperates the connotations of free-love inspired by her name (the comparisons with the 1960s pseudo-beat culture, Yéyé) – she is playing a guitar with a former boyfriend. Suddenly, in the 'real' world, and filmed through parallel editing, we see how Camino's mother is looking through the doors of the operating theatre and Camino's fantasy starts to crumble (this is just one of many examples where an adult bodily presence seems to annihilate the hopefulness represented by childhood – another is when Camino looks to the hospital room door in expectation of seeing her sister come from Salamanca, only to find yet another relation from Opus Dei). In the fantasy the water forms a whirlpool whilst Camino's features are frozen into a scream.

That there is a relationship between fantasy world and reality is clear.

Through one nightmarish sequence we learn that Camino had a baby brother who died. In her childish state she was told by her mother that he had been taken away by a guardian angel and now, when her mother evokes the guardian angel to take care of her at night, Camino suffers nightmares. We see a terrifying angel, with large outstretched wings chasing her down corridors and this evokes a history of didactic material for children which informed them, happily, that God would be coming for them – the popular Spanish saying at bedtime is 'hasta mañana, si Dios quiere' (see you tomorrow, God willing). Camino's chosen guardian angel is Mr Meebles, wearing a suit of vivid emerald-green, whose great problem, like that of Tinkerbell, is that people need to believe in him for his existence to continue (as already remarked, the parallels with believers who sustain Catholicism are clear). But if Alexia González-Barros declared that 'tengo un problema' (I have a problem) and the problem was cancer (Molins, 2008), in the film we are left to choose between two evils: death-bound cancer or death-bound Catholicism.

In a nod to *Alice's Adventures in Wonderland*, Camino's fantasy sequences can play with scale, such as in the nightmare scenario where Camino's mother towers over her, but in general it is in the 'real-life' scenes where Camino begins to find her movement restricted (like Alice when she grows and can no longer fit into the tunnel). Camino is uncomfortable and spatially restricted, in contrast to the spatial freedoms of her fantasy world. The fantasy sequences are Technicolor extravaganzas, like Aldous Huxley's mescaline-induced fantasies where even the books on his walls are 'red books, like rubies, emerald books [...] lapis lazuli books whose colour was so intense, so intrinsically meaningful, that they seemed to be on the point of leaving the shelves to thrust themselves more insistently on my attention' (Huxley, 2011: 6). Huxley felt that he had 'recovered some of the perceptual innocence of childhood' (Huxley, 2011: 6) through his drug-induced reveries. Like *The Wizard of Oz* (Victor Fleming, 1939), home is a colourless place which cannot compete with the vivid colours of the fantasy world. In *Camino*, the hospital is filmed in shades of white, the home-life is shades of brown and grey, while Yeye's life in the Opus Dei seems so drained of colour as to look like the familiar 'step back in time' as she cleans, sorts, irons or prays, amongst other women in the church, separated from the men – the notion that the world of religious belief is anachronistic is clear. As David Batchelor notes in *Chromophobia* (2000), the fall into colour in films represents the dangerous and disruptive and notes his disappointment when he learned that Dorothy's 'spectacular descent into brilliant Technicolor' was 'only' a dream state, a result of her fall into unconsciousness (2000: 39). He quotes Salman Rushdie's observations on *The Wizard of Oz* in which we are not so much caught up in a Fall as an uprooting and displacement into colour:

> At the heart of *The Wizard of Oz* is a great tension between these two dreams ... [of leaving and of having roots]. In its most potent emotional moment, this

is unarguably a film about the joys of going away, of leaving the greyness and entering the colour, of making a new life in the 'place where there isn't any trouble'. 'Over the Rainbow' is, or ought to be, the anthem of all the world's migrants, all those who go in search of the place where 'the dreams that you dare to dream really do come true'. It is a celebration of Escape, a great paean to the Uprooted Self, a hymn – the hymn – to elsewhere. (Rushdie, 1992: 16)[10]

Where Dorothy 'has to return from colour – to Home, Family, Childhood, Kansas and Grey', she chants 'East, West, Home is Best', although for Batchelor, 'without a chance of convincing anyone who has taken a moment to compare the land of Oz with the grey-on-grey of Kansas [...] Perhaps the implications of no returning, of not recovering from the Fall into colour, were too radical for Hollywood to contemplate' (Batchelor, 2000: 41). Camino appears to return to the harsh realities of her life and death in the hospital, the final scenes show a chaotic performance of *Cinderella* and her embrace of Jesús. There are parallels with Guillermo del Toro's *El laberinto del fauno*: just as Ofelia seems to depart, after her death, for a fantasy underworld of her own making, so Camino enjoys her fairy tale fantasy as a defence against the reality unfolding in the 'real' world. *Camino*, even more than *El laberinto del fauno*, draws on the ambiguities of the fantasy world/ afterlife parallels. But in *Camino* the role of the spectator draws out the full effect of the polysemic potential of the narrative. Where these fantasy sequences have provided much needed relief for the spectator as much as for Camino, are these final sequences nothing more than a narratively constructed sop to provide the spectator with a happy ending? *Camino* is manipulative and mawkish but its critical edge derives from its ability to reveal itself as such. Can Camino's flights of fantasy offer a 'true' access to childhood and, moreover, a true picture of the world (with all of its negative views of Catholicism), or are they, like the attempts of Opus Dei and Camino's family in the film, an endeavour to frame the child for the purposes of propaganda or ideological manipulation? In its 'double-voicedness' the film draws out binaries, from the body/soul divide, the saintly and the secular, fantasy and reality. But these binaries intertwine and overlap at each turn so that the secular Camino is as saintly as the religious construction, whilst her 'soul' is a secular flight of fantasy which cannot quite leave her physical body.

The politics of memory

While Fesser maintains that his film is based on the lives of various adolescent cancer victims and the lives of various saints and visionaries, the dedication at the end of the film is to Alexia González-Barros a girl who died of cancer and is in process of beatification. The film provoked a *carta al Director* of the newspaper *La Razón* by Alfredo González-Barros y González, the brother of Alexia. 'No debería hacer falta que te diga que mi hermana no murió rodeada de aplausos' (I shouldn't have to point out that my sister did not die to the sound of applause), he wrote, a reference to the deathbed scene in *Camino* where scenes of grief were supplemented by joy that Camino would be ascending to heaven. 'Murió rodeado de cariño' (she died surrounded by affection), he went on, 'cariño de sus seres queridos: padres y hermanos y con el silencio respetuoso de las enfermeras, doctores y enermos que motu propio se acercaron a la habitación de Alexia' (affection from her loved ones: parents and brothers and sisters and with the respectful silence of the nurses, doctors and patients who came of their own accord to Alexia's room). 'Te ruego que rectifiques públicamente tu aserto – que quiero creer fruto de un grave error inocente por tu parte – de que los padres y hermanos de Alexia se despidieron de su hija y hermana con un aplauso' (I ask that you rectify the assertion – that I believe to be the result of a serious but innocent error on your part – that the parents and brothers and sisters of Alexia bade farewell to their daugher and sister with applause). They had already asked, he said, for any explicit reference to Alexia to be removed before the film was released (González-Barros y González, 2008: 12). The letter was followed, some weeks later, by a letter from Teresa and Pablo, parents of a child named María Fernández, a seven-year-old girl suffering from cancer, who wrote, 'quien sabe si algún día Dios pondrá un hijo moribundo entre tus brazos, ¿serás capaz de repetirle lo que dices en tus entrevistas? Quizás el mundo te cambiaría de color' (who knows if one day you might have a dying child in your arms – will you be capable of repeating what you say in your interviews? Perhaps you'd see things in a different light?) (Fernández, 2008: 12). Fesser, in a reply published in *El Mundo*, was unrepentant: 'quizás algún día los hermanos, tíos y sobrinos de Alexia, que me envían dardos envenenados en formas de cartas al director, comprendan esta película y sientan la vergüenza de haberme maltratado ellos a mí' (perhaps one day the brothers and sisters, uncles and aunts and nieces and nephews of Alexia, who are sending me poisoned darts in the form of letters to the editor, will understand this film and will feel ashamed of having mistreated me in this way) (Fesser, 2008: 54). Fesser's diagnosis of the situation was not that he had angered the family and other members of Opus Dei with a false portrayal of Opus Dei, but rather that it was too similar, too close to the bone: he describes his film elsewhere as a 'radiografía' (X-ray) and further writes, 'la película no es una frivolidad sobre sus exóticas costumbres sino que va directa a su corazón (si lo hay) y les muestra tal y como son' (the film is not a frivolity on exotic customs but it goes to the heart (if there is one) and it shows [Opus Dei] as they are) (Fesser, 2008: 54). In an echoing of the themes of the film, propaganda wars raged over the body of the child Alexia which were every bit as dissecting as the operations performed on Camino's body.

Camino flaunts her status as a cinematic construction. Her face is permanently lit up with happiness, and in spite of her construction as a martyr, she is also reminiscent of the Disney heroines she so idolises. Camino is obviously a construct. But in 2011 Pedro Delgado made *Alexia*, a documentary produced with the consent of Alexia's family and friends which purported, through its Super 8 home videos and 'talking heads', to tell the truth about Alexia's story.[11] The film has a voice-over purportedly embodied by Alexia (Miriam Fernández) speaking to us from the dead, who enters into dialogue with Hugo, her guardian angel (voiced by Richard del Olmo). Given that one of the conditions for beatification is 'fama de santidad' (fame of sanctity) following death, the documentary seems like just one more way to publicise Alexia's death in the hope of speeding up the process of beatification. The film is restrained, particularly regarding the death of Alexia, which is related after the fact by a nurse at the hospital. The film is a touching story of a child using her faith to get through illness. But the overriding sense is that Alexia's story is shaped by traditional Catholic narratives of the lives of saints and martyrs. Thus, when Alexia claimed to have felt the presence of a demonic force shortly before her death (one that encouraged her to commit suicide), we are told that in this sense she recapitulates the story of Santa Teresa de Jesús, who saw a 'negrillo abominable' (abominable black demon), whilst even Miguel Angel Monge's story (admittedly he comes across as much more sympathetic than in Fesser's version) of how Alexia insisted on taking communion even when she was near death, recalls the story of Santa Rita, also mentioned by the disembodied voice of Alexia in the film, who was confined to bed during the last four years of her life, due to illness, and was unable to eat and drink but was 'sustained by the Eucharist alone' (Anon, 2007). Fesser states in the press-book for *Camino* that he based his film on a variety of similar stories: that of Montse Grases, who similarly asked to be admitted to Opus Dei from her deathbed; Bernadette Soubirous, the clair-voyant of Lourdes who did not wish to cure her own blindness; the three children Lucia, Francisco and Jacinta who the Virgin told her secrets to in confession (and whose life was made into a film version in Rafael Gil's *La señora de Fátima*, 1951); Mari Carmen García Velero who 'gave herself to God' and Saint Therese of Lisieux.[12] But the sense we have from *Alexia* is the sense that Alexia's story has been shaped by previous Catholic martyr narratives. How far this is due to Alexia's self-presentation through her diary (and based on her desire to elide herself with Catholic martyrs) and how far this has to do with her construction and framing by her family/documentary-makers, is less important than the repetitions of the model of martyrdom and suffering that are repeated through time.

What is at stake in the differing portrayals of the death of a little girl? Opus Dei representatives were furious at the film's portrayal of the organi-sation. Manuel Garrido, the group's Spanish spokesperson reported that 'it is a false and manipulative picture which offers a highly distorted view of Opus Dei' (Tremlett, 2008). Earlier, Tremlett had reported on the fact that 'Opus Dei's 84,000 members around the world deny [that the move-ment's founder, Escrivá] actively supported Franco', whilst the Opus Dei representative in the Vatican, Flavio Capucci, claimed that 'Escrivá should not be criticised for his silence on the Franco regime's abuses or for letting

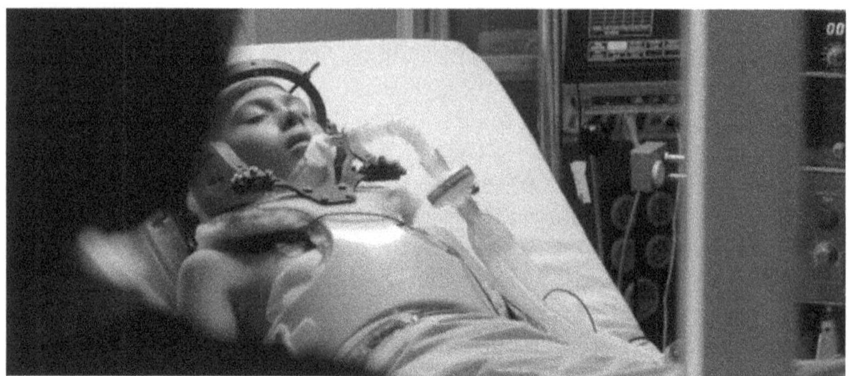

12 Martyrology in Javier Fesser's *Camino* (2008).

Opus members join the dictator's governments' (Tremlett, 2008). It was well known that neo-liberal Opus Dei technocrats had been responsible for presiding over the stabilisation programme in Franco's government in 1959 and influenced many state institutions during Francoism (Graham and Labanyi, 1996: 213, 273) and still hold positions of power.[13] But more recently, Opus Dei representatives have been implicated in the scandal of the stories of babies stolen from their families at birth. In fact, the involvement of Opus Dei in a variety of state-run organisations has always been clear, given Escrivá's close proximity to General Franco from the start of the regime. In *Camino*, the close links between Francoism and Opus Dei are intimated in the décor: the muted filtered greys of the room where Camino's sister, Yeye, does the ironing which aesthetically intimate the connection to 1940s Spain and the values of the *Sección Femenina* with their exaltation of the Virgin Mary and Isabel la Católica as role models for young women, and their rigid separation of gender roles. Alexia's family criticised Fesser for the portrayal of family members applauding Camino's death. But this is no more than the natural consequence of the ideology expressed in the film. Rather than being a portrayal of extremes, the film's articulation of the fetishisation of death is remarkably close to Spain under Franco with its exaltation of martyrdom and consumption of the lives of saints as a daily diet for children. More shocking is its legacy in the present day.

Aside from the entrenched legacies of extreme ideologies in contemporary Spain, the film articulates a critique of the narrativisation of versions of history. Spanish official history was construed as a Crusade of saints and martyrs united in a common cause. Only recently has 'historical memory' begun to redress the balance with alternative stories of heroism or of monstrous horrors of the past. There is a difficulty in that in some senses 'historical memory' may have become a war of who has the greatest claim to victimhood, as Labanyi (2006) and Crumbaugh (2007) have noted.[14] In its evoking of 'wound culture', *Camino* suggests that victimhood may be a collective problem requiring ethical, collective answers. It suggests a call for the examination of the legacies of the past and the way they endure in the present.

In Gutiérrez Albilla's excellent assessment of Pedro Almodóvar's *La mala educación* (Bad Education, 2004) (a film which depicts the child sexual abuse by Catholic clergy under Francoism), Gutiérrez Albilla suggests that the 'spectator's bodily and physical encounter with the film as an event, instead of as a static text, becomes a requirement for completion of the meaning of the filmic text' (Gutiérrez Albilla, 2013). The same can be said of *Camino* which depicts the 'exhibition and witnessing' of the 'endlessly reproducible display of wounded bodies and wounded minds in public' (Selzer, 1997: 3). As Gutiérrez Albilla (2013) notes, *La mala educación* turns on questions of prosthetic memory as it depicts the attempts of the protagonists to come to terms with the abuse suffered by one of the boys, Ignacio. As boys, Enrique and Ignacio found relief from the oppressive atmosphere of their Catholic upbringing in the local cinema, over a mutual desire for Sara Montiel (the folkloric singer of the day) and for each other. An intimate two-shot captures their spectatorship of the diva and their mutual masturbation. Later, caught in the cold blue hues of the night-time dormitory, Enrique wonders if they have sinned but Ignacio tells him that he enjoyed it and that, in any case, he is a hedonist. Earlier, Ignacio had been chosen by Father Manolo to sing in front of a panel of libidinous priests: Ignacio's angelic singing contorted Father Manolo's face into the picture of desire. But when, in a later scene, the boys' faces mutate into the adult versions of themselves (Fele Martínez as Enrique and Gael García Bernal as Ignacio), we will soon discover that this was no more than a self-conscious visual trick on the part of the film's director. For this is not Ignacio at all, but his brother Juan. The frontal shot of the two adults (Enrique and Juan) as they sit in the car is designed to remind us in a rhyming two-shot of the earlier scene (with Enrique and Ignacio) in the cinema. Enrique glances down towards his lap, a gesture which not only reveals that he is remembering the earlier scene, but also evokes the children's bodies – 'haunted by an earlier body image that was able to negotiate the childhood space with ease' (Weiss, 1999: 35). But the ease between the boys turns to awkwardness between the adults. Ignacio looks nonplussed and Enrique changes the subject. Later, when Enrique goes to the rural village to visit Ignacio's mother he will find out that Ignacio is dead and that the man in front of him is an imposter. Thus, as spectators we realise that some of the scenes of the film are memories of the past told in flashback but others are fictionalised accounts of the past which belong to the filmed version of events. Furthermore, if these are prosthetic memories, then they do not belong to Juan. The link between the adult haunted by the self as a child has been severed, as evidenced in the scene in the car. But it is not the case that these memories do not have a body, rather that the body lies elsewhere, in the drug-ridden body of Ignacio, collapsed over her typewriter, killed not over some trauma-related suicide but because of murder. Juan's memories are not his own but this does not invalidate them. Returning to Marita Sturken, and her article on 'false memory syndrome', she asks, 'what is an experience that we cannot remember? What is a memory that does not need an experience?' But she concludes that 'these memories belong to all of us. What we can learn from them will not come from calling them falsehood, but rather from examining the abuse they attest to, the fears they give rise to, and the desires they fulfil' (Sturken, 1999: 245). Dislodged from their creator, the prosthetic memories of child abuse in the film become those of the Spanish nation. In a similar way, *Camino* suggests that it matters little whether this film is really about the life of Alexia or one of the other manifestations of the phenomenon of saintly beatification or the construction of death as martyrdom. What is far more important is the entrenched culture of extreme ideology. If the child, finally, represents anything, it is the enduring image of the child as symbol for the future. The question, then, is how to overcome the spectres of the past to move forward into a brighter future.

Notes

1 Mariscal notes that the film caused her to lose money, which forced her to abandon her track record for direction in what was termed 'un cine interesante' (interesting cinema). In the same piece she says she turned to direction, 'porque no vi inconveniente en ello. Creo que somos capaces de hacer lo mismo que el hombre' (because there was no reason not to. I think we're capable of doing anything that men do) (Romo, 1963: 34).
2 Fouz-Hernández (2007) has written about youth films of 1990s Spain.
3 Ballesta cites the need to keep his face intact, 'me revientan la nariz se carga mi carrera' (they bust my nose and that's the end of my career), as the reason why he gave up FullContact, a form of Taekwondo, in 2005 (Ruíz, 2005). It is a rather depressing footnote that his star persona is the reason assumed for a series of beatings in various suburbs of Madrid (Hermoso, 2006). Ballesta was awarded a Goya for his performance in *El Bola*, at the time the youngest actor even to be given the award (later superseded by Andoni Erburu and Nerea Camacho). His 2005 film *Planta cuarta* (Fourth Four, Antonio Mercero), about young cancer victims, also offers an interesting meditation on the relationship of the physical body to masculinity. See Prout (2008).
4 Compare Duncan Wheeler's discussion of masculinities cast in a long tradition of Manichean opposites in the domestic violence film *Te doy mis ojos* (I Give You My Eyes, Iciar Bollaín, 2003) (Wheeler, 2012).
5 Alexia Ventura's *La secta de los misteriosos* (The Sect of the Mysterious Ones, 1914) might be included in this collection (see page 5 of the Introduction).
6 In her discussion of the trauma and sense memory of child sexual abuse, Bennett is in fact citing Charlotte Delbo's memories of Auschwitz (Bennett, 2005: 25).
7 In this sense, the film returns to the double-voicedness of Francoist religious cinema which aimed to harness the secular for sacred aims (Wright, 2007).
8 A boy is employed by a florist to delivery flowers and wreaths but he gets distracted by street-life and arrives late to all of his appointments. Speech is kept

to a minimum with Mickey-Mousing standing in for emotional expression – a lively march accompanies the workers streaming out of the Madrid metro, whilst drums record a cross lady's sentiments. The end of the film is the sign 'Se necesita chico' being restored to the florist's window. Mercero remarked that 'el niño de mi película ni canta, ni baila, ni espero que sea repipi, ni que entorne los ojos delicadamente, sino que espero que sea un niño español normal' (the child of my film doesn't sing or dance, nor is he affected, I hope, nor does he delicately lower his eyes. I hope he's a normal Spanish child' (Alonso Ibarrola, 1963: n.p.). One cannot help but feel that with Lolo García therefore he must have deliberately chosen a 'cute' child.

  9 It is interesting to note the censorship documents reveal that the film was passed by censors with no cuts.

10 In Stephanie Donald's lecture on *The Wizard of Oz*, which takes up the motif of Dorothy as migrant in world cinema, she muses that 'Oz is a fantastic representation of Kansas, of America and of the possibility of the Other in Technicolor, but with the same cast of principal characters, just more dangerous, more exotic, and yet oddly, more manageable. Best of all, the woman who terrifies her the most, can be melted with a bucket of water' (Donald, 2012).

11 Ninfa Watt, a childhood friend of Alexia's, who appears as a talking head in the film, had already written an article in which she claimed to correct some of the misperceptions created by Fesser's film.

12 For a discussion of the life and death of Mari Carmen González Valerio, see Harvey (2002). The 'sacrificial economy' she describes may remind us of Marcelino's trading of his life to be with his mother and the coming to life of the statue against the bringing to death of Marcelino.

13 For an analysis of Opus Dei's rise to power in Spain, see Artigues (1968).

14 Labanyi (2006) notes the proliferation of 'victim testimonies' from those who suffered under the Franco regime. Crumbaugh (2007) documents the framing and construction of Miguel Angel Blanco, the right-wing politician who was killed by ETA terrorists in 1997.

Conclusion

In 2011 the Spanish Academia de Cine announced that Goyas would not be awarded to any actor under the age of sixteen. Francesc Colomer and Marina Comas, recognised the previous year for their performances in *Pa negre*, would be the last child recipients of such an award. The reasons for such a decision, apparently, had to do with the protection of minors, but debates raged in the Spanish press concerning whether this was about anxieties over the seductiveness of the image of the child on screen (the child actor might steal the show leaving no opportunities for the adult actors to compete for a prize) or a sense that child performance had as much to do with their framing and construction by a film-making team than with acting talent.[1] Ana Torrent in particular was invoked – she had not won a prize (the scheme had not been in place when she was a child star) and she had famously commented that in the filming of *El espíritu de la colmena* she was not acting, just being. As Karen Lury has written of child stars, children are more 'valued for who or what they *are* – inevitably or inherently – than what they can *do*' (Lury, 2010: 150). In this book, we have seen how children's acting has in different ways involved an accessing of the real through fakery: Marcelino was offered sweets to make his face light up; Ana Torrent felt real fear at the monster.[2] The child nevertheless seems to introduce 'naturalness', a sense of authenticity, a contingent reference in the 'real world'.

The debates over the 'authenticity' and 'naturalness' of the cinematic child, as well as their 'seductiveness', speaks to anxieties concerning cinema's potential for capturing the real on screen as well as its capacity for fakery. In terms of the capturing of the Spanish past on screen, the cinematic child can be a powerful tool for the exploration of the recovery of memories even as it may usher in anxieties regarding the possible inauthenticity of these memories. Prosthetic memories created by cinema can be open to accusations of the implantation of images of the past that are nostalgic, inauthentic or ideologically slanted. Elsaesser calls these images 'traumatised' and sees them as inherently postmodern: these are the event without a trace (Elsaesser, 2001). Writing specifically of recreated images of the past on screen, Pam Cook acknowledges that there is always a melancholy around such images, a sense that something has been lost that is now irrecoverable. But she maintains that what has been lost is not reality itself, but a sense that an audience has 'somehow been duped into accepting inauthentic versions and forgetting the truth'. But she goes on, 'what has been lost, it seems, is the authority of history itself, and its ability to produce convincing and objectifiable accounts of the past which will serve as a consensus' (Cook, 2005: 3). In some senses, the contingency which the child affords might be seen to lend credence to the authenticity of the past represented. But anxieties regarding the potential for the child to fake, seduce or produce nostalgia never seem far away. The cinematic children under discussion here articulate anxieties that the past as depicted under Francoism (the endless retelling of the story of the victors of the war and the denial of an alternative memory) was a false, if seductive, reality, but also an awareness that recent filmic recreations of the past might be laid open to accusations of nostalgia or distortion. Moreover, the melancholia often associated with the child might have to do with the consciousness that memories are always already sutured and prosthetic. Furthermore, they provide a constant reminder of the lack of consensus regarding memory, history, Spain's past and how to interpret it. But Alison Landsberg's theories of prosthetic memory suggest that cinema can provide a powerful medium through which to engage with the past. As she dwells on the potential for cinema to evoke a sense of immediacy and to provide an 'experiential site' to engage with the past, a question that is never entirely resolved in her book, *Prosthetic Memory* (2004), is the extent to which cinema can provide the audience with a medium for reflection on the past.

In this book the films studied repeatedly return to the motif of the child and the monster. Víctor Erice's iconic *El espíritu de la colmena* is paradigmatic of the ways that Spanish films can engage with history through the figure of the child. As we have seen, throughout a series of films from Spain's filmic history, the monster can take on many allegorical guises, but in general comes to represent the relationship of the self to a (prosthetic) memory. The monster represents the horrors of Spain's recent past. In the sense that the cinematic children studied here retain traces of their mechanical origins (they are dolls, cyborgs, ventriloquist's dummies or cinematic monsters themselves), through them we can gain a critical distance on the past which can give cinema an ethical dimension. The child, then, is seer and witness to the past, but where Deleuze (1995) views this position as the inherently passive wide-eyed gaze of the child, the notion of the child and the monster as prosthetic allows for a critical reflection on the spectres and monsters of Spain's past. The cinematic child, then, does not necessarily suggest a politics of victimhood in representations of the past, but can imply critical engagement and confrontation. The moral positions of these films are not fixed but depend on engagement to produce meaning. Prosthetic memories therefore have a lot to contribute to 'memory wars', whilst the child is a potent motif both for the loss of historical memory (and its trauma) as well as its recuperation.

Chapter 1 interpreted the child in *Marcelino, pan y vino* as a passive victim of National Catholic ideology. But through the strangeness of the dubbing techniques used, the film was seen to open up a space for critical reflection on the way that the child has been used as a mouthpiece for the regime. The imaginative fantasy of that film and also its nightmarish baroque religious imagery are returned to in the discussion of *Camino* in Chapter 4, revealing that the question of the legacies of the Catholicism of Francoism still has the power to provoke explosive debate. In Chapter 2, Marisol's body was seen as an archive, not just of the ways she was called upon to promote Francoism's policies during the 1960s, but also of her exploitation under the patriarchal fantasy engendered by the Franco regime. If Marisol brings the representation of femininity under Francoism into sharp relief, Chapter 4 explored how masculinity in Spain is still labouring under the legacies left by Francoist patriarchal models. Chapter 3 saw the ways that the cinematic child might represent the burdens of Spanish history and the way that films since the Spanish Transition have offered up the lost child as a potent motif for the trauma and loss associated with historical memory. Finally, Chapter 4 explored the tortured teen body not as a 'traceless event', but as one marked by the imprints of the Spanish past.

What do we make of Spanish cinema's repetitive returns to the motif of the child and the monster throughout time? Thomas Elsaesser muses as to whether cinema's returns 'inhibit the narrative closure that story telling and narrative history' might allow. The way that cinema can transport us into an experiential relationship with the past, can bring that past to life, and might generate not historical amnesia, but in its place an inability to stop obsessing about the past. As Elsaesser writes, 'acts of re-telling, remembering and repeating all point [...] in the direction of obsession, fantasy, trauma' (Elsaesser, 1996: 145). But repetition can also denote a working through, as Elsaesser acknowledges. As we have seen in this book, the child's confrontation with the monster can stand for the sense of collective guilt following the death of the dictator that more had not been done to remove him in the final years of the regime. At the same time, it can also stand for the powerlessness of a nation subjected to years of ideological brainwashing. Prosthetic cinema, it seems, can provide a cathartic function for a nation attempting to come to terms with its past.

Finally, then, *The Child in Spanish Cinema* has explored the ways that the Spanish cinematic child comes to represent prosthetic memory. The films under discussion return to the theme of the child and the monster to allegorise the relationship of the self to the past, and to cinema. Spanish cinema can have an important role to play in offering the spectator the space to work through a critical engagement with the horrors of Spain's past. The child emerges as a potent motif not just for the loss of historical memory, but also for its recuperation through cinema. The child also provides a powerful way to work through the legacies of the dictatorship. The child's relationship to time can speak to nostalgia and loss, but it can also be a malleable icon to project forwards into the future.

Notes

1 Carlos Boyero and Kike Maíllo both suggested that this had to do with anxiety 'que un niño nos quite el premio' (that a child might rob us of a prize) (Boyero, 2011: n.p; Clemente, 2012: n.p.).
2 By contrast, Francesc Colomer was asked to imagine that his father was ill in order to bring on tears – acting, rather than 'being' (from the DVD extras).

Bibliography

Abajo de Pablos, J. J. (1996), *Mis charlas con José Luis Sáenz de Heredia* (Valladolid: Quirón Ediciones).

Abraham, N. and Torok, M. (1994), *The Shell and the Kernel: Renewals of Psychoanalysis* (Chicago: University of Chicago Press).

Affron, C. (1977), *Star Acting: Gish, Garbo, Davis* (London: Dutton).

Agamben, G. (1999), *Remnants of Auschwitz: The Witness and the Archive* (Michigan: Zone Books).

Agamben, G. (2007), 'Notes on Gesture', in *Infancy & History: Essays on the Destruction of Experience*, trans. L. Heron (London: Verso), pp. 133–140.

Aguilar, J. (2012), *Las estrellas del destape la transición: el cine español se desnuda* (Madrid: T&B Editores).

Aguilar, J. and Losada, M. (2008), *Marisol* (Madrid: Colección Portfolio).

Aguilar, P. (2004), 'Madres de cine: entre la ausencia y la caricatura', in A. de la Concha and R. Osborne (eds), *Las mujeres y los niños primero: discursos dela maternidad* (Barcelona: Icaria), pp. 179–200.

Aguilar, S. (1936), 'La estrella mayor y la estrella menor: Lina Yegros y Mari-Tere', *Cinegramas*, 78, 8 March: n.p.

Aguilar Fernández, P. (1996), *Memoria y olvido de la guerra civil española* (Madrid: Alianza).

Ahmed, S. (2004), *The Cultural Politics of Emotion* (Edinburgh: Edinburgh University Press).

Aizpún, I. (1989), 'Pablito Calvo, «Marcelino», vende pisos', *Ya*, 2 September, n.p.

Alonso Ibarrola, J. L. (1963), 'Mercero: se necesita chico', *La Estafeta Literaria*, 30 March, n.p.

Altman, R. (1980), 'Moving Lips: Cinema as Ventriloquism', *Yale French Studies*, 60: 67–79.

Amich Elías, C. (2005), *El poder y los derechos del niño en el franquismo* (Salamanca: Ediciones Universidad Salamanca).

Anderson, P. (2011), 'In the Name of the Martyrs: Memory and Retribution in Francoist Southern Spain, 1936–45', *Cultural and Social History*, 8 (3): 355–370.

Anon (1927a), 'Hablando con Antoñito Cabero', *El Imparcial*, 8 January, 6.

Anon (1927b), 'Una película barcelonesa: *La tía Ramona*', *España Cinematográfica*, 30 June, 6.

Anon (1936), 'Gran Concurso', *Proyector de Cine*, January, n.p.

Anon (1952), 'Pequeña batalla del doblaje', *Primer Plano*, 58, 27 January, n.p.

Anon (1960), *¿Sabes ir al cine?* Madrid: Talitha.

Anon (1961a), 'Marisol: 11 añitos', *Primer Plano*, 12 February, n.p.

Anon (1961b), 'La vida semanal de Marisol', *Primer Plano*, 19 February, n.p.

Anon (1961c), 'Marisol, ocho centímetros más', *Primer Plano*, 23 July, n.p.

Anon (1961d), 'Marisol ha cambiado de casa', *Primer Plano*, 27 August, n.p.

Anon (1962a), 'Pilarín Sanclemente: hacer cine es menos cansado pero el teatro, en cambio, es mucho más divertido', *Radiocinema*, 27 July, 18–19.

Anon (1962b), *Simpatía: la vida de Marisol contada por ella misma en 25 capítulos* (Bilbao: Editorial Fher).

Anon (1962c), 'Marisol cumple trece años', *Radiocinema*, 1 February, 16.

Anon (1962d), 'Marisol en Atenas', *Radiocinema*, 13 December, 15.

Anon (1962e), 'Franco vuelve a su casa', *Primer Plano*, 5 January, n.p.

Anon (1963a), 'El productor Benito Perojo contrata en exclusiva a las gemelas Pili y Mili', *Radiocinema*, 14 February, 15.

Anon (1963b), 'Cine de dos caras en la Argentina', *Primer Plano*, 22 March, n.p.

Anon (1965), 'La semana actualidad', *Fotogramas*, 895, 1 December, n.p.

Anon (1969), 'Carola de día, Carola de noche', *Nuevo Fotogramas*, 25 July, 5.

Anon (1979), 'La tobita de Lolo', *Interviú*, 4 January, 101.

Anon (2007), 'Santa Rita of Cascia: Saint of the Impossible', http://romancatholic blog.typepad.com/roman_catholic_blog/2007/05/saint_rita_of_c.html (accessed 09.09.2012).

Anon (2008a), 'Antena 3 resuelve hoy "El enigma de Marisol"', www.vertele.com/ noticias/antena-3-resuelve-hoy-el-enigma-de-marisol/ (accessed 06.09.2012).

Anon (2008b), 'La familia de la niña que inspiró la película Camino, molesta con Javier Fesser', *El Mundo*, 26 September, www.elmundo.es/elmundo/2008/09/26/ cultura/1222453715.html (accessed 14.09.2012).

Anon (2009), 'Elio Quiroga: Franco quería un parque de atracciones católico en España como Lourdes o Fátima', www.elconfidencial.com/cache/2009/06/02/ ocioytelevision_17_secretos.html (accessed 03.08.2012).

Anon (2012), 'Penélope Cruz Concerned About Spain's Financial Crisis and How It Could Affect Film Industry', *Washington Post*, 9 September, www. washingtonpost.com/entertainment/penelope-cruz-concerned-about-spains-finan cial-crisis-and-how-it-could-affect-film-industry/2012/09/09/a8ed6400–fa72–11e 1–a65a-d6e62f9f2a5a_story.html (accessed 09.09.2012).

Anzieu, D. (1989), *The Skin Ego* (New Haven, CT: Yale University Press).

Anzieu, D. (1993), *Psychic Envelopes*, trans. D. Nash (London: Karnac).

A. R. (1962), 'Una mañana de pesca con Marisol', *Radiocinema*, 11 October, n.p.

Arata, L. O. (1983), '"I Am Ana": The Play of Imagination in *The Spirit of the Beehive* and *Cría cuervos*', *Quarterly Review of Film Studies*, 8 (2): 27–33.

Arce, J. (2011), 'Kike Maíllo, director de *Eva*: "Me interesa explicar qué somos, cómo es la condición humana"', http://noticias.labutaca.net/kike-maillo-director- de-eva-me-interesa-explicar-que-somos-como-es-la-condicion-humana/ (accessed 20.08.2012).

Arconada, A. and Velayos, T. (2006), *Rodajes al borde de un ataque de nervios: el cine español se confiesa* (Madrid: T&B Editores).

Aries, P. (1965), *Centuries of Childhood: A Social History of Family Life* (London: Vintage).

Arnau, R. C. (2007), 'La recuperación de la versión para el mercado alemán de la secta de los misteriosos (Alberto Marro, 1917)', *Secuencias: revista de historia del cine*, 26: 66–80.

Artaud, A. (1978), 'Les souffrances du "dubbing"', in *Oeuvres completes*, vol. 3 (Paris: Gallimard), pp. 85–87.

Artigues, D. (1968), *El Opus Dei in España: su evolución ideológica y política 1928–57* (Madrid: Ruedo Ibérico).

Ascarza, V. F. (1945), *La niña instruida* (Madrid: Magisterio).

Asimov, I. (1983), *The Complete Robot Series* (London: Mass Market Paperback).

Avery, G. and Reynolds, K. (2000), *Representations of Childhood Death* (London: Palgrave Macmillan).

Baackman, S. (2004), 'Female Counter-memories of Nazi Germany: The Child as a Lieu de Mémoire in Marianne Rosenbaum's *Peppermint Frieden*', *Seminar*, 40 (1): 19–34.

Bachelard, G. (1969), *The Poetics of Reverie: Childhood, Language and the Cosmos* (Boston, MA: The Beacon Press).

Balázs, B. (1952), *Theory of the Film: Character and Growth of a New Art* (London: Dennis Dobson Ltd).

Balázs, B. (2010), 'Visible Man or the Culture of Film', in E. Carter (ed.), *Béla Balázs and Early Film Theory: Visible Man and the Spirit of Film*, trans. R. Livingstone (Oxford: Berghahn Books), pp. 1–84.

Ballester Casado, A. (2001), *Traducción y nacionalismo. La recepción del cine Americano en España a través del doblaje (1928–48)* (Granada: Editorial Comares).

Bandrés, J. and Llavona, R. (1997), 'Psicología en los campos de concentración de Franco', *Psicothema*, 8 (1): 1–11.

Barker, J. (2009), *The Tactile Eye: Touch and the Cinematic Experience* (Berkeley: University of California Press).

Barreiro, J. (1999), *Marisol frente a Pepa Flores* (Madrid: Plaza y Janés).

Batchelor, D. (2000), *Chromophobia* (London: Reaktion Books).

Bazin, A. (1997), *Bazin at Work: Major Reviews and Essays from the Forties and Fifties* (London: Routledge).

Begin, P. (2008), 'When Victim Meets Voyeur: An Aesthetic of Confrontation in Hispanic Social Issue Cinema', *Hispanic Research Journal*, 9 (3): 261–275.

Belinchón, G. (2010), 'La liberación de la mujer es una falacia: entrevista a Achero Mañas', *El País*, 6 September, www.elpais.com/articulo/cultura/liberacion/mujer/falacia/elpepucul/20100906elpepicul_4/Tes (accessed 16.04.2011).

Benjamin, W. (1968a), 'The Work of Art in the Age of Mechanical Reproduction', in H. Arendt (ed.), *Illuminations*, trans. H. Zohn (New York: Schocken), pp. 217–252.

Benjamin, W. (1968b) 'On Some Motifs in Baudelaire', in H. Arendt (ed.) *Illuminations* trans. H. Zohn (New York: Schocken), pp. 155–200.

Benjamin, W. (1996), 'A Child's View of Color', in M. P. Bullock, M. W. Jennings, H. Eiland and G. Smith (eds), *Selected Writings, 1913–1926*, vol. 1 (Cambridge, MA: Harvard University Press), pp. 50–51.

Bennett, J. (2001), 'Stigmata and Sense Memory: St. Francis and the Affective Image', *Art History*, 24 (1): 1–16.

Bennett, J. (2005), *Empathic Vision: Affect, Trauma and Contemporary Art* (Stanford, CA: Stanford University Press).

Bergeron, K. (1996), 'The Castrato as History', *Cambridge Opera Journal*, 8 (2): 167–184.

Bick, E. (1968), 'The Experiences of Skin in Early Object Relations', *International Journal of Psycho-Analysis*, 49: 484–486.

Bick, E. (1986), 'Further Considerations on the Function of the Skin on Early Object Relations', *British Journal of Psychotherapy*, 2: 292–299.

Bick, E. (2002), 'The Experience of the Skin in Early Object Relations', in A. Briggs (ed.), *Surviving Space: Papers on Infant Observation* (London: Karnac Books), pp. 55–59.

Bloom, M. (2000), 'Pygmalionesque Delusions and Illusions of Movement: Animation from Hoffmann to Truffaut', *Comparative Literature*, 52 (4): 291–230.

Borges, J. L. (1988), 'On Dubbing', in E. Cozarinsky (ed.), *Borges in/and/on Film*, trans. G. Waldman and R. Christ (New York: Lumen Books), pp. 62–63.

Borrás Llop, José María (ed.) (1996), *Historia de la infancia en la España contemporánea 1834–1936* (Madrid: Ministerio de Trabajo y Asuntos Sociales).

Boyero, C. (2008), 'Los monstrous imponen el "Camino"', *El País*, 26 September, http://elpais.com/diario/2008/09/26/cine/1222380002_850215.html (accessed 15. 09.2012).

Boyero, C. (2011), 'Dejar a los niños fuera de los Goya me parece un poco hipócrita', *El País*, 24 June, http://cultura.elpais.com/cultura/2011/06/24/videos/ 1308866401_870215.html (accessed 14.09.2012).

Boym, S. (2001), *The Future of Nostalgia* (London: Basic Books).

Burch, N. (1990), *Life to Those Shadows* (Berkeley: University of California Press).

Burgoyne, R. (2009), 'Prosthetic Memory/Traumatic Memory: *Forrest Gump* (1994)', in M. Hughes-Warrington (ed.), *The History on Film Reader* (London: Routledge), pp. 137–142.

Cabero, J. A. (1949), *Historia de la cinematografía española* (Madrid: Gráficas Cinema).

Cabrera, M. and del Rey, F. (2007), *The Power of Entrepreneurs: Politics and Economy in Contemporary Spain* (Oxford: Berghahn).

Camina, A. (1973), '*El espíritu de la colmena*', *Cine para leer* (Madrid: Razón y fe), pp. 120–123.

Camporesi, V. (2001), 'Cuentos de estrellas, valor y formalidad', *Archivos de la Filmoteca*, 38, June, 62–71.

Camporesi, V. (2007a), 'Para una historia social de lo no nacional en el cine español. Ladislao Vajda y el caso de los huidos de las persecuciones antisemitas en España', in N. Berthier, *Cine, nación y nacionalidades en España* (Madrid: Casa de Velázquez), pp. 61–74.

Camporesi, V. (2007b) 'Spain: Bipolar Visions, Unified Realities. A General Overview', in D. Ostrowska and G. Roberts (eds), *European Cinemas in the Television Age* (Edinburgh: Edinburgh University Press), pp. 55–70.

Carroll, J. C. (2006), *Saintly Youths of Modern Times* (Huntingdon, IN: Our Sunday Vision).

Castañeda, C. (2002), *Figurations: Child, Bodies, Worlds* (Durham, NC and London: Duke University Press).

Castro de Paz, J. L. (2004), 'En el balcón vacío (Jomi García Ascot, 1962). El film exiliado o la ventana del fanstasma', in *Cine y exilio. Forma(s) de la ausencia* (A Coruña: Vía Láctea), pp. 19–59.

Castro de Paz, J. L. and Cerdán, J. (eds) (2005), *Suevia Film. Cesáreo González: Treinta años de cine español* (Santiago de Compostela: Xunta de Galicia).

Cavell, S. (1979), *The World Viewed: Reflections on the Ontology of Film* (Cambridge, MA: Harvard University Press).

Cebollada, P. (1976), 'Intriga, terror y ciencia ficción con un tema insólito', *Ya*, 24 April, n.p.

Cenarro, A. (2008a), 'Francoist Nostalgia and Memories of the Spanish Civil War', *International Journal of Iberian Studies*, 21 (3): 203–217.

Cenarro, A. (2008b), 'Memories of Repression and Resistance: Narratives of Children Institutionalized by Auxilio Social in Postwar Spain', *History and Memory*, 20 (2): 39–59.

Cenarro, A. (2009), *Los niños del Auxilio Social* (Madrid: Espasa-Calpe).

Charnon Deutsch, Lou (2000), *Fictions of the Feminine in the Nineteenth-Century Spanish Press* (Pennsylvania: The Pennsylvania State University Press).

Chazelle, D. (2010), 'Truffaut's *The 400 Blows*', 20 September, www.wrongplanet. net/postt138293.html (accessed 07.06.2011).

Chion, M. (1999), *The Voice in Cinema*, trans. C. Gorbman (New York: Columbia University Press).

Christian, W.A. (1992), *Moving Crucifixes in Modern Spain* (Princeton: Princeton University Press).

Clarke, J. J. (2004), 'Doubly Monstrous? Female and Disabled', *Essays in Philosophy*, 9 (1): 3, http://commons.pacificu.edu/eip/vol9/iss1/3 (accessed 05.01.2012).

Clemente, J. M (2012), 'Kike Maíllo: A los mayores nos cuesta aceptar que un niño nos quite un premio', *Vanity Fair*, 18 February, http://blogs.revistavanityfair.es/ cinelandiavf/2012/02/18/kike-maillo-"a-los-mayores-nos-cuesta-aceptar-que-un-nino-nos-quite-un-premio"/ (accessed 14.09.2012).

Company, J. M. (1997), '*Marcelino, pan y vino* 1954 [1955]', in J. Pérez Perucha (ed.), *Antología crítica del cine español 1906–1995* (Madrid: Cátedra/ Filmoteca Española), pp. 355–357.

Connerton, P. (1989), *How Societies Remember: Thinking in the Social Sciences* (Cambridge: Cambridge University Press).

Connor, S. (2000), 'Sounding Out Film', www.bbk.ac.uk/english/skc/soundingout/ (accessed 22.08.2012).

Connor, S. (2001), *Dumbstruck: A Cultural History of Ventriloquism* (New York Oxford University Press).

Connor, S. (2002), 'A Skin That Walks', paper given at Royal Holloway, University of London, www.stevenconnor.com/skinwalks/ (accessed 08.09.2012).

Connor, S. (2004), *The Book of Skin* (Ithaca, NY: Cornell University Press).

Cook, D. T. (2004), *The Commodification of Childhood: The Children's Clothing Industry and the Rise of the Child Consumer* (Durham, NC: Duke University Press).

Cook, P. (2005), *Screening the Past: Memory and Nostalgia in Cinema* (London: Routledge).

Creed, B. (2005), 'Baby Bitches from Hell: Monstrous Little Women in Film', in J. Crew and R. Leonard (eds), *Mixed-up Childhood*, pp. 33–38, http://repository. unimelb.edu.au/10187/2078 (accessed 05.01.2012).

Crumbaugh, J. (2007), 'Are We All (Still) Miguel Ángel Blanco? Victimhood, the Media Afterlife, and the Challenge for Historical Memory', *Hispanic Review*, 75 (4): 365–384.

Crumbaugh, J. (2009), *Destination Dictatorship: The Spectacle of Spain's Tourist Boom and the Reinvention of Difference* (New York: State University Press).

Cruz, J. I. (2001), 'Por rutas imperials. Datos, imágenes y comentarios sobre los campamentos del Frente de Juventudes', *Archivos de la Filmoteca*, 38, June, 72–84.

Cueto, R. (1998), *Los desarraigados del cine español* (London: Nuer Ediciones).

Darke, C. (2010), '"Les Enfants et les Cinéphiles": The Moment of Epiphany in *The Spirit of the Beehive*', *Cinema Journal*, 49 (2): 152–158.

Davies, A. (2006), 'The Beautiful and Monstrous Masculine: The Male Body and Horror in *El espinazo del diablo*', *Studies in Hispanic Cinema*, 3 (3): 135–147.

Davies, A. (2011), 'The Final Girl and Monstrous Mother of *El orfanato*', in A. Davies (ed.), *Spain on Screen: Developments in Contemporary Spanish Cinema* (Basingstoke: Palgrave Macmillan), pp. 79–92.

Davies, A. (2012), *Spanish Spaces: Landscape, Place and Space in Spanish Culture* (Liverpool: Liverpool University Press).

Davies, T. (2004), *The Face on the Screen: Death, Recognition and Spectatorship* (Bristol: Intellect Books).

Deleuze, G. (1986), *Cinema I: The Movement-Image*, trans. H. Tomlinson and B. Habberjam (Minneapolis: University of Minnesota Press).

Deleuze, G. (2005), *Cinema II: The Time-Image*, trans. H. Tomlinson and B. Habberjam (Minneapolis: University of Minnesota Press).

Deleyto, C. (1993), 'Rewriting Spain: Metafiction and Intertextuality in Saura's *Carmen*', *Journal of Hispanic Research*, 2 (2): 237–247.

Delgado, M. (2008), 'The Young and the Damned', *Sight and Sound*, April. www.bfi.org.uk/sightandsound/review/4275 (accessed 05.01.2012).

Derrida, J. (1978), *Writing and Difference*, trans. A. Bass (Chicago: University of Chicago Press).

Derrida, J. (1995), *Archive Fever: A Freudian Impression*, trans. E. Preowitz (Chicago: University of Chicago Press).

Deslaw, E. (1955), 'Pablito Calvo juega en la playa y toma parta en la batalla de flores', *Primer Plano*, 761, 15 May, n.p.

Devillard, M. J., Pazos, A., Castillo, S. and Medina, N. (2001), *Los niños españoles en la URSS (1937–1997): narración y memoria* (Madrid: Ariel).

Dinesen, I. (1991), *Last Tales* (New York: Vintage).

Doane, M. A. (1985), 'The Voice in the Cinema: The Articulation of Body and Space', in E. Weiss and J. Belton, *Film Sound: Theory and Practice* (New York: Columbia University Press), pp. 162–176.

Doane, M. (1989), *The Desire to Desire* (Bloomington: Indiana University Press).

Doane, M. (2002), *The Emergence of Cinematic Time: Modernity, Contingency, the Archive* (Cambridge, MA: Harvard University Press).

Doane, M. (2003), 'The Close-Up: Scale and Detail in the Cinema', *differences: A Journal of Feminist Cultural Studies*, 14 (3): 89–111.

Dolar, M. (2006), *A Voice and Nothing More* (Cambridge, MA: MIT Press).

Donald, S. H. (2012), 'The Dorothy Project: Children, Film and Migration', manuscript for *Leverhulme Lecture*, University of Leeds.

Draaisma, D. (2000), *Metaphors of Memory: A History of Ideas About the Mind* (Cambridge: Cambridge University Press).

Dyer, R. (1986). *Heavenly Bodies: Film Stars and Society* (London: British Film Institute).

Edelman, L. (2004), *No Future: Queery Theory and the Death Drive* (North Carolina: Duke University Press).

Egido (1976), 'Detrás de la cortina no hay nada: ¿Quién puede matar a un niño?', 10 May (unreferenced source from the files of the Filmoteca Española, Madrid).

Elena, A. (2001), 'El canot del cine Rex: una revisión del cine de Joselito', *Archivos de la Filmoteca*, 38, June, 48–61.

Ellis, J. and Sánchez-Arce, A. M. (2011), 'The Unquiet Dead: Memories of the Spanish Civil War in Guillermo del Toro's *Pan's Labyrinth*', in A. Sinha and T. McSweeney (eds.), *Millennial Cinema: Memory in Global Film* (New York: Columbia University Press), pp. 173–191.

Elsaesser, T. (1996), 'Subject Positions, Speaking Positions: From *Holocaust, Our Hitler*, and *Heimat* to *Shoah* and *Schindler's List*', in V. Sobchack (ed.), *The Persistence of History: Cinema, Television, and the Modern Event* (New York: Routledge, 1995), pp. 145–183.

Elsaesser, T. (2001), 'Postmodernism as Mourning Work', *Screen*, 42 (2): 193–201.

Elsaesser, T. and Hagener, M. (2010), *Film Theory: An Introduction Through the Senses* (New York: Routledge).

E. M. (1963), 'Antoñita, "la singla"', *Primer Plano*, 26 April, n.p.

Escudero Alday, R. (2013), 'The Right to Know', in Francisco Espinosa Maestre, *Shoot the Messenger: From the Pact of Silence to the Trial of Baltasar Garzón* (Brighton: Sussex Academic Press), pp. i–iv.

Estivill, J. (2001), 'La infancia en el cine políticamente instructivo de posguerra', *Archivos de la Filmoteca*, 38, June, 16–27.

Evans, J. (1995–96), 'A Myth in Time: Víctor Erice's *El sur*', *Journal of Hispanic Research*, 4: 147–157.

Evans, P. (1982), '*El espíritu de la colmena*: The Monster, the Place of the Father and Growing Up in the Dictatorship', *Vida Hispánica*, 32 (3): 13–17.

Evans, P. W. (2000), 'Cheaper by the Dozen: *La gran familia*, Francoism and Spanish Film Comedy', in D. Holmes and A. Smith, *100 Years of European Cinema: Entertainment or Ideology?* (Manchester: Manchester University Press), pp. 77–88.

Evans, P. W. (2004), 'Marisol: The Spanish Cinderella', in A. Lázaro-Reboll and A. Willis (eds), *Spanish Popular Cinema* (Manchester: University of Manchester Press), pp. 129–151.

Evans, P. and Fiddian, R. (1987), 'Erice's *El sur*: A Narrative of Star Cross'd Lovers', *Bulletin of Hispanic Studies*, 64 (2A): 127–135.

Farnegaes, A. (1962), 'Dos gemelas españolas dispuestas a eclipsar la popularidad de las famosas hermanas Kessler', *Radiocinema*, 18 October, 39–41.

Faulkner, S. (2005), 'Ageing and Coming of Age in Carlos Saura's *La caza* (The Hunt 1965)', *MLN*, 120 (2): 457–484.

Faulkner, S. (2006), 'Franco's Great Family: *La gran familia* (*The Great Family*, Palacios, 1962)', in *A Cinema of Contradiction: Spanish Film in the 1960s.* (Edinburgh: Edinburgh University Press), pp. 27–46.

Faulkner, S. (2011), '*El príncipe destronado* (Miguel Delibes 1973) / *La guerra de papá* (Antonio Mercero 1977) and Third Way Spanish Cinema', *Revista Arbor (Centro Superior de Investigaciones Científicas)*, 187 (748): 279–285.

Faulkner, S. (2013), *A History of Spanish Film: Cinema and Society 1900–2010* (London and New York: Continuum).

Fernández, T. and P. (2008), 'Carta a Fesser', *La Razón*, 6 November, 12.

Ferrán, O. (2007), *Working Through Memory in Contemporary Spanish Narrative* (Bucknell: Bucknell Unversity Press).

Fesser, J. (2008), 'Carta abierta a Opus Dei', *El Mundo*, 24 October, 58.

Fiestas, J. (1963), 'San Sebastián. Un festival con buen tiempo', *Primer Plano*, 14 June, n.p.

Flores, J. (1983), 'Réplica de Marisol', *El País*, 28 October, http://elpais.com/diario/1983/10/28/opinion/436143611_850215.html (accessed 06.09.2012).

Fouz-Hernández, S. (2007), 'Boys Will Be Men: Teen Masculinities in Recent Spanish Cinema', in Timothy Shary and Alexandra Seibel, *Youth Culture in Global Cinema* (Austin, TX: University of Texas Press), pp. 222–237.

García, P. (1952), 'Niños en el cine', *Primer Plano*, 588, 20 January, n.p.

García, T. (2011), 'Eva seduce en Venecia', *El País*, 7 September, http://cultura.elpais.com/cultura/2011/09/07/actualidad/1315346404_850215.html (accessed 20.08.2012).

García Escudero, J. M. (1956), 'Convertir un rayo de luz en un rayo de dios', *Film Ideal*, 1, October, 16.

García Lorca, F. (1991), 'Canciones de cuna' in *Obras Completas* III (Mexico: Aguilar), pp. 282–300.

Gibert, F. J. (1936), 'La Shirley Temple española es andaluza', *Proyector de Cine*, May, 4–5.

Gil Pecharromán, J. (1990), 'El accidente de caza de Franco', in J. M. Martínez (ed.), *La vida cotidiana en la España de los 60* (Madrid: Ediciones del Prado), p. 18.

Giménez, C. (2000), *Paracuellos* (Barcelona: Glénat).

González-Barros y González, A. (2008), 'Carta abierta a Fesser', *La Razón*, 27 September, 12.

González del Pozo, J. (2008), 'Al cerrar la puerta: violencia contra niños y ruptura del silencio en *El Bola* de Achero Mañas', *Letras Hispanas*, 5 (1): 50–62.

González Duro, E. (2008), *Los psiquiatras de Franco: los rojos no estaban locos* (Barcelona: Ediciones Península).

Graham, H. and Labanyi, J. (eds) (1996), *Spanish Cultural Studies: An Introduction* (Oxford: Oxford University Press).

Grainge, P. (2002), *Monochrome Memories: Nostalgia and Style in Retro America* (Westport, CT: Greenwood Press).

Greene, N. (1999), *Landscapes of Loss: The National Past in Postwar French Cinema* (Princeton, NJ: University of Princeton Press).

Gros, J. and Raguer, P. (1954), *Niños santos: Siluetas de vidas edificantes para la infancia y la juventud* (Barcelona: Editorial La Hormiga de Oro).

Gubern, R. (1977), *Raza, un ensueño del General Franco* (Madrid: Ediciones 99).

Gubern, R. (2001), 'Teoría y práctica del star-system español', *Archivos de la Filmoteca*, 38, June, 8–15.

Gubern, R. and P. Hammond (eds) (2012), *Luis Buñuel: The Red Years, 1929–39* (Wisconsin: University of Wisconsin Press).

Gutiérrez Albilla, J. D. (2011), 'Children of Exile: Trauma, Memory and Testimony in Jaime Camino's Documentary *Los niños de Rusia* (2001)', in A. Davies (ed.), *Spain on Screen: Developments in Contemporary Spanish Cinema* (London: Palgrave), pp. 129–150.

Gutiérrez Albilla, J. D. (2013), 'Inscribing/Scratching the Past on the "Surface" of the "Skin": Embodied Inter-subjectivity, "Prosthetic Memory" and Witnessing in Almodóvar's *La mala educación*', in M. D'Lugo and K. M. Vernon (eds), *A Companion to Pedro Almodóvar* (London: Wiley-Blackwell), pp. 322–344.

Gutiérrez Lanza, C. (2011), 'Censors and Censorship Boards in Franco's Spain

(1950s–60s): An Overview Based on the TRACE Cinema Catalogue', in D. Asimakoulas and M. Rogers (eds), *Translation and Opposition* (Bristol: Multilingual Matters), pp. 305–320.

Haase, D. (2000), 'Children, War and the Imaginative Space of Fairy Tales', *The Lion and the Unicorn*, 24 (3): 360–377.

Hansen, M. (1993), 'With Skin and Hair: Kracauer's Theory of Film, Marseilles, 1940', *Critical Inquiry*, 19 (3): 437–469.

Hansen, M. B. (1996), '*Schindler's List* Is Not *Shoah*: The Second Commandment, Popular Modernism and Popular Memory', *Critical Inquiry*, 22 (2): 292–312.

Hansen, M. B. (2008), "Benjamin's Aura", *Critical Inquiry*, 34 (2): 336–375.

Hardcastle, A. E. (2005), 'Ghosts of the Past and Present: Hauntology and the Spanish Civil War in Guillermo del Toro's *The Devil's Backbone*', *Journal of the Fantastic in the Arts*, 15: 119–131.

Harris, D. (2001), *Cute, Quaint, Hungry and Romantic: The Aesthetics of Consumerism* (Cambridge, MA: Da Capo Press).

Harvey, J. (2001), 'The Value of Nostalgia: Reviving Memories of National-Catholic Childhoods', *Journal of Spanish Cultural Studies*, 2 (1): 109–118.

Harvey, J. (2002), 'Good Girls Go to Heaven: The Venerable Mari Carmen González Valerio y Sáenz de Heredia', in J. Labanyi (ed.), *Constructing Identity in Contemporary Spain: Theoretical Debates and Cultural Practice* (Oxford: Oxford University Press), pp. 113–127.

Harvey, J. (2004), 'Death and the Adorable Orphan: *Marcelino, pan y vino* (1954; 1991; 2000)', *Journal of Romance Studies*, 4 (1): 63–77.

Harvey, J. (2008), 'Domestic Queens and Warrior Wives: Heroines in Spanish Schoolbooks for Girls (1940–1960)', *History of Education*, 37 (2): 277–293.

Heredero, C. F. (1993), *Las huellas del tiempo: cine español 1951–61* (Valencia: Ediciones Documentos Filmoteca).

Heredero, C. F. (2000), 'Una mirada limpia y directa', *Diario 16*, 20 October, 59.

Hermoso, B. (2006), '"El Bola" pasea por el lado salvaje', *El Mundo*, 6 October, www.elmundo.es/elmundo/2006/10/06/cultura/1160091680.html (accessed 07.06.2011).

Heywood, C. (2001), *A History of Childhood: Children and Childhood in the West from Medieval to Modern Times* (Cambridge: Polity).

Higonnet, A. (1998), *Pictures of Innocence: The History and Crisis of Ideal Childhood* (London: Thames and Hudson).

Hirsch, M. (2008), 'The Generation of Post-Memory', *Poetics Today*, 29 (1): 103–128.

Hoffman, A. R. (2010a), '"This Movie Is Like a Rorschach Test": Disrupted Allegory and the Image of the Child in *Pan's Labyrinth* (Del Toro)', *Genre*, 43 (1–2): 137–162.

Hoffman, E. (2010b), 'The Long Afterlife of Loss', in Susannah Radstone and Bill Schwarz, *Memory: Histories, Theories, Debates* (New York: Fordham University Press), pp. 406–415.

Holland, P. (2004), *Picturing Childhood: The Myth of the Child in Popular Imagery* (London: I. B. Tauris).

Holliday, C. (2012), 'Emotion Capture: Vocal Performances by Children in the Computer-Animated Film', *Alphaville: Journal of Film and Screen Media*, 3 (Summer), www.alphavillejournal.com/Issue%203/HTML/Index%20(text).html (accessed 23.09.2012).

Huxley, A. (2011), *The Doors of Perception* and *Heaven and Hell* (London: Thinking Ink).

Huyssen, A. (2000), 'Of Mice and Mimesis: Reading Spiegelman with Adorno', *New German Critique*, No. 81, Dialectic of Enlightenment (Autumn), 65–82.

Ivy, M. (1993), 'Have You Seen Me? Recovering the Inner Child in Late Twentieth-Century America', *Social Text*, 37: 227–252.

Jablonski, Nina G. (2006), *Skin: A Natural History* (Berkeley: University of California Press).

Jaen, A. (1936), 'Mari-Tere: estrella infantile de la pantalla española', *Cinegramas*, 76, 23 February, n.p.

Jameson, F. (1991), *Postmodernism, Or the Cultural Logic of Late Capitalism* (Durham, NC: Duke University Press).

Jenkins, H. (ed.) (1998), *The Children's Culture Reader* (New York and London: New York University Press).

Jenks, C. (1996), *Childhood* (London: Routledge).

Johnson, W. (2009), 'Hollywood's Hot Voodoo', in J. Radway, A. Gaines, K. Kevin, B. Shank and P. von Eschen (eds), *American Studies: An Anthology* (Oxford: Blackwell), pp. 329–345.

Jolivet, A.-M. (2001), 'Pablito Calvo/Marcelino', *Archivos de la Filmoteca*, 38, June, 28–48.

Jolivet, A.-M. (2004), *La pantalla subliminal: Marcelino, pan y vino según Vajda* (Valencia: Generalidad de Valencia).

Jones, O. (2001), '"Before the Dark of Reason": Some Ethical and Epistemological Considerations on the Otherness of Children', *Ethics, Place & Environment: A Journal of Philosophy & Geography*, 4 (2): 173–178.

Jones, O. (2003), '"Endlessly Revisited and Forever Gone": On Memory, Reverie and Emotional Imagination in Doing Children's Geographies. An "Addendum" to "'To Go Back Up the Side Hill': Memories, Imaginations and Reveries of Childhood" by Chris Philo', *Children's Geographies*, 1 (1): 25–36.

Jordan (1963), '1963 será', *Radiocinema*, 17 January, 36.

Kaes, A. (1989), *From Hitler to Heimat: The Return of History as Film* (Cambridge, MA: Harvard University Press).

Kayser, W. (1957), *The Grotesque in Art and Literature* (New York, Columbia University Press).

Kelleher, J. (1998), 'Face to Face with Terror: Children in Film', in K. Lesnik-Oberstein (ed.), *Children in Culture: Approaches to Childhood* (London: Palgrave Macmillan), pp. 29–56.

Kilbourn, R. (2010), *Cinema, Memory, Modernity: The Representation of Memory from the Art Film to Transnational Cinema* (New York: Routledge).

Kim, Y.-S. (2005), *The Family Album: Histories, Subjectivities and Immigration in Contemporary Spanish Culture* (Bucknell: Bucknell University Press).

Kincaid, J. (1992), *Child-Loving: The Erotic Child and Victorian Culture* (New York: Routledge).

Kinder, M. (1983), 'The Children of Franco in the New Spanish Cinema', *Quarterly Review of Film Studies*, 8 (2): 57–76.

Kinder, M. (1993), *Blood Cinema: The Reconstruction of National Identity in Spain* (Berkeley: University of California Press).

Kirby, L. (1997), *Parallel Tracks: The Railroad and Silent Cinema* (Durham, NC and London: Duke University Press).

Kracauer, S. (1940), 'Marseilles Notebooks', *Kracauer Papers, Dokumente zum Exil in Frankreich und den Verienigten Staaten* (Marbach am Neckar: Deutsches Literaturarchiv).

Kristeva, J. (1985), 'Stabat Mater', *Poetics Today* 6:1–2: 133–152.

Kuhn, A. (2010), 'Cinematic Experience, Film Space and the Child's World', *Canadian Journal of Film Studies/Revue Canadienne d'Études Cinematographiques*, 19 (2): 82–98.

Kulka, T. (1996), *Kitsch and Art* (Philadelphia: Pennsylvania State University Press).

Kundera, M. (1987), *The Unbearable Lightness of Being* (New York: Harper).

Kuznets, L. R. (1994), *When Toys Come Alive: Narratives of Animation, Metamorphosis and Development* (New Have and London: Yale University Press).

L. A., C. (1962), 'Caras nuevas de TV = caras nuevas de nuestro cine', *Radiocinema*, 30 August, 15.

Labanyi, J. (2000) 'History and Hauntology, or What Does One Do with the Ghosts of the Past?', in J. R. Resina (ed.), *Disremembering the Dictatorship: The Politics of Memory in the Spanish Transition to Democracy* (Amsterdam: Rodopi), pp. 65–82.

Labanyi, J. (2001), 'Internalisations of Empire: Colonial Ambivalence and the Early Francoist Missionary Film', *Discourse*, 23 (1): 25–42.

Labanyi, J. (2004), 'Buñuel's Cinematic Collaboration with Sáenz de Heredia 1935–36', in I. Santaolalla, P. D'Allemand, J. Díaz Cintas, P. W. Evans, C. Sanmateu, A. Whyte and M. Witt (eds), *Buñuel, siglo XXI* (Zaragoza: Prensas Universitarias de Zaragoza), pp. 203–301.

Labanyi, J. (2005a), 'The Mediation of Everyday Life: An Oral History of Cinema-going in 1940s and 1950s Spain. An Introduction to a Dossier', *Studies in Hispanic Cinema*, 2 (2): 105–108.

Labanyi, J. (2005b), 'El cine como lugar de memoria en las películas, novelas y autobiografías de los años setenta hasta el presente', in J. R. Resina and U. Winter (eds), *Casa encantada: Lugares de memoria en la España constitucional* (Madrid: Iberoamericana), pp. 157–171.

Labanyi, J. (2006), 'Historias de víctimas: la memoria histórica y el testimonio en la España contemporánea', *Iberoamericana*, 6 (24): 87–98.

Labanyi, J. (2008), 'The Politics of Memory in Contemporary Spain', *Journal of Spanish Cultural Studies*, 9 (2): 119–125

LaCapra, D. (2001), *Writing History, Writing Trauma* (Baltimore: Johns Hopkins University Press).

Lacoue-Labarth, P. and J.-L. Nancy (1990), 'The Nazi Myth', *Critical Inquiry*, 16: 291–312.

Landsberg, A. (1995), 'Prosthetic Memory: *Total Recall* and *Blade Runner*', *Body and Society*, 1 (3–4): 175–189.

Landsberg, A. (2004), *Prosthetic Memory: The Transformation of American Remembrance in the Age of Mass Culture* (New York: Columbia University Press).

Lastra, J. (2000), *Sound Technology and the American Cinema: Perception, Representation, Modernity* (Film and Culture Series) (New York: Columbia University Press).

Latorre, J. (2006), *Tres décadas de El espíritu de la colmena (Víctor Erice)* (Madrid: Ediciones Internacionales Universitarias).

Lázaro-Reboll, A. (2007), 'The Transnational Reception of *El espinazo del diablo* (Guillermo del Toro 2001)', *Hispanic Research Journal*, 8 (1): 39–51.

Lebeau, V. (2008), *Childhood and Cinema* (London: Reaktion).

Levine, M. (2006), *The Belated Witness: Literature, Testimony and the Question of Holocaust Survival* (Palo Alto, Stanford University Press).

Lijtmaer, L., Maíllo, K. and Fernández, E. (2011), *Eva: Así se hizo la película* (Madrid: Ocho y medio).

Lingis, A. (1983), *Excesses: Eros and Culture* (Albany: State University of New York Press).

Llorente Hernández, A. (2002–3), 'La construcción de un mito: la imagen de Franco en las artes plásticas en el primer franquismo (1936–1945)', *Archivos de la Filmoteca (Materiales para una iconografía de Francisco Franco)*, V. Sánchez Biosca (coord), 42–43: 46–75.

López García, J. R. (2008), 'Las verdaderas historias de las muertes de Francisco Franco: para una revisión ucrónica del franquismo', in T. López Pellisa and F. Á. Moreno Serrano (eds), *Ensayos sobre ciencia ficción y literatura fantástica: actas del Primer Congreso Internacional de literatura fantástica y ciencia ficción* (Madrid: Asociación Cultural Xatafi: Universidad Carlos III de Madrid), pp. 653–673.

Lopez-Palacios, M. (1962), 'De la nueva generación: Conchita Goyanes', *Radiocinema*, 6 September, 18.

Lough, F. (2007), '*La lengua de las mariposas*: Symbolic Structures in Social and Ideological Contexts', *The Journal of Symbolism. An International Annual of Critical Aesthetics*, 7: 149–168.

Lury, K. (2010), *The Child in Film: Tears, Fears and Fairy Tales* (London: I. B. Tauris).

Lury, K. (2011), 'Cinephilia and the "Contingent Performance" in Bill Douglas's My Childhood and Daniel Reeves Obsessive Becoming', unpublished paper.

Madrid, F. (1948), 'Rossellini ha llevado a la pantalla una novela de Valle-Inclán', *El Hogar* (Buenos Aires), 2029, 3 September, 6.

Marí, J. (2003), 'El Umbral del destape', in C. X. Ardavín, *Valoración de Francisco Umbral: Ensayos críticos en torno a su obra* (Gijón: Llibros del Pexe), pp. 242–260.

Marks, L. (1999), *The Skin of the Film: Intercultural Cinema, Embodiment and the Cinema* (Durham, NC: Duke University Press).

Marmol, F. (2012) 'La hija de Marisol hereda la honestidad de su madre', *El Mundo*, 9 July, www.elmundo.es/elmundo/2012/07/09/andalucia_malaga/1341833500. html (accessed 20.08.2012).

Marshall, L. (2008), '*Camino*: Screen International Review', *Screen International*, 25 September.

Martin, C. (2003) 'Defying Common Sense: Casting Pepa Flores/Marisol as Mariana Pineda', *Journal of Iberian and Latin American Studies*, 9 (2): 149–161.

Martín, J. (1976), 'El bello camino hacia la democracia: Marisol', *Interviú*, 1 (16): 30–38.

Martínez, E. (1977), 'Una película en la que no pasa nada', *Última Hora*, 29 October, n.p.

Martin-Jones, D. (2011), *Deleuze and World Cinemas* (London and New York: Continuum).

Martin-Márquez, S. (1996), 'Monstrous Identity: Female Socialization in *El espíritu de la colmena*', *New Orleans Review*, 2.

Martin-Márquez, S. (1999), 'Culture and Acculturation in Manuel Summer's *Del rosa al amarillo*', in P. W. Evans (ed.), *Spanish Cinema: The Auteurist Tradition* (Oxford: Oxford University Press), pp. 55–75.

Massumi, B. (2002), *Parables for the Virtual: Movement, Affect, Sensation* (Durham, NC: Duke University Press).

Mate, R. (2010), 'From History and Memory – and Back: Factuality, Knowledge and Morality', in Antonio Gómez López-Quiñones and Susanne Zepp (eds), *The Holocaust in Spanish Memory. Historical Perceptions and Cultural Discourse* (Leipzig: Simon-Dubmow-Institut für jüdische Geschichte und Kultur), pp. 15–30.

Mavor, C. (1996), *Pleasures Taken: Performances of Sexuality and Loss in Victorian Photographs* (London: I. B. Tauris).

McDannell, C. (1995), *Material Christianity: Religion and Popular Culture in America* (New Haven: Yale University Press).

M. Ceja, A. B. (1957), 'Novedades del cine mexicano', *Primer Plano*, 13 October, n.p.

Medialdea, S. (1989), Sánchez Silva: «Escribí el cuento para que los padres lo contasen a sus hijos», *Ya*, 25 August, n.p.

Medina Domínguez, A. (2001), *Exorcismos de la memoria: políticas y poéticas de la melancolíaa en la España de la transición* (Madrid: Ediciones Libertarias).

Mejías, L. (1943), 'Voces de alquiler', *Primer Plano*, 151, 5 September, n.p.

Merish, L. (1996), 'Cuteness and commodity aesthetics: Tom Thumb and Shirley Temple', in R. Garland Thompson (ed.), *Freakery: Cultural Spectacles of the Extraordinary Body* (New York and London: New York University Press), pp. 185–203.

Michaud, P.-A. (2004), *Aby Warburg and the Image in Motion*, trans. S. Hawkes (Cambridge, MA: MIT Press).

Miles, R. (2011), 'Reclaiming Revelation: Another Look at *Pan's Labyrinth* and *The Spirit of the Beehive*', *Quarterly Review of Film and Video*, 28 (2): 195–203.

Miller, T. (2003), 'The Burning Babe: Film Narrative and the Figures of Historical Witness', in A. Douglass and T. A. Vogler (eds), *Witness and Memory: The Discourse of Trauma* (New York: Routledge), pp. 207–232.

Mitchell, T. (1990), *Passional Culture: Emotion, Religion and Society in Southern Spain* (Philadelphia: University of Pennsylvania Press).

Mitchell, T. (1998), *Betrayal of the Innocents: Desire, Power and the Catholic Church in Spain* (Philadelphia: University of Pennsylvania Press).

Molins, M. V. (2008), *Alexia: experiencia de amor y dolor vivida por un adolescente* (Madrid: Planeta).

Montero, R. (1984), 'Prosoviética', *El País*, 15 December, http://elpais.com/diario/1984/12/15/ultima/471913204_850215.html (accessed 06.09.2012).

Montero, R. (2011), 'Never Mind the Bullfights', *The Guardian*, 30 March, www.guardian.co.uk/commentisfree/2011/mar/30/spains-changed-national-character (accessed 08.02.2012).

Morales (1961), 'Pepito Moratalla y Jaime Blanch de ayer a hoy', *Radiocinema*, 20 April, 22–23.

Morales, J. L. (1979a), 'Marisol nos cuenta su vida (1)', *Interviú*, 169: 25–28.

Morales, J. L. (1979b), 'Marisol nos cuenta su vida (2)', *Interviú*, 170: 28–31.

Morcillo, A. (2010), *The Seduction of Modern Spain: The Female Body and the Francoist Body Politic* (Bucknell: Bucknell University Press).

Moreno-Nuño, C. (2009), 'The Comic-strip of Historical Memory: An Analysis of Paracuellos by Carlos Giménez, in the Light of *Persépolis* by Marjane Satrapi and *Maus* by Art Spiegelman', *España en armas: Culture of Wars/War of Cultures*, ed. Antonio Gómez López-Quiñones, *Vanderbilt Journal of Luso-Hispanic Studies*, 4: 177–195

Morreall, J. and Loy, J. (1989), 'Kitsch and Aesthetic Education', *Journal of Aesthetic Education*, 2 (4): 63–73

Mortimore, R. (1975), 'Buñuel, Sáenz de Heredia and Filmófono', *Sight and Sound*, 44, Summer, 180–182.

Mulvey, L. (1975), 'Visual Pleasure and Narrative Cinema', *Screen*, 16 (3): 6–18.

Mulvey, L. (2005), *Death 24x a Second: Stillness and the Moving Image* (London: Reaktion Books).

Murray, A. (2010), *Giorgio Agamben* (London: Routledge).

Nágera, A. V. (1941), *Niños y jóvenes anormales*, Sociedad de Educación 'Atenas' (Madrid: S.A.).

Naremore, J. (1988), *Acting in the Cinema* (Berkeley: University of California Press).

Nash, M. (1994), 'Pronatalism and Motherhood in Franco's Spain', in G. Bock and P. Thane (eds), *Maternity and Gender Policies. Women and the Rise of the European Welfare States 1880s-1950s* (New York: Routledge), pp. 160–177.

Nora, P. (1989), 'Between Memory and History: Les Lieux de Mémoire', *Representations: Special Issue on Memory and Counter-memory*, 26, Spring, 7–24.

Nornes, A. M. (2007), *Cinema Babel: Translating Global Cinema* (Minneapolis: University of Minnesota Press).

Otero, L. (1999), *Mi mamá me mima* (Madrid: Plaza y Janés).

Palacios Lis, I. (2003), *Mujeres ignorantes: madres culpables. Adoctrinamiento y divulgación materno-infantil en la primera mitad del siglo XX* (Valencia: Universitat de Valencia).

Patino, B. M. (n.d.), 'Notas sobre *Canciones para después de una guerra*', www. basiliomartinpatino.com/escritos.htm (accessed 20.09.2012).

Pavlović, T. (2003), *Despotic Bodies and Transgressive Bodies: Spanish Culture from Francisco Franco to Jesús Franco* (New York: SUNY Press).

Pavlović, T. (2011), *The Mobile Nation: España cambia de piel* (London: Intellect).

Perriam, C. (2003), *Stars and Masculinities in Spanish Cinema* (London: Palgrave Macmillan).

Perriam, C. (2008), '*El espíritu de la colmena* (Víctor Erice, 1973)', in J. R. Resina (ed.), *Burning Darkness: A Half Century of Spanish Cinema* (New York: SUNY Press), pp. 61–82.

Philo, C. (2003), '"To Go Back Up the Side Hill": Memories, Imaginations and Reveries of Childhood', *Children's Geographies*, 1 (1): 7–23.

Pinto, D. (2004), 'Indoctrinating the Youth of Post-war Spain: A Discourse Analysis of a Fascist Civics Textbook', *Discourse Society*, 15 (5): 649–667.

Pío, G. V. (1962), 'Luis Lucia presenta a Rocío Durcal', *Primer Plano*, 26 January, n.p.

Pollock, G. (2009), 'Art/Trauma/Representation', *Parallax*, 15 (1): 40–54.

Preston, P. (2012), *The Spanish Holocaust: Inquisition and Extermination in Twentieth-Century Spain* (London: Harper Press).

Prout, R. (2005), '*Marcelino, pan y vino*/The Miracle of Marcelino', in A. Mira, *The Cinema of Spain and Portugal* (London: Wallflower), pp. 71–78.

Prout, R. (2008), 'Cryptic Triptych: (Re)Reading Disabilities in Spanish Film 1960–2003: *El cochecito*; *El jardín de las delicias* and *Planta cuarta*', *Arizona Journal of Hispanic Cultural Studies*, 22: 165–187.

Pulver, A. (2000), 'Butterfly's Tongue', *The Guardian*, 28 July. http://film.guardian.co.uk/News_Story/Critic_Review/Guardian_review/0,,347809,00.html (accessed 05.01.2012).

Quesada, L. (1962), 'Marisol, operada', *Primer Plano*, 19 January, n.p.

Radstone, S. (2000), 'Screening Trauma: *Forrest Gump*, Film and Memory', in S. Radstone (ed.), *Memory and Methodology* (Oxford: Berg), pp. 79–107.

Rebello, S. (1990), *Hitchcock and the Making of Psycho* (New York: W. W. Norton).

Renshaw, L. (2011), *Exhuming Loss: Memory, Materiality and Mass Graves of the Spanish Civil War* (Walnut Creek, CA: Left Coast Press).

Richards, M. (2005), 'Ideology and the Psychology of War Children in Franco's Spain, 1936–1945', in K. Ericsson and E. Simonsen (eds), *Children of World War II: The Hidden Enemy Legacy* (Oxford: Berg), pp. 115–137.

Riley, E. C. (1984), 'The Story of Ana in *El espíritu de la colmena*', *Bulletin of Hispanic Studies*, 61 (4): 491–497.

Rollan (1969), 'Rocío Durcal: un "pichi" de nuevo estilo', *Miss: Semanario de actualidad*, 113, 30 May, 12–14.

Rollan (1970), 'La boda de Rocío Durcal y Junior', *Miss*, 147, 23 January, 20–30.

Romano, J. (1936), 'El cine ha convertido en realidad los sueños de los niños porque todos quieren ser como Spanky', *Cinegramas*, 77, 1 March, n.p.

Romo, A. (1962), 'Estrellita: nueva tracción de nuestro cine', *Radiocinema*, 1 November, 28–29.

Romo, A. (1963), '23 años de cine con Ana Mariscal', *Radiocinema*, 31 January, 35–38.

Rose, J. (1992), *The Case of Peter Pan, or the Impossibility of Children's Fiction* (Philadelphia: University of Pennsylvania Press).

Rose, J. (2009), *Studying The Devil's Backbone* (London: Auteur).

Ruíz, R. (2005), '*El Bola* se hace mayor', *El País*, 9 October, www.elpais.com/articulo/portada/Bola/hace/mayor/elpeputec/20051009elpepspor_2/Tes (accessed 07.06.2011).

Rushdie, S. (1992), *The Wizard of Oz* (London: BFI).

Sánchez-Silva, J. M. (1969), *Marcelino pan y vino y otras narraciones* (Madrid: Salvat).

Sánchez Vidal, A. (1991), *El cine de Florián Rey* (Aragón: Caja de Ahorros de la Inmaculada).

Sanghera, R. (2010), 'Bow Wow', in S. Steinberg, M. Kehler and L. Cornish (eds), *Boy Culture: An Encyclopedia*, vol. 2 (Santa Barbara, CA: Greenwood Press), pp. 347–349.

Santa Eulalia, M. G. (1978), 'La era de los "niños prodigio" ha terminado', *ABC*, 4 January, 56.

Santner, E. (1990), *Stranded Objects: Mourning, Memory and Film in Postwar Germany* (Ithaca: Cornell University Press).

Savater, F. (1976), 'Prólogo', *El espíritu de la colmena. Víctor Erice and Ángel Fernández Santos* (Madrid: Elías Querejeta Producciones), pp. 9–26.

Schober, A. (2004), *Possessed Child Narratives in Literature and Film: Contrary States* (London: Palgrave Macmillan).

Segal, N. (2009), *Consensuality: Didier Anzieu, Gender and the Sense of Touch* (New York: Rodopi).

Seguin, J.-C. (1990), 'Joselito: la voix inhumaine', PhD thesis from the University of Bordeaux III.

Selzer, M. (1997), 'Wound Culture: Trauma in the Pathological Public Sphere', *October*, 80, Spring, 3–26.

Serrano, R. (1996), 'En busca del gen rojo', *El País*, 7 January, http://elpais.com/diario/1996/01/07/espana/820969222_850215.html (accessed 14.09.2012).

Shaviro, S. (2010), *Post-Cinematic Affect* (Winchester and Washington: O-Books).

Simmel, G. (1959), 'The Aesthetic Significance of the Face', in K. H. Wolff (ed.), *Essays, Philosophy and Aesthetics* (New York: Harper Torchbooks), pp. 276–281.

Sinyard, N. (1992), *Children in the Movies* (London: B. T. Batsford).

Skal, D. J. (1993), *The Monster Show: A Cultural History of Horror* (London: W.W. Norton & Co).

Smith, P. J. (2000a), *The Moderns: Time, Space and Subjectivity in Contemporary Spanish Culture* (Oxford: Oxford University Press).

Smith, P. J. (2000b), 'Butterfly's Tongue', *Sight and Sound*, September, 39–40.

Smith, P. J. (2003), 'El Bola', *Sight and Sound*, June, 38.

Smith, P. J. (2006), *Spanish Visual Culture: Cinema, Television, Internet* (Manchester: Manchester University Press).

Smith, P. J. (2007), '*Pan's Labyrinth* (El laberinto del fauno)', *Film Quarterly*, 60 (4): 4–9.

Smith, P. J. (2010), 'Students of Genre', *Film Quarterly*, 63 (4): 12–13.

Sobchack, V. (1990), '"Surge and Splendour": A Phenomenology of the Hollywood Historical Epic', *Representations*, 29, Winter, 24–49.

Sobchack, V. (1991), *The Address of the Eye: A Phenomenology of the Film Experience* (Princeton: Princeton University Press).

Sobchack, V. (1996), 'Introduction: History Happens', in V. Sobchack (ed.), *The Persistence of History: Cinema, Television and the Modern Event* (London: Routledge), pp. 1–14.

Sobchack, V. (2004), *Carnal Thoughts: Embodiment and Moving Image Culture* (Berkeley: University of California Press).

Sobchack, V. (2006), 'On (Not) Watching Horror Films', *Film Comment*, 235, July/August, 38–41.

Sobchack, V. (2008), 'Embodying Transcendence: On the Literal, the Material and the Cinematic Sublime', *Material Religion: The Journal of Objects, Art and Belief*, 4 (2): 194–203.

Solomon, R. C. (2004), 'On Kitsch and Sentimentality', in *In Defense of Sentimentality* (Oxford: Oxford University Press), pp. 235–254.

Sprengler, C. (2011), *Screening Nostalgia: Populuxe Props and Technicolor Aesthetics in Contemporary American Film* (Oxford: Berghahn Books).

Staiger, J. (1985), 'The Eyes Really Are the Focus: Photoplay Acting and Film Form and Style', *Wide Angle*, 6 (4): 14–23.

Steedman, C. (1995), *Strange Dislocations: Childhood and the Idea of Human Interiority 1780–1930* (London: Virago Press).

Steinberg, L. (1984), *The Sexuality of Christ in Renaissance Art and in Modern Oblivion* (London: Faber and Faber).

Steinberg, S. (2006), 'Franco's Kids: Geopolitics and Postdictatorship in *¿Quién puede matar a un niño?*', *Journal of Spanish Cultural Studies*, 7 (1): 23–36.

Stewart, G. (2007), *Framed Time: Toward a Postfilmic Cinema* (Chicago: University of Chicago Press).

Stewart, S. (1993), *On Longing: Narratives of the Miniature, the Gigantic, the Souvenir, the Collection* (Durham, NC: Duke University Press).

Stoichita, V. (2008), *The Pygmalion Effect: From Ovid to Hitchcock* (Chicago: University of Chicago Press).

Stone, R. (2001), *Spanish Cinema* (London: Longman).

Studlar, G. (2001), '"Oh Doll Divine!": Mary Pickford, Masquerade and the Pedophilic Gaze', *Camera Obscura*, 16 (3): 197–227.

Sturken, M. (1997), *Tangled Memories: The Vietnam War, the AIDS Epidemic, and the Politics of Remembering* (Berkeley: University of California Press).

Sturken, M. (1999), 'Narratives of Recovery: Repressed Memory as Cultural Memory', in M. Bal, J. Crew and L. Spitzer (eds), *Acts of Memory, Cultural Recall in the Present* (London: University Press of New England), pp. 231–248.

Taussig, M. (1999), *Defacement: Public Secrecy and the Labor of the Negative* (Palo Alto: Stanford University Press).

Taylor, D. (2003), *The Archive and the Repertoire: Performing Cultural Memory in the Americas* (Durham, NC and London: Duke University Press).

Taylor, J. R. (1972), *Graham Greene's Films* (New York: Simon and Schuster).

Tello, A. (1978), 'Antonio Mercero: Lolo García me imita como un animal mimético', *El periódico de Catalunya*, 24 December, 19.

Thomson, M. (2000), 'Reviews: Butterfly's Tongue', www.bbc.co.uk/films/2000/07/26/butterflys_tongue_review.shtml (accessed 05.01.2012).

Toboso, P. (2000), *Pepín Fernández 1891–1982. Galerías Preciados. El pionero de los grandes almacenes* (Madrid: Lid).

Torreiro, C. (1997), 'Cerca de la ciudad, 1952', in Julio Pérez Perucha (ed.), *Antología crítica del cine español 1906–1995* (Madrid: Cátedra), pp. 312–314.

Torres, M. (1983), 'El puño de Marisol', *El País*, 21 October, http://elpais.com/diario/1983/10/21/ultima/435538804_850215.html (accessed 06.09.2012).

Tremlett, G. (2008), 'Opus Dei Fury at Film of Saintly Girl's Death', *The Guardian*, 5 October, www.guardian.co.uk/world/2008/oct/05/religion.spain (accessed 08.08.2012).

Tremlett, G. (2011a), 'Hundreds of Spanish Babies "Stolen from Clinics and Sold for Adoption"', *The Guardian*, 27 January, www.guardian.co.uk/world/2011/jan/27/spanish-babies-stolen-clinic?INTCMP=SRCH (accessed 13.02.2012).

Tremlett, G. (2011b), 'Carlos Saura: Franco Took So Long to Die We Had Time to Buy Champagne', *The Guardian*, 24 June, www.guardian.co.uk/film/2011/jun/24/carlos-saura-raise-ravens-franco-spain (accessed 20.08.2012).

Triana-Toribio, N. (2003), *Spanish National Cinema* (London: Routledge).

Turkle, S. (2011), *Alone Together: Why We Expect More from Technology and Less from Each Other* (New York: Tantor Media).

Tusell, J. (1988), *La dictadura de Franco* (Madrid: Alianza Editorial).

Umbral, F. (1963), 'Fin de semana: Marisol', *Mundo Hispánico*, 180, March, 26–31.

Umbral, F. (1976), 'Marisol vista por Francisco Umbral', *Interviú*, 20.

Umbral, F. (1991), 'Marisol, sociología de una ninfa', in *Crónica de esa guapa gente: memorias de la jet* (Barcelona: Planeta), pp. 17–19.

Unamuno, M. de (1998), *Recuerdos de niñez y mocedad* (Madrid: Alianza Editorial).

Uzal, M. (2007), 'Le Regard fixe de l'enfance: à propos de *L'Ésprit de la ruche*', in S. Pras (ed.), *Víctor Erice, Abbas Kiarostami: Correspondances* (Paris: Editions du Centre Pompidou), p. 60.

Valentine, G. (1996), 'Angels and Devils: Moral Landscapes of Childhood', *Environment and Planning D: Society and Space*, 14 (5): 581–599.

Valentine, G. (2004), *Public Space and the Culture of Childhood* (London: Ashgate).

Van-Alphen, E. (2002), 'Caught by Images: On the Role of Visual Imprints in Holocaust Testimonies', *Journal of Visual Culture*, 1 (2): 205–221.

Vattimo, G. (1992), *The Transparent Society* (Baltimore: Johns Hopkins University Press).

Vázquez Montalbán, M. (1986), *Crónica sentimental de España* (Madrid: Espasa Calpe).

Vicent, A. (1981), *Retratos de la transición* (Madrid: Penthalon).

Vilarós, T. (2005), 'Banalidad y biopolítica: la transición española y el nuevo orden del mundo', *Desacuerdos*, 2: 29–56.

Vincent, M. (1999), 'The Martyrs and the Saints: Masculinity and the Construction of the Francoist Crusade', *History Workshop Journal*, 47: 68–98.

Vinyes, R. (2010), *Irredentas: Las presas políticas y sus hijos en las cárceles franquistas* (Madrid: Ediciones Planeta).

Vinyes, R., Armengou, M. and Belis, R. (2003), *Los niños perdidos del franquismo* (Barcelona: Plaza & Janés).

Walker Bynum, C. (2011), *Christian Materiality: An Essay on Religion in Late Medieval Europe* (Cambridge, MA: MIT Press).

Wardi, D. (1992), *Memorial Candles: Children of the Holocaust* (London: Routledge).

Warner, M. (2000), *No Go, The Bogeyman: Scaring, Lulling and Making Mock* (London: Vintage).

Watt, N. (2008), 'Camino de Javier Fesser y la verdadera historia de Alexia', 24 October, www.zenit.org/es/articles/camino-de-javier-fesser-y-la-verdadera-histo ria-de-alexia (accessed 08.08.2012).

Weiss, G. (1999), *Body Images: Embodiment as Incorporeality* (London: Routledge).

Wheeler, D. (2009), 'Godard's List: Why Spielberg and Auschwitz are Number One', *Media History*, 15 (2): 185–203.

Wheeler, D. (2012), 'The Representation of Domestic Violence', *Modern Language Review*, 107: 438–500.

Whittaker, T. (2012), 'Soundscapes of Resistance in the Quinqui Film', in R. Stone and L. Shaw (eds), *Singing Signs: Screening Songs in Hispanic and Lusophone Cinema* (Manchester: University of Manchester Press).

Willemen, P. (1994), 'Through the Glass Darkly: Cinephilia Reconsidered', in *Looks and Frictions: Essays in Cultural Studies and Film Theory* (London and Bloomington: British Film Institute and Indiana University Press), pp. 223–258.

Wilson, E. (2003), *Cinema's Missing Children* (London: Wallflower).

Wilson, E. (2005), 'Children, Emotion and Viewing in Contemporary European Film', *Screen* (special edition on the child, ed. K. Lury), 46 (3): 329–340.

Winnicott, D. W. (1980), *Playing and Reality* (New York: Penguin).

Wojcik-Andrews, I. (2007), *Children's Films: History, Ideology, Pedagogy, Theory* (London: Taylor and Francis).

Wood, G. (2002), *Edison's Eve: A Magical History of the Quest for Mechanical Life* (London: Random House).

Wright, S. (2005), 'Dropping the Mask: Theatricality and Absorption in Sáenz de Heredia's *Don Juan* (1950)', *Screen*, 46 (4): 415–431.

Wright, S. (2007), 'Haunting, "Doubling" and the Undoing of Francoist Aesthetics in Albert Boadella's *¡Buen viaje, Excelencia!* (2003)', *Contemporary Theatre Review*, 17 (3): 313–320.

Wright, S. (2008), 'El niño en peligro y otras piezas de lo real en *El cebo* (1958) de Ladislao Vajda', *Secuencias*, 28: 27–45.

Wright, S. (2013a), 'Ana Torrent as Palimpsest in Elio Quiroga's *No Do/The Haunting* (2009)', in F. Canet and D. Wheeler (eds), *New Trends in Contemporary Spanish Cinema* (Bristol: Intellect).

Wright, S. (2013b), 'De Alexia Ventura a Pitusín: Género, nación y actuación en dos estrellas infantiles del primer cine español', in F. Vilches-de Frutos and P. Nieva-de la Paz (eds), *Imágenes Femeninas en la Literatura Española y las Artes Escénicas (Siglos XX – XXI)* (Temple, Philadelphia: Society of Spanish and Spanish-American Studies), pp. 121–134.

Yampolsky, M. and Joseph, L. P. (1993), 'Voice Devoured: Artaud and Borges on Dubbing', *October*, 64: 57–77.

Yarza, A. (2004), 'The Petrified Tears of General Franco: Kitsch and Fascism in José Luis Sáenz De Heredia's *Raza*', *Journal of Spanish Cultural Studies*, 5 (1): 49–66.

Young, I. M. (2005), *On Female Body Experience: 'Throwing Like a Girl' and Other Essays* (New York and Oxford: Oxford University Press).

Young-Bruehl, E. (2002), *Freud On Women: A Reader* (London: Vintage).

Yubero, C. and Conde, J. (1996), *La España de Mariquita Pérez* (Madrid: Aguilar).

Zelizer, V. A. (1985), *Pricing the Priceless Child: The Changing Social Value of Children* (Princeton: Princeton University Press).

Ziolkowski, E. (2001), *Evil Children in Religion, Literature and Art* (London: Palgrave Macmillan).

Žižek, S. (1996), '"I Hear You With My Eyes", or The Invisible Master', in R. Salecl and S. Žižek (eds), *Gaze and Voice as Love Objects* (Durham, NC and London: Duke University Press), pp. 90–128.

Zornado, J. (2006), *Inventing the Child: Culture, Ideology and the Story of Childhood* (London: Routledge).

Index

Note: 'n.' after a page reference indicates the number of a note on that page

Abadal, Baltasar 19n.11
   Tenacidad /Tenacity 19n.11
Alice in Wonderland 122, 148
Alonso, Luis R. 7
   buenaventura de Pitusín, La/Pitusín's
      Good Fortune vi, 5, 6, 7,
      19n.13, 19n.17
Almodóvar, Pedro 11, 19, 20n.23, 50,
      55n.20, 74, 75, 122, 128n.32,
      153
   Hable con ella/Talk to Her 128n.32
   Matador 74, 75
   Mujeres al borde de un ataque de
      nervios/Women on the Verge of
      a Nervous Breakdown 50
   piel que habito, La/The Skin I Live In
      122
   Todo sobre mi madre/All About My
      Mother 19, 55n.20, 137, 140
Alvarez, Paquito 7
   Vidas rotas/Broken Lives see
      Fernández Ardavín, Eusebio
Amadori, Luis César 66
   Como dos gotas de agua/Like Two
      Peas in a Pod 66
   Cristina Guzmán 66
Amenábar, Alejandro 4, 118
   The Others 4, 118
Amnesty Law 13
Amo, Antonio del 52
   ¿Chico o chica?/Girl or boy?
      87n.10
   gemelas, Las/The Twins 87n.10
   pequeño ruiseñor, El/The Little
      Nightingale 52, 53

'Angelito' (Angel Gómez Matteo)
      87n.10
   Pachín see Ruiz Castillo, Arturo
Aranda, Vicente 87n.16
   Fata Morgana 87n.16
archive 3, 13, 15, 61, 85, 86n.7, 125,
      158
Armendáriz, Montxo 19, 107, 132
   Historias del Kronen/Stories from the
      Kronen 132
   Secretos del corazón/Secretos of the
      Heart 19, 107, 108, 110, 123
Armiñán, Jaime de 76, 80
   Carola de día, Carola de noche/
      Carola By Day, Carola By Night
      76
   nido, El/The Nest 80
Asimov, Isaac 1, 18n.1
automata 1, 2, 3, 11, 12, 13, 17, 18,
      20n.24, 20n.25, 35, 143
Avelina (Avelina Ruiz) 7
   ¡Muñecas!/Dolls! see Roncoroni,
      Mario
   virgen del mar, La/The Virgin of the
      Sea see Roncoroni, Mario
Aznar, Adolfo 7
   Pupín y sus amigos/Pupín and His
      Friends 7

Baby Peggy (Diana Serra Carey) 6
Balañá, Pedro 130
   último sábado, El/The Last Saturday
      130
Ballesta, Juan José 11, 131, 133, 141,
      154n.3

Ballesta, Juan José *(cont.)*
    Bola,El/Ball-bearing see Mañas,
      Achero
    Planta cuarta/The Fourth Floor see
      Mercero, Antonio
Baquero, Ivana 11, 120
    laberinto del fauno, El/Pan's
      Labyrinth see Toro, Guillermo
      del
Bardem, José Antonio 76
    corrupción de Chris Miller, La/The
      Corruption of Chris Miller
      76–7
    poder del deseo, El/The Power of
      Desire 77
Bayona, Juan Antonio vi, 4, 11
    orfanato, El/The Orphanage vi, 4,
      11, 17, 112, 113, 116, 118
Becker, Wolfgang 11
    Goodbye Lenin 11
Belén, Ana 11, 17, 66
    Zampo y yo/Zampo and Me see
      Lucia, Luis
Beringola, Francisco 7
    Corazón de reina/Heart of a Queen 7
Berlanga, Luis García 55
    Plácido 55
Blanch, Jaime 36, 53, 56n.25
    Caballero andaluz. El/An Andalusian
      Gentleman see Lucia, Luis
Boadella, Albert 21
    ¡Buen viaje, Excelencia!/Have a
      Good Trip Your Excellency! 21
Bollaín, Iciar 154
    Te doy mis ojos/I Give You My Eyes
      154
Buchs, José 5, 20
    abuelo, El/The Grandfather 5,
      19n.12
    medalla del torero, La/The Matador's
      Medal 20
Buñuel, Luis 8, 20n.19
    ¡Centilela alerta! /Attention on the
      Watch! see Gremillón, Jean
    ¿Quién me quiere a mí?/Who Loves
      Me? see Sáenz de Heredia, José
      Luis
    Tierra sin pan/Land Without Bread
      8

Cabello Lapiedra, Javier 20n.17
    pata del muñeco, La/The Doll's Foot
      20n.17
Cabero, Antoñito 6
Cabero, Juan Antonio 7
    Estudiantes y modistillas/Students
      and Seamstresses 7
Calvo, Pablito vi, 4, 10, 19, 23, 28, 32,
    35, 42, 44, 45, 47, 48, 49, 52,
    55n.14, 56n.26, 89
    Marcelino, pan y vino/The Miracle of
      Marcelino see Vajda, Ladislao
    Mi tío Jacinto/My Uncle Jacinto see
      Vajda, Ladislao
Camacho, Nerea vi, 11, 142, 143,
    154n.3
    Camino see Fesser, Javier
Camus, Mario 83, 130
    días del pasado, Los/Days of the Past
      83, 84
    Young Sánchez 130
Cantudo, María José 78, 81
Caravaggio
    Narcissus 124
Castro, Maleni 87n.10
    ¿Chico o chica?/Boy or Girl see Amo,
      Antonio del
    gemelas, Las/The Twins see Amo,
      Antonio del
caza, La/The Hunt see Saura, Carlos
censorship 10, 15, 25, 43, 44, 50, 66,
    76, 143, 155n.9
Chaplin, Charles 5, 66, 76
    The Kid 5
Chaplin, Geraldine 97, 116
    Cría cuervos/Raise Ravens see Saura,
      Carlos
    Orfanato, El/The Orphanage see
      Bayona, Juan Antonio
child evacuees 10, 14
    Children of Spain 10
    Elai-Alai see Sobrevila, Nemesio
    Guernika see Sobrevila, Nemesio
    Llegada de niños españoles a
      Veracruz/Arrival of Spanish
      Children in Veracruz 10
    Niños españoles en Méjico/Spanish
      Children in Mexico 10
    Nuevos amigos/New Friends 10

children's sexuality 19n.2, 34, 55n.19,
    57n.36, 80, 101, 104, 105
child sexual abuse 14, 21n.30, 60, 85,
    122, 153, 154, 154n.6
'Chispita' (Román González) 9
    Aurora de esperanza/Dawn of Hope
      see Sau, Antonio
Chomón, Segundo de 2, 4, 18n.5
    hotel eléctrico, El/The Electric Hotel
      2
    Magic Bricks 2
    Metempsychose 2
    teatro eléctrico de Bob, El/ Bob's
      Electric Theatre 2
Cinderella 62, 71, 142, 149
Civil Guard 108, 123, 124
Cloche, Maurice 25
    Monsieur Vincent 25
    Peppino e Violetta/Never Take No
      For An Answer 25
Colomer, Francesc vi, 11, 123, 156,
    159n.2
    Pa negre/Black Bread see Villaronga,
      Agustí
commodity culture 27, 28, 32, 38, 39,
    40, 41, 47, 63, 64, 69
    Corte Inglés, El (department store)
      56n.27
    Galerías Preciados (department store)
      39, 40, 56n.27
Comas, Marina 156
    Pa negre/Black Bread see Villaronga,
      Agustí
Connor, Steven 3, 42, 133, 134
Coogan, Jackie 5, 6
    Coogan Law 6
Cuerda, José Luis 107, 109, 110, 123
    girasoles ciegos, Los/ The Blind
      Sunflowers 123, 126
    lengua de las mariposas, La/
      Butterfly's Tongue 107, 109,
      110, 124, 125, 126
cute 6, 32, 35, 36, 37, 38, 40, 41,
    55n.19, 67, 109, 127n.21, 155n.8
cyborg 3, 12, 17, 131, 139, 143, 157

Dalí, Salvador 59, 60
    The Metamorphosis of Narcissus
      114, 115, 116

Shirley Temple, The Youngest, Most
    Sacred Monster of Her Time 59
Deleuze, Gilles 16, 17, 28, 95, 100,
    127n.13, 138, 157
Delgado, Fernando 10
    granujas, Los/The Rogues 19n.17
    Lluvia de hijos/Raining Kids 10
Delgrás, Gonzalo 10
    Cristina Guzmán 10
desarrollismo 27, 29, 71, 72
destape 11, 17, 77, 80, 81, 88n.21,
    130
Díez del Corral, Pedro 11, 145
Doane, Mary Ann 2, 28, 29, 41, 42, 45,
    46, 48, 61
dolls 3, 7, 17, 18, 20n.19, 21n.25, 26,
    28, 37, 38, 60, 62, 63, 65, 118,
    157
    Mariquita Pérez 60, 62, 63
    Mariví 63
dubbing viii, 17, 27, 41–52, 57n.31,
    57n.32, 57n.33. 64, 158
    Artaud on 45, 49
dubbing artists 42, 44, 45, 52, 57n.31,
    58n.42
    anonymity of 44–5
    Conesa, Matilde 45
    Ovíes, José María 42
    Torcal, Sélica 44, 45, 52, 58n.42
    Vilariño, Matilde 42, 44, 45
Durcal, Rocío 11, 17, 66, 74, 78,
    87n.10, 87n.11, 88n.18

Elorrieta, José María 88n.19
    Milagro del sacristán, El/The Altar
      Boy's Miracle 88n.19
Elsaesser, Thomas 18n.7, 21n.33, 42,
    61, 62, 93, 95, 119, 121, 156,
    158
Erburu, Andoni 107, 154n3
    Secretos del corazón/Secrets of the
      Heart see Armendáriz, Montxo
Erice, Víctor vi, 4, 11, 17, 18n.10,
    19n.10, 89, 90, 91, 94, 95,
    96, 97, 98, 99, 101, 120, 121,
    127n.6, 140, 152
    espíritu de la colmena, El/The Spirit
      of the Beehive vi, 4, 11, 17,
      18n.10, 19, 43, 89–102, 107,

Erice, Víctor *(cont.)*
    109, 111, 117, 122, 124, 156,
    157
    sur, El/The South 19n.10, 96
España, Pepito 7
    calumnia, La/Slander see Ruiz
      Rivelles, Luis
españolada 8, 72, 88n.17, 106
Estrellita (Isabel Rincón Bautista) 11,
    17, 66, 87n.13
    Han robado una estrella/A Star Has
      Been Stolen see Setó, Javier

Fabrizi, Aldo 24
    Maestro, El/The Teacher 24, 33, 34,
      36, 38, 44, 46, 52
face 2, 5, 6, 8, 10, 11, 13, 16, 18n.3,
    26–8, 32, 34, 35, 39, 42, 46, 48,
    49, 56n.26, 60, 67, 71, 72, 75,
    83, 89, 95, 96, 99, 101, 102,
    104, 105, 109, 110, 112, 120,
    121, 125, 126, 127n.3, 128n.31,
    132, 133, 134, 141, 143, 147,
    150, 154, 154n.3, 156
Fellini, Federico 25
    Dolce Vita, La 103
Fernández Ardavín, César 34, 44, 46,
    130
    Lazarillo de Tormes, El(1959)/
      Lazarillo of Tormes 34, 44, 46,
      130
Fernández Ardavín, Eusebio 7
    Forja de almas/Forging Souls 10
    Vidas rotas/Broken Lives 7
Fernán Gómez, Fernando 57n.33, 76,
    99, 109, 124
Ferrer, Mel 60
    Cabriola/Prancer 60
Fesser, Javier vi, 11, 130, 141, 142, 144,
    149, 150, 151, 152, 155n.11
    Camino 11, 130, 141–53, 155n.11
    gran aventura de Mortadelo y
      Filemón, La/Mortadelo and
      Filemón's Great Adventure 141
Fleming, Victor 49, 148
    The Wizard of Oz 49, 78, 122, 148,
      155n.10
Franco, Carmencita (María del Carmen
    Franco y Polo) 50

Franco, Francisco 10, 29, 30, 31, 36,
    50, 56n.27, 67, 68, 83, 87n.14,
    90, 93
    death of 13, 15, 21, 77, 78, 93, 94,
      97, 102, 105, 106
    death wish towards 15, 21, 93, 106
    nostalgia for Francoism 14, 15,
      21n.28, 61
Frankenstein 3, 18, 91, 94, 95, 96, 97,
    98, 99, 100, 101, 115, 127
    Frankenstein (James Whale) 3, 89,
      95, 97, 100, 101
      Dr Frankenstein 97
      cinema as 'Frankensteinian
        dream' 2, 17
      Frankenstein's monster 3, 18, 91,
        94, 95, 96, 98, 99, 100, 115, 127
    Frankenstein (Mary Shelley) 91
Freud, Sigmund 15, 21n.36, 35, 91, 97,
    105, 118
Fuente, Valeria de la 7
    Estudiantes y modistillas/Students
      and Seamstresses see Cabero,
      Juan Antonio

Gades, Antonio 74, 77, 80, 83, 84
Galbó. Cristina 11, 145
    Del rosa al amarillo/From Pink… To
      Yellow see Summers, Manuel
García, Lolo 11, 43, 80, 81, 82, 83, 88,
    155
    guerra de papá,La/Daddy's War see
      Mercero, Antonio
    Tobi, el niño con alas/Toby, the
      Boy With Wings see Mercero,
      Antonio
García Ascot, Jomi 98
    balcón vacío, El/The Empty Balcony
      98
García Cardona, Angel 4
    ciego de la aldea, El/The Blindman of
      the Village 4
Gargallo, Francisco 6–7
    Sor Angélica/Sister Angelica 7
Gargallo, Luisita 6
    tía Ramona, La/Aunt Ramona see
      Winter, Nick
Gay, Cesc 132, 135
    Krámpack 132, 135

Gil, Miguelito 10, 32, 34, 39, 47
  Recluta con niño/Recruit With Child
    see Ramirez, Pedro Luiz
  traje blanco, Un/The Miracle of the
    White Suit see Gil, Rafael
Gil, Rafael 24, 51, 119
  Murió hace quince años/He Died
    Fifteen Years Ago 51, 119
  señora de Fátima, La/Our Lady of
    Fatima 151
  traje blanco, Un/The Miracle of the
    White Suit 51, 119
Gimpera, Teresa 73, 87n.16, 99
Girelli, Arturito 7
  Sor Angélica/Sister Angelica see
    Gargallo, Luisita
golfos, Los/The Delinquents see Saura,
  Carlos
González, Valentín, R. 8, 9
  ¡Nosotros somos así/That's How We
    Are! 8, 9
González Barros, Alexia 142, 144,
  148, 149, 150, 151, 152, 154,
  155n.11
Goya, Francisco 136
  Saturn 136
Goyanes, Carlos 74, 76
Goyanes, Manuel 59, 60, 61, 66, 68, 76
Goyas 11, 44, 55n.11, 122, 123,
  127n.7, 131, 141, 154n.3, 156
Grau, Jorge 77–8
  Trastienda, La/The Backroom 77–8
Greene, Grahame 20n.22, 59
Gremillón, Jean 8
  ¡Centinela, alerta!/Attention on the
    Watch! 8
Guerra, Armando 8
  Carne de fieras/Wild Beasts 8

historical consciousness 14, 92, 93, 94,
  102, 127n.8
  historical memory 14, 119, 121, 122,
    125, 152, 157, 158
Hitchcock, Alfred 49, 66, 76, 87n.12
  Psycho 49, 76, 87n.12
  Vertigo 66
horror genre 27, 49, 89, 94, 97, 99,
  101, 102, 104, 105, 116, 122,
  127n.19

horrors of Spain's past 17, 94, 97, 102,
  117, 119, 124, 152, 157, 158

Ibáñez Serrador, Narciso 102
  Historias para no dormir/Stories to
    Keep You Awake 102
  residencia, La/The Dorm 102
  ¿Quién puede matar a un niño?/Who
    Can Kill a Child? 102–4, 116,
    119
Iglesia, Alex de la 20n.23, 128n.31
  Balada triste de trompeta/The Last
    Circus 20n.23, 128n.31
innocence 4, 17, 28, 30, 31, 39, 48, 64,
  82, 85, 89, 90, 94, 102, 104,
  105, 106, 107, 109, 110, 112,
  126, 129, 133, 148
Intertextuality 4, 74, 94, 111, 112, 114,
  116, 118, 122
Iquino, Ignacio 130
  Camino cortado/Closed Exit 130
  golfo que vio una estrella, El/The
    Good-For-Nothing Who Saw a
    Star 33, 34, 35, 38, 47
  travesuras de Morucha, Las/
    Morucha's Mischief 56n.21

Joselito (José Jiménez Fernández) 4, 10,
  19, 23, 52–3, 58n.42, 71
  pequeño ruiseñor, El/The Little
    Nightingale see Amo, Antonio
    del

Labanyi, Jo 8, 14, 20n.21, 21n.27,
  21n.35, 32, 33, 34, 35, 92, 93,
  152, 155n.14
Landsberg, Alison 12, 13, 14, 15, 100,
  101, 107, 108, 117, 157
  see also memory, prosthetic
  memory
Lang, Fritz 143
  Metropolis 143
Lanzman, Claude 93
  Shoah 93, 112
Larrañaga, Carlitos 33
  Pequeñeces/Little Trifles see Orduña,
    Juan de
Law of Historical Memory (2007) 14,
  93

Law of Political Responsibilities (1939) 13
Lazaga, Pedro 31
   Aprendiendo a morir/Learning To Die 88
   Operación plus ultra/Operation Beyond 31, 56n.27
León de Aranoa, Fernando 128, 132
   Barrio/Neighbourhood 132
   lunes al sol, Los/Mondays in the Sun 128
ley de género 131
Lozano, Manuel vi, 109, 127n.
   lengua de las mariposas, La/Butterfly's Tongue see Cuerda, José Luis
Lucia, Luis vi, 24, 47, 53, 62, 63, 66, 67
   caballero andaluz, Un/An Andalusian Gentleman 53, 130
   Canción de juventud/Song for Youth 66, 87n.10
   Cerca de la ciudad/Close to the City 24, 33, 34, 35, 39, 47, 51, 129
   Ha llegado un ángel/An Angel Has Appeared 56n.22, 63, 68, 71, 86n.4
   novicia soñadora, La/The Dreaming Novice 66
   piyayo, El 130
   rayo de luz, Un/A Ray of Light vi, 60, 62, 63, 67, 68, 86n.4
   Solos los dos/Just the Two of Us 74
   Tómbola/Tombola 66, 68, 69, 70, 71
   Zampo y yo/Zampo and Me 66
Lumière, Louis 2, 18n.4, 139
   Arrival of a Train at a Station 138
   Repas de bébé/Feeding the Baby 2

Madonna and Child 6, 35, 36, 38, 46, 55n.20, 87n.15, 137, 138
Maíllo, Kike 1, 2, 11, 12, 159n.1
   Eva 1, 2, 3, 11, 12, 13
Mañas, Achero 11, 130, 131, 136, 138
   Bola, El/Ball-bearing 11, 130, 131–41, 154n.3

Todo lo que tú quieras/Your Heart's Desire 137
Marey, Etienne-Jules 2, 60
Mariscal, Ana 130, 154n.1
   camino, El/The Path 80
   Segundo López, aventurero urbano/Segundo Lopez, Urban Adventurer 130, 154n.1
Marisol (Pepa Flores) vi, 4, 11, 17, 19, 23, 59–80, 83–6, 86n.2, 86n.3, 86n.4, 86n.5, 86n.6, 86n.8, 87n.13, 88n.18, 88n.21, 126n.1, 158
   Búsqueme a esa chica/Get that girl for me see Palacios, Fernando
   Cabriola/Prancer see Ferrer, Mel
   Ha llegado un ángel/An Angel Has Appeared see Lucia, Luis
   nueva Cenicienta, La/The New Cinderella see Sherman, George
   rayo de luz, Un/A Ray of Light see Lucia, Luis
   Solos los dos/Just the Two of Us see Lucia, Luis
   Tómbola/Tombola see Lucia, Luis
Mari Tere (Antoñita Barboso) 8, 20n.19, 20n.20
   ¿Quién me quiere a mí?/Who Loves me? see Sáenz de Heredia, José Luis
Marro, Alberto 5, 19n.11
   Alexia o la niña del misterio/Alexia, child of mystery 19n.11
   beso de la muerta, El/The Kiss of the Dead Woman 19n.11
   Elva 19n.11
   misterios de Barcelona, Los/The Barcelona Mysteries 19n.11
   secta de los misteriosos, La/The Mysterious Sect 5, 154n.4
   testamento de Diego Rocafort, El/Diego Rocafort's Will 19n.11
Martínez, Luisito 10
   Cristina Guzmán see Delgrás, Gonzalo
Martinez Beringola, Pepito 7
   Corazón de reina/Heart of a Queen see Beringola, Francisco

martyrdom 24, 141, 142, 147, 150, 151, 152, 154
Masó, Pedro 31
  familia bien, gracias, La/The Family's Fine, Thanks 31
Méliès, Georges 2, 18
  Pygmalion 18
memory 1, 4, 11, 12, 13, 14, 15, 16, 18n.9, 21n.25, 41, 50, 65, 69, 74, 84, 89, 90, 154, 157
  amnesia 14, 21n.27, 69, 112, 158
  false memory 85–6, 101, 122, 154
  implanted memory 1, 12, 13, 15, 85
  prosthetic memory 1, 3, 12, 13, 14, 15, 17, 18, 21n.33, 85, 92, 94, 97, 100, 101, 107, 108, 115, 120, 122, 125
Mercero, Antonio 11, 80, 81, 82, 88n.20, 146, 154n.3, 155n.8
  guerra de papá, La/Daddy's War 11, 80, 81, 88n.20
  Planta cuarta/The Fourth Floor 154n.3
  Se necesita chico/Boy Wanted 146, 154–5n.8
  Tobi, el niño con alas/Toby, the Boy with Wings 11, 80, 81, 82
Mills, Hayley 66, 86n.3, 87n.13
  Parent Trap, The see Swift, David
  Pollyanna see Swift, David
Millais, John Everett 77
  Cherry Ripe 77
Moreno Alba, Rafael 83
  Mariana Pineda 83, 84
Moratalla, Pepe 10, 32, 33, 34, 35, 36, 47, 56n.25
  Cerca de la ciudad/Close to the City see Lucia, Luis
  golfo que vio una estrella, El/The Good-For-Nothing Who Saw a Star see Iquino, Ignacio
  Sucedió en mi aldea/It Happened In My Village see Santillán, Antonio
'Morucha' 56n.21
  travesuras de Morucha, Las/Morucha's Mischief see Iquino, Ignacio

Mulvey, Laura 3, 16, 61
  Death, 24 x Per Second 3, 61
Murillo, Bartolomé Esteban 40
  Adoration of the Magi, The 40
musical 4, 8, 9, 23, 52–3, 60, 71, 72, 78
Muybridge, Eadweard 2, 99

Nieves Conde José Antonio 10, 129
  Surcos/Furrows 10, 129
niño perdido (lost child) 14, 21, 119, 152
NO-DO (Noticiarios y Documentales) 28, 30, 48, 52, 106, 116, 119, 128n.23, 128n.25
Nuri, Alicia 6

Opus Dei 130, 142, 143, 147, 148, 149, 150, 151, 152, 155n.13
  Escrivá de Balaguer, José María 142
Orduña, Juan de 33
  Pequeñeces/Little Trifles 33
orphan 6, 14, 23, 24, 25, 26, 32, 34, 36, 47, 50, 51, 53, 55n.18, 57n.40, 60, 66, 93, 98, 107
  orphaned nation 107
  orphanage 4, 39, 47, 112, 113, 114, 115, 118, 119
Ozon, François 81
  Ricky 81

Pabst, G.W. 25
  Pandora's Box 25
  Pequeñeces/Little Trifles 33
pact of silence 13
Padrós, Antoni 78
  Shirley Temple Story 78
Palacios, Fernando 30
  Búsqueme a esa chica/Get That Girl For Me 73
  familia y uno más, La/The Great Family Plus One 30
  gran familia, La/The Great Family 30, 39, 57n.28
  Marisol, rumbo a Río/Marisol, destination Rio see Palacios, Fernando
Palacios, Manuel 61
  Marisol, la película/Marisol, The Film 61

Patino, Basilio Martín 50, 57n.39
   *Canciones para después de una
      guerra/Songs For After a War*
      57n.39
   Caudillo 50
Paoletti, Marcos 10, 32, 34, 44, 46
   Lazarillo de Tormes, El(1959)/
      Lazarillo of Tormes see
      Fernández Ardavín, César
   maestro, El/The Teacher see Fabrizi,
      Aldo
performance 6, 8, 27–8, 36, 46–8, 59,
      62, 63–4, 89–90, 95–6, 98–102,
      104–5, 125–6, 126n.1, 127n.21,
      132, 140–1, 143, 159n.2
Perojo, Benito 20
   Corazones sin rumbo/Drifting Hearts
      20
   Malvaloca/Hollyhock 20
Picasso, Pablo 114
   Guernica 114
Pickford, Mary 5, 19n.12
Pili y Mili (Aurora and Pilar Bayona)
      11, 17, 65, 66
   *Como dos gotas de agua/Like Two
      Peas in a Pod see* Amadori, Luis
      César
Pinocchio 2, 3, 18, 46
'Pitusín' (Alfredo Hurtado) vi, 5–6, 7,
      19n.13, 19n.17
   *Agustina de Aragón/Agustina of
      Aragon see* Rey, Florián
   *buenaventura de Pitusín, La/Pitusín's
      Good Fortune see* Alonso, Luis
      R.
   chavala, La/The Lass see Rey, Florián
   Dolores, La/Dolores see Rey, Florián
   granujas, Los/The Rogues see
      Delgado, Fernando
   *Lazarillo de Tormes, El/Lazarillo of
      Tormes* (1924) *see* Rey, Florián
   *medalla del torero, La/The
      Bullfighter's Medal see* Buchs,
      José
   *novio de mamá, El/Mum's Boyfriend
      see* Rey, Florián
   *pilluelo de Madrid, El/*The Urchin
      from Madrid *see* Rey, Florián
   revoltosa, La/The Mischief Maker

as assistant director
   Chimes After Midnight see
      Welles, Orson
as director
   *abrigo a cuadros, Un/A checked
      suit* 20n.17
Polo, Carmen (María del Carmen Polo
      y Martínez Valdés) 50, 56n.27
Ponce de León, Alfonso 7
   Niños/Children 7
Porto, Juan José 44
   *florido pensil, El/The Flower-Filled
      Garden* 44
Príncep, Roger 118, 126
   *girasoles ciegos, Los/ The Blind
      Sunflowers see* Cuerda, José Luis
   orfanato, El/The Orphanage see
      Bayona, Juan Antonio
pro-natalism 29, 30, 31
pygmalion motif 2, 18n.6, 60, 62

quinque 100
Quiroga, Elio 112, 116, 128n.23
   NO-DO/The Haunting 112, 116,
      117, 128n.23

Radványi, Géza von 24
   Somewhere in Europe 24
Ramirez, Pedro Luis 34, 39
   Recluta con niño/Recruit with Child
      34, 39
religious cinema (*cine religioso*) 10, 11,
      17, 23–58, 129
Rey, Fernando 23, 41, 66
Rey, Florián 10, 19n.17
   *Agustina de Aragón/Agustina of
      Aragon* 20n.19
   aldea maldita, La/The Cursed Village
      (1930) 10, 33
   aldea maldita, La/The Cursed Village
      (1942) 10, 33, 34
   chavala, La/The Lass 19n.17
   Dolores, La/Dolores 20n.19
   *Lazarillo de Tormes, El/Lazarillo of
      Tormes* (1924) 20n.17
   *pilluelo de Madrid, El/*The Urchin
      from Madrid 20n.19
   novio de mamá, El/Mum's Boyfriend
      20n.19

revoltosa, La/The Mischief Maker
20n.19
Sierra de Ronda/The Ronda
Mountains 20n.19
Rilla, Wolf 104
Village of the Damned 104
robot *see* automata
Roldán, Fernando 20n.19
Paloma de mis amores/Paloma of My
Heart 20n.19
Roncoroni, Mario 7
¡Muñecas!/Dolls! 7
virgen del mar, El/The Virgin of the
Sea 7
Rooney, Mickey 7, 47
Rossellini, Roberto *24*
Germany Year Zero 24
Miracolo, Il/The Miracle 25, 54n.6
Rome, Open City 24
Rovira-Beleta, Francisco 87n.10, 130
atracadores, Los/The Robbers 130
Ruiz Castillo, Arturo 87n.10
Pachín 87n.10
Ruiz Rivelles, Luis 7
calumnia, La/Slander 7

Sáenz de Heredia, José Luis 8, 10,
20n.19
!No me mire usted!/Don't Look At
Me! 10, 20n.19, 52
Raza 10, 33, 36
¿Quién me quiere a mí?/Who Loves
Me? 8
saints 23, 25, 26, 142, 143, 147, 149,
151, 152
child saints 25, 144
Sanclemente, Pilarín 56n.22
Santillán, Antonio 33
Sucedió en mi aldea/It Happened In
My Village 31, 34, 35, 38
Sau, Antonio 9
Aurora de esperanza/Dawn of hope
9
Saura, Carlos 4, 11, 21n.32, 68, 73, 90,
97, 102, 118, 128n.27, 130
Carmen 73, 74
caza, La/The Hunt 68
Cría cuervos/Raise ravens 4, 11, 19,
97, 106, 111, 116, 124, 125

Deprisa, deprisa/Hurry, hurry 130
golfos, Los/The Delinquents 130
science-fiction 11, 12
Seaton, George 143
Bernadette's Song 143
Sección Femenina (Female Division of
the Falange) 60, 108, 152
Setó, Javier 66
Han robado una estrella/A Star Has
Been Stolen 66
Sherman, George 71, 72
Búsqueme a esa chica/Get that girl
for me see Palacios, Fernando
nueva Cenicienta, La/The New
Cinderella 71, 72
Sica, Vittorio de 24
Shoeshine 24
Silvestre, Miguel 7
niños del hospicio, Los/The Children
of the Poorhouse 7
skin 1, 122, 131–41, 145, 147
tattoo 133, 134, 137, 138
Smart, Ralph 25
Peppino e Violetta/Never Take No
For An Answer 25
Smith, Paul Julian 19, 79, 80, 81,
89, 91, 92, 94, 95, 109, 120,
126n.1, 127n.6, 128n.32, 129,
132, 133, 133, 138, 142
Sobrevila, Nemesio 10
Elai-Alai 10
Guernika 10
social-realism 128n.32, 131, 141
Spanish Civil War 8, 9, 10, 14, 21n.29,
24, 25, 30, 51, 57n.28, 68,
69, 73, 75, 80, 83, 90, 91, 93,
97, 98, 101, 108, 109, 112,
114, 115–16, 119, 124, 125,
128n.31, 147, 157
Spielberg, Steven 2, 43, 93
A.I. 2
E.T. 43
Schindler's List 93, 112, 127n.10
Summers, Manuel 11, 80, 81, 145
Adiós, cigüeña, adiós/Goodbye,
Stork, Goodbye 80
Del rosa al amarillo/From Pink... To
Yellow 11, 80, 145, 146
niño es nuestro, El/It's Our Child 80

Swift, David 66
  Parent Trap, The 66
  Pollyanna 60, 86n.3

Temple, Shirley 7, 8, 20n.19, 20n.22,
    32, 59, 64, 65, 68, 78
Tielve, Fernando 11, 114
  *espinazo del diablo, El/The Devil's
    Backbone see* Toro, Guillermo
    del
Toro, Guillermo del vi, 4, 11, 18n.8,
    115, 120, 121, 122, 149
  *espinazo del diablo, El/The Devil's
    Backbone* 11, 17, 112, 113, 114,
    119
  *laberinto del fauno, El/Pan's
    Labyrinth* vi, 4, 11, 17, 18n.8,
    94, 119, 120–22, 123, 125, 149
Torrent, Ana vi, 4, 11, 18n.9, 19n.10,
    43, 55n.13, 79, 80, 89, 90–6,
    97, 99–100, 107, 112, 116–18,
    122, 126n.1, 127n.4, 156
train 5, 68, 96, 111, 132, 134, 139,
    140, 141
transition to democracy 13, 14, 19n.10,
    55n.20, 61, 122, 158
trauma 1, 12, 14, 19, 61, 62, 69, 74,
    75, 76, 80, 85, 92, 93, 96, 97,
    98, 99, 100, 101, 102, 108, 111,
    112, 115, 117, 119, 121, 124,
    125, 127n.18, 130, 153, 154n.6,
    156, 157, 158
Truffaut, François 89
  *quatre cents coups, Les/The Four
    Hundred Blows* 89, 132
'two Spains' 75

Umbral, Francisco 60, 77, 78, 79
  dream of Susan Estrada 76, 78
  on Ana Torrent 79, 126n.1
  on Marisol 60, 77, 78, 79, 80, 85,
    126n.1
Urgoitia, Ricard 8, 9
Uribe, Imanol 108
  Viaje de Carol, El/Carol's Journey 108

Vallejo-Nájera, Antonio 14, 35, 51,
    119
  'red gene' 14, 51

Vajda, Ladislao 19, 23, 24, 25, 26,
    28, 29, 43, 52, 53n.2, 54n.8,
    55n.11, 94
  cebo, El/The bait 55n.11
  *Marcelino, pan y vino/The Miracle of
    Marcelino* 4, 17, 19, 23–9, 32–6,
    39, 41–3, 44, 45, 47, 48, 49,
    51, 52, 53, 54n.4, 54n.5, 55n.9,
    55n.14, 56n.26, 57n.36, 94,
    111, 124, 129, 142, 155n.12,
    156, 157
  Mi tío Jacinto/My Uncle Jacinto 52
ventriloquism 17, 42, 45, 47, 48, 51,
    52
  ventriloquist's dummy 3, 17, 45, 47,
    48, 50, 70, 157
Ventura, Alexia 5, 19n.11, 19no.13,
    154n.5
  *Alexia o la niña del misterio/Alexia,
    child of mystery see* Marro,
    Alberto
  *beso de la muerta, El/The Kiss of
    the Dead Woman see* Marro,
    Alberto
  Elva see Marro, Alberto
  *misterios de Barcelona, Los/The
    Barcelona Mysteries see* Marro,
    Alberto
  *secta de los misteriosos, La/The
    Mysterious Sect see* Marro,
    Alberto
  Tenacidad /Tenacity see Abadal,
    Baltasar
  *testamento de Diego Rocafort, El/
    Diego Rocafort's Will see*
    Marro, Alberto
Vidal, Armando 7
  *héroes del barrio, Los/The Heroes of
    the Neighbourhood* 7
Vilarós, Teresa 67, 71, 73
Villaronga, Agustí vi, 11, 122, 124, 126
  mar, El/The Sea 108–9
  niño de la luna, El/Moonchild 122
  Pa negre/Black Bread vi, 11, 122–6,
    156
  Tras el cristal/In a glass cage 122
Viñoly Barreto, Román 56n.26
  Barcos de papel/Paper Boats
    56n.26

voice 27, 41, 42, 43, 44, 45, 46, 47,
48, 49, 51, 52, 53, 57n.34,
58n.42, 62, 89, 93, 108, 111,
117, 151
see also dubbing

Welles, Orson 20n.19
Chimes after midnight 20n.19
Weston, Edward 82
Neil 82
Winnicott, Donald 22n.39, 26

Winter, Nick 6
tía Ramona, La/Aunt Ramona 7
witness 16, 70, 89, 90, 94, 95, 100,
101, 102, 107, 120, 123,
127n.18, 145, 153, 157
wounds 14, 53, 54n.8, 75, 82, 107,
123, 130, 135, 141, 144, 153
'wound culture' 130, 141, 152, 153

Zemeckis, Robert 85
Forest Gump 85, 110

EU authorised representative for GPSR:
Easy Access System Europe, Mustamäe tee 50,
10621 Tallinn, Estonia
gpsr.requests@easproject.com

www.ingramcontent.com/pod-product-compliance
Ingram Content Group UK Ltd.
Pitfield, Milton Keynes, MK11 3LW, UK
UKHW021911060726
6981IPUK00004B/79